DATE			

Opposing Viewpoints®

Other Books of Related Interest in the Opposing Viewpoints Series:

American Foreign Policy
Central America
Terrorism

Additional Books in the Opposing Viewpoints Series:

Abortion
AIDS
American Government
The American Military
American Values
America's Prisons
The Arms Race
Biomedical Ethics
Censorship
Chemical Dependency
Constructing a Life Philosophy
Crime & Criminals
Criminal Justice
Death and Dying
The Death Penalty
Drug Abuse
Economics in America
The Environmental Crisis
Male/Female Roles
The Mass Media
The Middle East
Nuclear War
The Political Spectrum
Problems of Africa
Religion and Human Experience
Science and Religion
Sexual Values
Social Justice
The Soviet Union
The Vietnam War
War and Human Nature
The Welfare State

Opposing Viewpoints®

David L. Bender & Bruno Leone, *Series Editors*

Bonnie Szumski, *Book Editor*

OPPOSING VIEWPOINTS SERIES ®

Greenhaven Press   577 Shoreview Park Road   St. Paul, Minnesota 55126

No part of this book may be reproduced or used in any other form or by any other means, electrical, mechanical or otherwise, including, but not limited to photocopy, recording or any information storage and retrieval system, without prior written permission from the publisher.

Library of Congress Cataloging-in-Publication Data

Latin America: opposing viewpoints.

  (Opposing viewpoints series)
  Includes bibliographies and index.
  1. Latin America—Foreign relations—United States.
2. United States—Foreign relations—Latin America.
3. Latin America—Politics and government—1948-   .
4. Human rights—Latin America.   5. Latin America—
Economic policy.   6. Debts, External—Latin America.
I. Szumski, Bonnie, 1958-   .   II. Series.
F1418.L3555   1988   327.7308   87-21088
ISBN 0-89908-399-4 (lib. bdg.)
ISBN 0-89908-374-9 (pbk.)

© Copyright 1988 by Greenhaven Press, Inc.

"Congress shall make no law... abridging the freedom of speech, or of the press."

First Amendment to the US Constitution

The basic foundation of our democracy is the first amendment guarantee of freedom of expression. The *Opposing Viewpoints Series* is dedicated to the concept of this basic freedom and the idea that it is more important to practice it than to enshrine it.

Contents

Why Consider Opposing Viewpoints?

"It is better to debate a question without settling it than to settle a question without debating it."

Joseph Joubert (1754-1824)

The Importance of Examining Opposing Viewpoints

The purpose of the Opposing Viewpoints books, and this book in particular, is to present balanced, and often difficult to find, opposing points of view on complex and sensitive issues.

Probably the best way to become informed is to analyze the positions of those who are regarded as experts and well studied on issues. It is important to consider every variety of opinion in an attempt to determine the truth. Opinions from the mainstream of society should be examined. But also important are opinions that are considered radical, reactionary, or minority as well as those stigmatized by some other uncomplimentary label. An important lesson of history is the eventual acceptance of many unpopular and even despised opinions. The ideas of Socrates, Jesus, and Galileo are good examples of this.

Readers will approach this book with their own opinions on the issues debated within it. However, to have a good grasp of one's own viewpoint, it is necessary to understand the arguments of those with whom one disagrees. It can be said that those who do not completely understand their adversary's point of view do not fully understand their own.

A persuasive case for considering opposing viewpoints has been presented by John Stuart Mill in his work *On Liberty*. When examining controversial issues it may be helpful to reflect on this suggestion:

> The only way in which a human being can make some approach to knowing the whole of a subject, is by hearing what can be said about it by persons of every variety of opinion, and studying all modes in which it can be looked at by every character of mind. No wise man ever acquired his wisdom in any mode but this.

Analyzing Sources of Information

The Opposing Viewpoints books include diverse materials taken from magazines, journals, books, and newspapers, as well as statements and position papers from a wide range of individuals, organizations and governments. This broad spectrum of sources helps to develop patterns of thinking which are open to the consideration of a variety of opinions.

Pitfalls To Avoid

A pitfall to avoid in considering opposing points of view is that of regarding one's own opinion as being common sense and the most rational stance and the point of view of others as being only opinion and naturally wrong. It may be that another's opinion is correct and one's own is in error.

Another pitfall to avoid is that of closing one's mind to the opinions of those with whom one disagrees. The best way to approach a dialogue is to make one's primary purpose that of understanding the mind and arguments of the other person and not that of enlightening him or her with one's own solutions. More can be learned by listening than speaking.

It is my hope that after reading this book the reader will have a deeper understanding of the issues debated and will appreciate the complexity of even seemingly simple issues on which good and honest people disagree. This awareness is particularly important in a democratic society such as ours where people enter into public debate to determine the common good. Those with whom one disagrees should not necessarily be regarded as enemies, but perhaps simply as people who suggest different paths to a common goal.

Developing Basic Reading and Thinking Skills

In this book carefully edited opposing viewpoints are purposely placed back to back to create a running debate; each viewpoint is preceded by a short quotation that best expresses the author's main argument. This format instantly plunges the reader into the midst of a controversial issue and greatly aids that reader in mastering the basic skill of recognizing an author's point of view.

A number of basic skills for critical thinking are practiced in the activities that appear throughout the books in the series. Some of the skills are:

Evaluating Sources of Information The ability to choose from among alternative sources the most reliable and accurate source in relation to a given subject.

Separating Fact from Opinion The ability to make the basic distinction between factual statements (those that can be demonstrated or verified empirically) and statements of opinion (those that are beliefs or attitudes that cannot be proved).

Identifying Stereotypes The ability to identify oversimplified, exaggerated descriptions (favorable or unfavorable) about people and insulting statements about racial, religious or national groups, based upon misinformation or lack of information.

Recognizing Ethnocentrism The ability to recognize attitudes or opinions that express the view that one's own race, culture, or group is inherently superior, or those attitudes that judge another culture or group in terms of one's own.

It is important to consider opposing viewpoints and equally important to be able to critically analyze those viewpoints. The activities in this book are designed to help the reader master these thinking skills. Statements are taken from the book's viewpoints and the reader is asked to analyze them. This technique aids the reader in developing skills that not only can be applied to the viewpoints in this book, but also to situations where opinionated spokespersons comment on controversial issues. Although the activities are helpful to the solitary reader, they are most useful when the reader can benefit from the interaction of group discussion.

Using this book and others in the series should help readers develop basic reading and thinking skills. These skills should improve the readers' ability to understand what they read. Readers should be better able to separate fact from opinion, substance from rhetoric and become better consumers of information in our media-centered culture.

This volume of the Opposing Viewpoints books does not advocate a particular point of view. Quite the contrary! The very nature of the book leaves it to the reader to formulate the opinions he or she finds most suitable. My purpose as publisher is to see that this is made possible by offering a wide range of viewpoints which are fairly presented.

David L. Bender
Publisher

The Countries of Latin America

Introduction

"The question of US culpability for Latin America's problems affects the debate over US policy."

Many of the countries of Latin America are rich with natural resources and cultural tradition. As Carlos Alberto Montaner, a Latin American commentator, remarked, "We Latin Americans, with more inhabitants than the United States, possess as much or more potential wealth. Spawned by Europe—just as the United States—we have universities that are more than four hundred years old. We have urban centers that were already established when Chicago was a prairie overrun by buffalo." Why, then, are most of the countries of Latin America plagued by poverty, violent repression, and economic corruption and despair?

Many commentators argue that these problems stem from US interference in Latin America: The history of US economic and military intervention is long, they argue, and has severely hampered Latin America's ability to become autonomous. Sergio Bitar, an economist, argues the US's imperialistic attitude undermines Latin America's economic and political objectives: "The United States' supremacy and Latin America's economic vulnerability have been the principal reasons for the subordination of Latin American aims to those of the United States." Because the US defines Latin America's problems in terms of US goals, these critics argue, Latin America has not been allowed to develop.

Furthermore, any attempts on the part of Latin Americans to change their plight is tenaciously opposed by the US. US support of the contras against the Sandinistas, its attempt to oust Fidel Castro, and its support of oppressive dictators like Pinochet in Chile are all proof that US policy is defined not in terms of what is good for Latin America, but what is good for the US. Those that argue that the US is responsible for Latin America's troubles urge that the US stay out of Latin American affairs. Some, like Bitar, go even further and contend that since the US is unlikely to allow Latin America autonomy, Latin Americans must use military force against the US, if necessary.

Others take issue with this argument and believe that blaming the US for Latin America's problems oversimplifies the situation. Luis Burstin, editor of a Costa Rican newspaper, is just one Latin American who does not agree that the US is responsible for Latin

American strife: "All the revolutionary groups in Latin America base their political action on the premise that poverty, chaos, and dictatorships—all . . . endemic phenomena around here for many centuries now—have their origin in the exploitation of our countries by the United States." Burstin and others counter that it is Latin Americans themselves who must change their societies, and the only way to do this is to accept responsibility for their own destinies. As former US government official Lawrence Harrison argues, "Latin America's future progress will depend importantly on its ability to see itself objectively; to suppress the tendency to seek foreign scapegoats; to work toward the kinds of cultural change that will improve the prospects for democratic progress; and to assume responsibility for its own future." Those that favor this side of the debate see the US as a benefactor and a model. They contend that the future of Latin America would greatly improve if, instead of rejecting the US, these countries actively sought its help and its democratic example.

The question of US culpability for Latin America's problems affects the general debte over US policy: If US involvement is the cause, then any attempt to intervene in Latin America, including economic aid, is correctly to be viewed suspiciously by Latin Americans as a further attempt at domination and subjugation. If Latin America is responsible for its own fate, then asking for economic and military aid is acceptable, as proponents of this view believe the US can be a true friend and ally.

The authors included in *Latin America and US Policy: Opposing Viewpoints* concern themselves with these issues while they debate the implications of current US involvement in Latin American affairs. Five chapter topics are debated: Is US Intervention the Cause of Latin America's Problems? How Should the US Deal with Latin American Human Rights Conditions? Are Latin American Revolutions a Threat to the US? What Form of Government Is Best for Latin America? How Serious Is the Latin American Debt? As readers discuss the implications of US policy in Latin America they should bear in mind the attitudes and actions that add to the complexity of this important relationship.

Is US Intervention the Cause of Latin America's Problems?

Chapter Preface

Historically, the United States' relationship with Latin America has been punctuated with US intervention. This intervention has taken a number of forms including direct military involvement in countries like Nicaragua and Grenada; economic aid through programs like the Alliance for Progress, a massive plan meant to revitalize Central American economies, and covert activities, such as the Bay of Pigs invasion of Cuba.

Debate over US intervention focuses on US motivation and the impact of US involvement on Latin American development. Many Latin Americans and US citizens believe US intervention is the result of imperialist tendencies: a desire to dominate Latin America as though these countries were colonies of the US. These people argue that the policy of the US is self-serving and based primarily on US economic benefit. To protect US corporate and business interests, the US supports friendly dictators in spite of human rights violations. On the other hand, the US government argues that economic and military aid is humanitarian and that without such aid Latin American economies would crumble and oppressive communist regimes would proliferate. Still a third view is that Latin Americans are to blame for their own economic and political oppression and that US intervention has little effect. Blaming the US for indigenous problems, a historical tolerance of violent dictators, and complacency are all reasons Latin Americans cannot wrest themselves from the stagnating conditions that plague them.

Whether or not US intervention is helpful to Latin America, it is sure to continue. Ongoing US military aid to the contras and massive bank loans to various Latin American countries testify to this. The authors in this chapter debate an issue that is sure to remain important and controversial.

"The United States will not tolerate any constructive development in the nations under its domination."

US Intervention Is the Cause of Latin America's Problems

Noam Chomsky

Noam Chomsky is an outspoken critic of US foreign policy, especially of its policy toward Latin America. His articles have appeared in several leftist publications and his most recent book is *Turning the Tide: U.S. Intervention in Central America.* In the following viewpoint, Chomsky traces US involvement in Latin America to prove that the US supports political oppression and poverty there. He concludes with a call for the US public to oppose this destructive intervention.

As you read, consider the following questions:

1. What does Chomsky believe is the reason behind US tolerance of Latin American poverty?
2. Why does the author believe that the US continues to support Latin American dictators?
3. Why does Chomsky argue that the Alliance for Progress was a failure?

Noam Chomsky, "How America Controls the Caribbean," *Against the Current,* May/June 1986. Reprinted with permission.

Why are we concerned about Central America today and were not concerned 10 years ago? Was democracy flourishing in Central America then, and was the population happy, free, prosperous, and well fed? Obviously not. Ten years ago Central Americans were living under brutal military dictatorships. The U.S. was directly responsible for what was happening to them then, exactly as we are now. But order reigned and profits flowed, and therefore there was no interest in Central America. A second question: Why are we concerned about Central America now and not the Caribbean? Is it that nothing is happening in the Caribbean? Of course not. Haiti, for example, has been in the news [since Jean-Claude Duvalier's overthrow]. But two years ago it wasn't in the news, although interesting and important things were happening. The Haitian legislature unanimously passed a law that reads: "Every political party must recognize in its statutes the President for Life as the supreme arbiter of the nation." The new electoral law excluded the Christian Democrats, and it declared that the state can suspend any political party without reason. This was ratified by 99.98 percent of the vote. The American ambassador described the new law as "an encouraging step forward." The Reagan administration then certified that Haiti's democratic development was proceeding, which allowed Congress to release $50 million in military and economic aid. This primarily aided Jean-Claude "Baby Doc" Duvalier; it went straight into his bank accounts.

Haiti is a country of about six million people in which 4,000 families have 80 percent of the wealth. Eighty-seven percent of the children suffer malnutrition, 82 percent of the population is illiterate, and 60 percent has an annual per capita income of $60. Torture, terror, and slave labor conditions were the common lot in Haiti until recently. But that was perfectly okay with the U.S. government.

An Interesting Comment

By December of 1985, things began to change. There were demonstrations and killings. At that point the United States began to show some concern. Here is the way it was described in the *Wall Street Journal:* The White House concluded that the regime was unraveling. U.S. analysts learned that ruling inner circles had lost faith in Duvalier. As a result, U.S. officials, including Secretary of State George Shultz, began openly calling for a "democratic process in Haiti."

Well, that's an interesting comment. The point is that earlier, everything was quite satisfactory, while now we suddenly needed a democratic process. The same cynicism was illustrated in our behavior in the Philippines at roughly the same time.

Now there is an official explanation for the lack of U.S. attention to other countries when order reigns and profits flow. One

Dan Wasserman. © 1987, The Boston Globe. Reprinted by permission of The Los Angeles Times Syndicate.

version was given by Jeane Kirkpatrick in a 1979 article that propelled her to fame and into the Reagan administration.

> *Because the miseries of traditional life are familiar, they are bearable to ordinary people who, growing up in the society, learn to cope.*

So therefore our lack of concern is quite proper; indeed, quite decent and moral because the lower orders feel no pain. That, incidentally, is a classic view of imperial power. But in the case of Central America, problems began brewing in the late '70s, when ordinary people forgot that their burdens were supposed to be bearable and attempted to change things. Suddenly there was a threat to order and profits in Nicaragua, El Salvador, and Guatemala. Therefore there was great concern in the U.S. and much rhetoric about the need for democracy in the region. . . .

The Iron Grip

Central America and the Caribbean have been in the iron grip of the United States for a century, and therefore this region tells us a lot about ourselves. What you find is starvation, slave labor, and torture. Virtually every effort to bring about some constructive change has led to a new dose of U.S. violence.

The Council on Hemispheric Affairs in its 1985 human rights report selected El Salvador and Guatemala as the worst governments in Latin America. They were the only two governments in Central America "that abducted, killed, and tortured political opponents on a systematic and widespread basis." This, incidentally, is the sixth successive year that these two nations were given that honor, and in that period their governments killed roughly 150,000 people.

There was one other contender for first place in Central America in the report—namely, the contras. They also murdered and tortured thousands of civilians. In fact, they carry out no other noteworthy military operations.

It is significant that we are talking about three close U.S. allies, all of which have been supported with military aid. (In the case of Guatemala, direct military aid was impeded by Congress, but indirect means were used to aid the bloody dictatorship, including reliance on the Argentine junta, Taiwan, and Israel.). . .

Supporting Dictators

What is the reason for this longstanding and systematic U.S. support of dictators in the Caribbean and Central America? There is an official answer to that, given in perhaps its clearest form by John F. Kennedy. He said that we would be in favor of decent democratic regimes, as he put it, but if there is a danger of a Fidel Castro we will always support a Rafael Trujillo.

What do those terms mean? What did he mean by a Castro? It is important to understand that he did not mean a communist or an ally of the Russians. The category of Castro is vastly broader. As for Trujillo, we know what he meant by that. Trujillo was the brutal dictator of the Dominican Republic who was installed with U.S. support and then tortured, murdered, and robbed for 35 years with American support until we finally turned against him because his robbery began to extend to U.S. corporations.

The Dominican Republic can serve as a case study for understanding America's role in this region. The first Marine landing on the island was in the year 1800, so there's a long history. . . .

15,000 Haitians Massacred

When the Marines left, they placed the country in the hands of a National Guard trained by the United States. Trujillo quickly emerged from this group as a leader and he became dictator. Everything was okay for 30 or 35 years. Trujillo was praised in the United States as a forward-looking leader; for example, he massacred some 15,000 Haitians in one month in 1937 and carried out similar actions against his own population. However by the late 1950s America's attitude toward Trujillo was beginning to sour. At that time he owned 70 to 80 percent of the economy, which meant that American-based corporations were being pushed out. The CIA was authorized to carry out an assassination plot. Whether it was the CIA's doing or not, Trujillo was assassinated in 1962.

Supporting Repression

Several regimes that receive support and help from the United States, violate every type of human rights and represent a dominating oligarchy that does not serve in any way the interests of the majority of the people, and are repressive and criminal dictatorships.

The multiple foreign interventions in the Latinamerican countries during this century have often had "the threat of international communism" as justification. The tendency has been to decide beforehand "what these countries need." Of course, that need agrees with the interests of foreign powers. Those Latinamerican countries have not had the liberty to find their own paths, that is, solutions to their social, economic and political problems. For some Northamerican sectors it has been very difficult to understand or accept that in the Latinamerican reality the same plans and solutions that are used in a developed country cannot be applied.

Esdras A. Rodriguez, *e/sa*, December 1983.

At that point there was a democratic election and Juan Bosch, a Kennedy-style liberal, was elected. He fought corruption, defended civil liberties, and stopped police repression. He began programs to educate peasants and workers for true democratic participation. He actually succeeded, under awful conditions, in initiating an economic revival.

Kennedy committed himself to undermining and destroying Bosch. U.S. aid was stopped. The United States blocked the removal of officers loyal to Trujillo from the Dominican government and kept close ties with them. Soon there was a military coup, quickly supported by the United States. Bosch was ousted and economic decline set in. Corruption and repression increased.

That incident helps us get some understanding of the meaning of the term *Castro*. Juan Bosch was one of those Castros who we had to oppose in favor of a Trujillo. Bosch was not a communist; he was a liberal democrat. He tried to institute a capitalist democracy and that was intolerable to U.S. interests. . . .

More Repression

In El Salvador in 1932, there was a huge massacre they called "the Matanza." Some 10,000 to 30,000 peasants were murdered in a few weeks. The United States Navy was off shore at the time but, as the Chief of Naval Operations testified before Congress, it was not necessary to intervene because the situation was well in hand.

Turning to Nicaragua, the first major U.S. military intervention there was in 1854. At that time the U.S. Navy burned down a town to avenge an alleged insult to American millionaire Cornelius Vanderbilt. Throughout much of the first half of this century, the country was under the rule of U.S. Marines, followed by the Somoza dictatorship.

In Guatemala there had been only one reprieve from a history of brutal military dictatorships. From 1944 to 1954, Juan José Arévalo modeled his government on Roosevelt's New Deal and immediately aroused American enmity. In 1954 that experiment was ended by a CIA coup, setting off 30 years of dictatorship that probably resembled Nazi Germany more closely than any other government in the contemporary world.

Death Squads and US Policy

This tradition of repression and murder was an essential component of John F. Kennedy's Alliance for Progress. In 1962 the Kennedy administration made a decision which, in terms of its consequences, is one of the most important in recent history, although barely known here. The U.S. effectively switched the mission of the Latin American military from hemispheric defense to *internal security*. Internal security means war against a country's own population. In El Salvador, for instance, the Kennedy administration established the basic structure of the death squads.

The Alliance for Progress, which is much lauded in the U.S. as another example of our benevolence, was a totally cynical operation. It was initiated in order to stop "the virus" of Castro from spreading contagion throughout the region. The alliance also favored a certain kind of economic development, geared to export crops grown for the benefit of U.S.-based agribusiness companies.

That kind of economic development carries a corollary: It inevitably arouses dissent, which requires an apparatus of repression to silence. Therefore the death squads are an essential component of the Alliance of Progress.

Exploiting Resources

Through all of this, American rhetoric has been very noble and elevated. Our presence in the Caribbean and Central America is explained as an effort to bring development to these backward lands and defend them against the creeping influence of our enemies. Kennedy called the enemy a "monolithic and ruthless conspiracy that is attempting to thwart our benevolence." Ronald Reagan renamed it "the Evil Empire." But the real enemy in these countries has always been the aspirations of the people themselves. And the principle under which we have defended ourselves from these enemies has been our right to exploit the resources and labor of these nations.

If we cannot destroy popular resistance movements by force, as we typically try to do, the next best thing is to drive them into the arms of the Russians so we have justification for the violence and terror that we launch against them. This very familiar story is being re-lived in Nicaragua today. The United States is not concerned by the useless Soviet tanks in the streets of Managua, nor is it concerned by the censorship of a newspaper that is funded by the U.S. and supports contra terrorism in Nicaragua. What the U.S. is concerned about is the early substantial success of social reforms—which have been aborted, thanks to the contra war.

The Threat of a Good Example

Julia Preston wrote in the *Boston Globe* that "few U.S. officials now believe the contras can drive out the Sandinistas soon. Administration officials say they are content to see the contras debilitate the Sandinistas by forcing them to divert scarce resources towards the war and away from social programs."

The cruelty and savagery of that policy is impossible to discuss. The point is, the United States will not tolerate any constructive development in the nations under its domination—any developments that will harm the interests of the elites who run this country. The real concern is the threat of a good example.

There is no reason at all for us to allow this horror story to continue. In a country as free as this one, there is a great deal that can be done to reverse this course. It basically requires two things. The first is a certain amount of honesty. Enough honesty to learn what we do in the world and to realize that we've been doing it for a long, long time. Second, it requires a certain degree of courage and commitment, namely that we devote ourselves to changing a world of terror and suffering that we have helped to create and now maintain.

23

"The idea that the United States is the cause of our backwardness, and that the prosperity of the United States rests on plunder does not fit with reality."

US Intervention Is Not the Cause of Latin America's Problem

Luis Burstin

Luis Burstin is a doctor and the editor of a newspaper in Costa Rica. He is at work on a book entitled *Latin American Political Mythology*. In the following viewpoint, excerpted from an interview in *Commentary* magazine, Burstin explains that both conservatives and liberals in the United States and Latin America blame the US for the region's poverty and political and social backwardness. Burstin argues that this is a "myth of guilt" and that Latin Americans themselves must stop blaming the US and begin to solve their own problems.

As you read, consider the following questions:

1. Why does Burstin believe that the myth that the US is the cause of Latin America's problems enjoys such widespread support?
2. Why does the author think Carlos Fuentes is wrong about the reasons for Latin American poverty?
3. Who is responsible for social injustice in Latin America, according to the author?

Luis Burstin, "A Few Home Truths About Latin America." Reprinted from *Commentary*, February 1985, by permission; all rights reserved.

American friend: We Americans seem to be growing very interested in Latin America these days.

Burstin: I have to disagree with you. There is certainly a great deal of what resembles interest, but it isn't really that at all. In the past, the amount of writing about Latin America, say in the American press, was negligible, except when we had a good revolution or an outstanding earthquake. . . . As for the current outpouring of books, essays, articles, and news stories about Central America, it reflects not an authentic intellectual or political interest, but perplexity spiced with pious worries and guilt feelings.

Two Kinds of Guilt

A: Could you be more specific about those "worries and guilt feelings"?

B: In the United States, at least in a sector of your academic and political classes, you seem to be experiencing, first, the feeling that perhaps you should have paid attention to us in the past, that it is this lack of interest which is now producing our convolutions; and, second—this is more common among liberal and leftist intellectuals—there is the belief that the poverty and the social and political nightmares of Latin America have been produced by the United States, by the exploitation of our countries by American corporations, and the intervention in our internal affairs of the United States government and politicians. So there are two distinctive kinds of guilt associated with this perplexity. . . .

A: What about the guilt feelings originating from the belief that the poverty and the social and political nightmares of Latin America have been produced by the United States?

B: This belief is at the heart of everything that is happening here. All the revolutionary groups in Latin America base their political action on the premise that poverty, chaos, and dictatorships—all, as you know, endemic phenomena around here for many centuries now, even before the United States emerged as a unified country— have their origin in the exploitation of our countries by the United States and in the interventionism and colonialism of the United States in Latin America. This premise, which does not have to be proved but only accepted, not only finds stimulus in some academic and left-wing political circles in the United States; it also gets joyful and enthusiastic support from many political leaders of the Third World, as well as most of the social-democratic and democratic-socialist political parties of Europe. . . .

We Are Poor Because the US Is Rich

A: I always thought that this American idea of responsibility for your troubles was the exclusive property of the Left, but I gather that you think it also involves the Right and sometimes even the democratic Center.

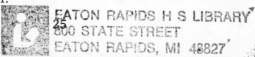

B: Yes, although not many on the Right or in the democratic Center express it explicitly. You see, thousands of tons of printed paper and thousands of hours of radio and television—not to mention the uninterrupted sequence of seminars on "dependence and underdevelopment"—tell our citizens daily, persistently, and unequivocally: *we are poor because the United States is rich; the United States is rich because it exploits us; let's fight against the United States.* As simple as that. And the message goes on: we live in chaos and under dictatorships because the United States intervenes in our countries; the support that the United States has traditionally given to our dictators proves this; American corporations are the godfathers of all the brutality and the killings that for decades the Latin American dictators, their puppets, have perpetrated. All we have to do is fight against the United States and all this will come to an end. And the implicit assertions are equally important: if the United States hadn't intervened in our countries, Latin America would not only have developed economically but we would also be enjoying perfect social justice and pure Jeffersonian democracy.

Blaming the US of Little Help

Guilt is a useful concept in child rearing, but not in social analysis. It is a fact of life that some Latin Americans tend to ascribe blame to the United States for many of their ills: either we are not importing enough or we are importing too much and making them more dependent; either we are not sending enough money to meet the needs or we are sending so much that we increase their dependency. It is a useful game for political purposes in Latin America. Except for explaining some of the political dynamics, this concept of guilt really helps us very little in understanding economic relationships.

William P. Glade, *Latin America: Dependency or Interdependence,* 1985.

A: Do they really go *that* far?
B: What do you mean "really"? Listen to this example. On March 5, 1981, one of our foremost novelists, the Mexican writer Carlos Fuentes, who is a leftist but certainly not a Communist, wrote in the New York *Times*: "Is not this the other fundamental reason, along with colonialism, of turmoil, instability, terrorism, hunger, and weakness in the area: United States interventionism, always, only, United States interventionism?" So now you can see what your interventionism has produced in our countries: *turmoil*, something we never knew before the United States started messing up things down here; *instability*, which of course is also completely alien to our tradition of centuries-old stable governments; then you have also provoked in our peaceful societies *terrorism*,

which the Montoneros, the Tupamaros, the Sendero Luminosos, and our native fascist gangs had to learn from American textbooks provided by the CIA; and as if all that weren't enough, add to the list *hunger*, a completely new social catastrophe in Latin America, because, as is universally known, for centuries we were such big producers of agricultural products that for the last two hundred years one of our main public-health problems has been the prevalence of obesity among our peasants; not only that, but worse, because, as is also universally accepted, our land had been fairly distributed among our obese farmers, who always used advanced agricultural techniques until the United States brought all this to an abrupt end by taking away our techniques and fertilizers and then reorganizing things in such a way that a few landlords ended up with all the land and began paying those miserable wages of a few cents and two tortillas a day; and, of course, *weakness*, a sad situation because we still remember the old times when we were strong and progressive countries, an example for all humanity to follow. . . .

Promoting Communism

The premise that the United States is responsible for the hunger, the instability, and the brutality in our countries unites well-meaning American leftists, independent anti-imperialistic Latin American intellectuals and politicians, and hard-core Marxist-Leninists. And when this assorted group gets together and is really able to get somewhere, by some strange repetitive coincidence, the Marxist-Leninists always turn out to be the major shareholders of the whole business.

A: Does all this go back a long way in Latin American history?

B: No. It is a relatively new political phenomenon. In the last century, for example, our greatest thinkers and politicians—men like Simón Bolívar and Benito Juárez—not only were great admirers of the United States but also wanted to emulate its example.

A: So things have changed a lot.

B: Yes; instead of old-fashioned liberal democrats, we now have these professional blamers. They should be forced to read the writings of P. T. Bauer. So should everyone else. You may not agree with him about everything, but how are you going to deny the overwhelming facts he puts before you? If colonialism were the original cause of our backwardness—and, along this line of thought, also of that of Africa and Asia—why is it that the so-called Fourth World, the least-developed countries of the Third World such as Afghanistan, Chad, Bhutan, Burundi, Nepal, and Sikkim, did not until very recently have any external economic contacts, and how is it that most of them were never Western colonies? . . .

A: The other argument which is used within this context is that the dependency of your countries has not exactly produced the backwardness—the backwardness was there—but the dependency has prevented your countries from developing and has perpetuated the backwardness.

B: Well, as Jean-François Revel has cleverly asked, why is it that here, in our hemisphere, the dependency of Latin America on the United States has produced backwardness, while in Canada, which is a country "dependent" on the United States to a degree that has no equal in the world, this relationship has produced not backwardness but a modern, progressive, and rich country? Or take Hong Kong, Taiwan, Singapore, and South Korea, poor and backward countries three decades ago but now among the most prosperous and vital in the world. They were invaded by foreign capital and technology; they became dependent on Western "imperialism" and markets; and yet in just three decades they left all their backwardness behind and are now jumping into the era of the highest technology. So there they are, working hard and studying hard and inventing things, and bringing in foreign capital, and becoming dependent and all that; and here we are, poor, rancorous, and blaming others for our social brutality and historical evils. . . .

Latin American "Luck"

Latin Americans do not value the same moral qualities North Americans do. The two cultures see the world quite differently. Latin Americans seem to feel inferior to North Americans in practical matters but superior in spiritual ones. In Latin American experience, powerful personages control almost everything. From this experience, it is easy to imagine that the whole world must work this way, and to project such expectations upon North America. It must be said, then, that relations between North and South America are emotional as well as economic. The "Catholic" aristocratic ethic of Latin America places more emphasis on luck, heroism, status, and *figura* than the relatively "Protestant" ethic of North America, which values diligence, regularity, and the responsible seizure of opportunity. Given two such different ways of looking at the world, intense love-hate relations are bound to develop. Looking at North America, Latins are likely to attribute its more advanced status to luck—and also to a kind of aristocratic power. In their experience, wealth is relatively static, and what is given to one is taken from another.

Michael Novak, *The Atlantic Monthly*, March 1982.

A: Now that you have recovered from the disease and acquired your immunity, what are some of the things you have learned?

B: I have already told you about some of them. Here is another and one of the most important: revolutions are not caused by poverty and social injustice. Until a few years ago, poverty and social injustice in Central America were regarded by almost everybody as part of the landscape. Now, there is almost no one who does not affirm that poverty and social injustice are the causes of our tumult. Yet history gives no solid evidence for such an assertion. If the direct cause of the violence in Latin America were social injustice, El Salvador and Guatemala would hardly be the only countries where guerrillas threaten the government. We can all think of several other Latin American nations with masses of poor people—countries that, according to the myth, should be excellent candidates for revolution. But you see, in those Latin American countries where a more or less cyclical mechanism permits the exercise of power to pass regularly from one ruling group to another, the possibilities of revolution diminish markedly—despite persisting poverty and social injustice. No. Neither Fidel nor the Sandinistas came to power because the Cuban *guajiro* or the Nicaraguan *campesino* was chronically poor. . . .

The Hope of Democracy Ends

The Communist parties attached to Moscow have always been accused by their more radical leftist competitors of being reformist, bourgeois, and ineffective. They are not. They are the only really effective revolutionary force in Latin America. The other groups and individuals are usefully noisy and belligerent, and they can sometimes overthrow a dictator like Batista or Somoza. But they are not capable of delivering the knockout blow, the blow that consolidates the process, that makes for *the real thing*. It is only when the Moscow-attached Communists and their sponsors come onto the stage that the real performance begins. And once it begins, the hope of democracy ends, and we who live down here not only have to suffer a new form of political oppression, which is bad enough, but we also have to suffer the arguments of our "friends" in the United States and Europe who tell us that we have no democratic tradition anyway and at least a dictatorship of the Left will "improve our social conditions."

29

"U.S. security depends on preventing fundamental economic transformation in Latin America."

Latin America Must Break with the US

Sergio Bitar

Sergio Bitar is an economist, author, and consultant. He served as minister of mining in Chile in 1973, has worked as general manager of a private manufacturing company, and was a consultant to the Sistema Economica Latinoamerica in Venezuela. Bitar has been a visiting fellow at the Harvard Institute for International Development and a fellow at the Latin American Program of the Woodrow Wilson International Center. In the following viewpoint, Bitar argues that Latin America's fundamental economic and social problems are primarily a result of US resistance to Latin America's efforts to change them. The US perceives every event in Latin America as a security threat, he argues, which effectively stops governments from making any fundamental improvements.

As you read, consider the following questions:

1. How does the US relationship with the Soviet Union affect its relationship with Latin America, according to the author?
2. What are some of the reasons the author gives to support his argument that the US does not allow change to occur in Latin America?

This work appears as "Economics and Security: Contradictions in U.S.–Latin American Relations" by Sergio Bitar in THE UNITED STATES AND LATIN AMERICA IN THE 1980s: CONTENDING PERSPECTIVES ON A DECADE OF CRISIS, Kevin J. Middlebrook and Carlos Rico, Editors. Published 1986 by the University of Pittsburgh Press. Used by permission of the publisher.

Shifts in economic power between Latin America and the United States have not been accompanied by similar changes in security relations. This imbalance has caused increasing divergence between Latin America's strategic interests and the limits imposed by U.S. security objectives in the hemisphere. Whereas the United States has given priority to its security aims in Latin America, Latin America has stressed its development goals.

This divergence has usually been resolved in favor of U.S. objectives. The United States' supremacy and Latin America's economic vulnerability have been the principal reasons for the subordination of Latin American aims to those of the United States. However, the degree of subordination is changing. Latin America's increased economic capacity has created new leverage. At the same time, the decline in the United States' relative economic power has limited the U.S. government's ability to impose its own criteria on Latin American governments. Both processes have produced conditions leading to a less asymmetrical realignment in strategic interests. . . .

Security from the US Perspective

To explain U.S. governmental actions in Latin America, one must consider the United States' strategic interests throughout the world. The United States' fundamental concern is its global rivalry with the Soviet Union. All other security issues are evaluated in this context. The United States' policy goal in developing countries is to prevent the Soviet Union from winning any advantage. Some analysts have even suggested that the United States should concentrate its efforts on containing subversion rather than expanding its nuclear arsenal. The U.S. government has emphasized the importance of political stability in developing countries on the assumption that stability reduces opportunities for Soviet influence. This emphasis is especially intense in Latin America due to the United States' great influence in the region. The United States is even less willing to accept risks in the Western Hemisphere than elsewhere, which means less autonomy for Latin America.

The U.S. government understands that security threats do not originate *in* Latin America; rather, they occur *through* Latin America. Events in the region do not necessarily pose security threats in their own right. Instead, U.S. concern is with Soviet actions that take advantage of unstable circumstances, perhaps using a Latin American country as a base from which to attack the United States.

The priority that the United States gives to its relations with the Soviet Union is not new. It dates from the early post-World War II period. But the projection of that global rivalry on U.S.-

Latin American relations has grown increasingly intense over time. The Cuban revolution dramatically changed the United States' perception of its postwar position in the hemisphere. After 1959 the United States considerably increased its pressure on Latin America so as to prevent any similar occurrence in the future. At about the same time, toward the end of the 1960s, the Soviet Union achieved overall strategic military parity with the United States. Technological, economic, and military progress also gave the great powers rapid access to all parts of the world. The Soviet Union now has the capability to project military force into Latin America. As a result of these factors, U.S. security policy has been increasingly—indeed, almost exclusively—concerned with the Soviet Union. . . .

Instability: Poverty or Subversion?

Because the United States' principal concern is with threats occurring *through* Latin America, its goal is to prevent the emergence of conditions that would favor Soviet influence. This objective is expressed in the search for internal "stability" in each Latin American country. The United States does not pretend that Latin America should play an active military role in a global conflict with the Soviet Union. Rather, it should avoid disturbances that might distract U.S. military attention. Latin America must remain "stable." The region's contribution to U.S. security is, therefore, its passivity. . . .

Latin America Must Find Its Own Way

Latin America is struggling to find its place in the world. It is undergoing social, political, and cultural transformations. At the same time, the United States is losing its hegemony in the world. The United States must adapt to that loss as well as accept a Latin America that is transforming.

Carlos Fuentes, *The Center Magazine*, January/February 1987.

The United States' understanding of the way in which "stability" is achieved has great impact on Latin America. In this regard, two points of view coexist in the United States: (1) that political and social instability has domestic causes, such as poverty and oppression; and (2) that instability is provoked by subversive groups with foreign support, principally from the Soviet Union and Cuba. These two views are often merged in different proportions, depending upon the observer's ideological perspective, the Latin American country in question, and the kind of crisis at issue. Different policies derive from each point of view. From the first perspective, economic and social development is necessary to ensure political stability; economic assistance and respect for human rights are the most appropriate means through which to achieve this goal. In contrast, the second perspective emphasizes the role of subversive elements and proposes the use of police, military, and ideological weapons to combat them. This second perspective also favors the formation of political alliances with Latin American groups such as the military, the land-owning oligarchy, and the national business elite, whose interests coincide with U.S. priorities abroad.

Each U.S. administration has combined these two approaches in different proportions, giving rise to a double-faceted policy toward Latin America. However, in recent years the policy emphasis on economic and social development has decreased, and the priority given to combating subversion has risen. This shift strengthens the military and police aspects of the security question. The reasoning behind U.S. policy can be articulated in the following manner: although poverty and repression are at the root of political instability, these problems are centuries old and have deep cultural, institutional, economic, and social bases. There is little that the United States can do to correct this situation in the immediate future. Poverty-stricken masses have always existed, but open political conflicts and social struggles have not broken out because of this. Therefore, if Latin America's economic and social problems are to persist for a long time, and if their solution ultimately depends on far-reaching transformations that are more the responsibility of each Latin American country than of the United States, then it is better for the U.S. government to concentrate its resources on resisting subversive forces. . . .

It follows, therefore, that problems of economic and social development—the fight against poverty, unemployment, the concentration of income and wealth, and economic dependence—are not and cannot be the top priority for U.S. security policy in Latin America. Thus U.S. efforts to maintain political stability in the region rely more on political, ideological, and counterinsurgency actions than on economic and social measures. The U.S. government believes that the former offer greater chances for immediate influence. . . .

The Subordination of Latin America's Economic Interests

When defined in this way, U.S. security goals clash with Latin American economic objectives. Because economic issues have major influence on Latin American security, the region's security interests diverge significantly from those of the United States. This divergence reflects different perspectives regarding the nature of change in Latin America.

Those responsible for the formulation of U.S. foreign policy perceive that socioeconomic change in the region results in the loss of U.S. control over Latin American countries. Some see social change leading to growing polarization, and polarization producing an environment that could attract a Soviet and/or Cuban presence. When an armed uprising against a dictatorship occurs, the common reaction of the dominant elite in the United States is to assume a connection between the insurgent forces and Marxism-Leninism. If the armed revolt should be successful, the strong concern is that the new rulers might establish a "totalitarian" regime with ties to the Soviet Union and Cuba and with an internationalist commitment to encourage subversion in other countries. The United States thus pursues policies intended to prevent such developments, but which in practice produce a self-reinforcing cycle of self-fulfilling prophecy. Even when social change occurs in a democratic context without armed struggle, some U.S. policymakers may fear that politics will eventually become polarized. If a strong Communist party and/or other Marxist groups are present, it is presumed there is a high probability that they will finally resort to violence. It is also assumed that even an elected "Marxist" government will in time be rejected by the people, and therefore the government will attempt to maintain power through the use of force. Consequently, it is necessary to act before this process is far advanced. . . .

US Contempt for Latin America

Past contempt for Latin America by the U.S. is revitalized by today's contempt. Latin America has come to the U.S. offering viable diplomatic solutions to the temporary crisis in Central America. The U.S. has consistently undermined such attempts. Has not the time come for Washington to listen seriously to what the governments of Latin America have to say about themselves, their histories, their laws, and their future?

Carlos Fuentes, *World Press Review*, April 1987.

A similar perception of change is implicit in the so-called domino theory. This image suggests that the example of one country must necessarily shape events in another, thus acquiring further momentum. It does not distinguish among cases: armed struggle, socioeconomic change effected by democratic means, or progressive military regimes. The domino theory has been applied to cases as divergent as Nicaragua under the Sandinistas, Chile under Allende, and Peru under Velasco, although this interpretation has been sustained most vigorously with regard to Nicaragua.

These widely held perceptions in the United States have important economic consequences for Latin America because they link economic transformations in the region with U.S. security concerns. Major changes in Latin America in financial or industrial ownership, in state activities, and in the role of the private sector or foreign capital are perceived in U.S. circles as a threat to the United States' security interests. . . .

From this perspective, U.S. security depends on preventing fundamental economic transformations in Latin America. Of course, the definition of what constitutes a "fundamental" transformation is based less on economic considerations than on a political evaluation of the Latin American government undertaking the measure. For example, the nationalizations of the banking system in Mexico (1982) and petroleum in Venezuela (1976) were viewed with concern, but these actions were not considered to be part of a process of radical social and political change. These countries thus enjoyed greater freedom of action in this regard.

Preventing Structural Change

In the final analysis, the United States' foreign policy toward Latin America is intended to prevent structural transformations. The means available to accomplish this goal include military, ideological, political, and economic policies. Some general comments on these other subjects are necessary to place the question of economic policies in proper perspective.

In military affairs, the United States has attempted to strengthen its relations with Latin American armed forces through training and joint study programs, specialized courses in the United States (and in Panama until 1984), trips abroad for Latin American officers, and personal contacts. The most important development in this area has been the proliferation of "national security doctrines" throughout the region. As a result, Latin American militaries are less concerned with defense against external aggressors than with combating internal enemies. This emphasis became especially pronounced following the Cuban revolution, and during the 1960s national security doctrines evolved to reflect differences among Latin American armed forces. Direct links between the Pentagon and Latin American officers have focused principally on imposing political regimes whose essential function is to fight domestic insurgency.

Latin American armed forces have at their disposal human and material resources disproportionate to any realistic external threat. The concept of internal security embedded in national security doctrines opened up new perspectives to the military, creating much broader opportunities and providing new justifications for exercising political power. These options diverted even more military attention toward political issues and paved the way to military dictatorships. In many cases, even under democratic regimes, the armed forces have become a kind of parallel government.

The United States has also promoted alliances with those sectors of the national economic elite that support large private holdings and foreign capital and that pursue a significant reduction in the role of the state. In Chile, Argentina, and Uruguay during the 1970s, the alliance between the military and the economic elite produced brutally repressive regimes and the application of rigidly monetarist, free-market economic schemes that in the end harmed the national interest.

United States' efforts to prevent change in Latin America also involve ideology. This is because the United States perceives its rivalry with the Soviet Union to be, in part, an ideological struggle. Indiscriminate ideological campaigns against "communism" become particularly damaging to Latin America when they advocate extremist ideas, or concepts that become extremist in the hands of national ruling minorities. One example of this phenomenon is the criticism now being directed against the Catholic church, which some senior U.S. government officials have suggested is an ally of Marxism. Ideological attacks have also had an effect on economic issues by creating a negative image of the state, administrative controls, import substitution, the regulation of foreign investment, and even agreements concerning regional economic integration.

Preserving Dominance

U.S. policies toward Latin America have been interventionist politically, often protectionist in economic terms, increasingly restrictive of immigration, patronizing in style, and unilateral in implementation. These policies have been grounded in insecurity and ultimately aimed at preserving dominance. . . .

The United States should recognize and accept Latin America's many changes instead of ignoring or resisting them. It should regard Latin America's nations as potential partners for confronting shared problems.

Abraham F. Lowenthal, *Minneapolis Star and Tribune*, May 31, 1987.

In the political sphere, the United States has pursued a number of policies intended to slow or inhibit change in Latin America, ranging from attempts to affect electoral campaigns, to so-called covert actions, to the conditioning of governments' foreign policies. . . .

United States policies limit the range of domestic Latin American economic choices concerning issues such as forms of ownership and relations with U.S. banks and corporations; affect particular political and social forces' opportunities to participate in government; and reduce Latin American countries' foreign policy options. For example, with varying degrees of intensity, the United States opposes producer-country agreements to defend the price of raw materials, tariff barriers, agreements among debtor countries intended to obtain more favorable terms of financing, relations with socialist countries, participation in the nonaligned country movement, the procurement of military supplies from non-U.S. sources, and so forth. Although the effectiveness of these actions depends upon the size of the Latin American country and the timing of their application, these different dimensions together constitute a limiting threshold for Latin American political, economic and military initiatives.

To what extent does this limiting threshold really reflect U.S. security interests? There are four kinds of developments that may be considered a threat to the United States: Soviet military bases or a Soviet or Cuban military presence in other Latin American countries; an internal political struggle in which leftist forces have independent military capabilities and may be assumed to have military connections with the Soviet Union and/or Cuba; situations in which there is a strong, dominant Communist party in a governing political coalition, or in which such a party may come to power by electoral means; and international policies that are systematically hostile to the U.S. government.

Because situations such as these allow the U.S. government to hold a broad range of interpretations, it is of utmost importance to define the threshold in U.S.-Latin American security relations more precisely. However, because the United States' goal is to prevent the emergence of threatening situations, an administration often reacts before specific facts and trends are fully known. Rapid responses require that the U.S. government hold a "theory" about the possible evolution of events. It is at this level that subjective views regarding potential security threats become important. The security threshold thus remains uncertain for Latin America, and the region's relative autonomy depends upon a particular U.S. administration's ideological orientation.

The fact that this threshold is blurred constrains Latin America's behavior precisely because it is uncertain when the United States may react forcefully to perceived security threats and what means it may employ. This uncertainty causes Latin American governments to proceed with extreme caution. One might argue that uncertainty is an integral part of U.S. security policy insofar as it constitutes a deterrent. . . .

Constraints on US Policy

To the extent to which U.S. policies confuse security with control and the maintenance of past relationships, any significant advance in Latin American autonomy will be seen as a threat to U.S. security. In contrast, a less hegemonic U.S. posture that recognizes changes in relative economic power would reduce tensions and encourage the development of a more mature hemispheric relationship. The growing interrelationship between Latin American economies and the economies of the United States and other developed capitalist countries makes extremely unlikely a political-economic rupture that would bring Latin America under Soviet influence. This closely woven network of economic ties with Latin America provides the United States with a system of coordination and cooperation that is a much more effective guarantee of U.S. security interests in the region than political and ideological pressures that attempt to enforce a rigid East-West alignment. . . .

The subordination of Latin America's strategic interests to those of the United States was largely due to a severe imbalance in economic power. Consequently, improving Latin America's strategic position depends on its becoming stronger economically. Latin American countries have undertaken a number of collective initiatives intended to achieve greater relative power, including both economic agreements and some forms of political coordination. Attempts at regional economic integration, joint industrial programing, financial and commercial agreements, laws regulating foreign investment, and the coordination of foreign economic policies in international forums are all examples of such actions in the economic field. The defense of principles of nonintervention and self-determination have also helped limit U.S. intervention in Latin American countries' internal affairs.

However, these measures have not fully succeeded in transforming economic potential into economic power. Latin America has enlarged its productive base, but when each country acts alone it cannot realize the full significance of this change. There is no collective Latin American vision of economic security, and Latin American perceptions of the region's subordination have scarcely been altered. Collective actions by Latin American countries are rare, and few Latin Americans think of the region in Latin American terms.

Greater Autonomy

A collective strategy to defend national and regional interests must be accompanied by efforts to strengthen relative economic power. A shift in relative power might then allow Latin America to achieve greater autonomy vis-à-vis the United States. Latin America's attempts to strengthen its international economic position should focus on measures that correct the basic asymmetry of the region's economic relations with industrialized countries; establish a multipolar global economic framework; and strengthen developing countries' coordination mechanisms, especially those multilateral organizations in which they have the most influence.

"[Latin America must] open the borders wide to foreign influence."

Latin America Must Imitate the US

Carlos Alberto Montaner

Carlos Alberto Montaner is Cuban-born and has had articles published in dozens of newspapers in the United States, Latin America, and Spain. His books include *Two Hundred Years of Gringos* and *Cuba and Castro*. In the following viewpoint, Montaner argues that Latin Americans have "renounced their contribution to shaping their own destiny." Latin Americans must recognize that they themselves are responsible for economic and social stagnation. In order for Latin America to change, he argues, individual countries must humble themselves and imitate the West.

As you read, consider the following questions:

1. What evidence does the author give to illustrate that Latin Americans are intellectually backward?
2. What does Montaner believe that Latin Americans must do to start becoming more innovative?
3. What role should the US play in Latin America's development, according to Montaner?

Why does Latin American society give up its spiritual autonomy and join itself like a parasite to another society that begins to mold it and endow it by increasingly handing down its accomplishments? One reasonable answer is this: the essential feature of North American society is the search for change, the construction of an ever different destiny. In this quest, North Americans consider only their own society as a point of reference. To be a permanent center of new initiatives governed by its own internal dialectic, the United States does not follow the lead of Europeans. Europe and the rest of the planet are yoked to the American engine, which sometimes advances in the direction of astral space, and other times gets immersed in the microuniverse of biogenetics. The United States drags with it the other countries of the world in the direction of innovation and toward the acceleration of growing technological complexity.

We Latin Americans, with more inhabitants than the United States, possess as much or more potential wealth. Spawned by Europe—just as the United States—we have universities that are more than four hundred years old. We have urban centers that were already established when Chicago was a prairie overrun by buffalo. Unconsciously, we have renounced our contribution to shaping our own destiny. Today we treat and tomorrow we will cure those illnesses that some foreign laboratory could already fight effectively. We will live longer because of advances in geriatrics in California or Texas. We will have fewer children because of birth control methods perfected in New York or Tokyo. We will learn better if our teaching methods come to terms with computer technology, devised by multinational corporations. We will be taller or shorter or we will have fewer abnormal children, if genetic transmission chains are correctly deciphered at Harvard or Stanford. We will have more fun if the video recorder is perfected and made cheaper in the Silicon Valley. All of these things are given or sold to us ready-made. Everything that we are and will be is given to us because we do not control our own lives. We move along indifferently without even a plan against the essential immorality that tolerates this paralysis of creativity. In the bloody history of our social struggle, no group has had as its main goal the assumption of an active role in the shaping of our national destiny.

Passing on Guilt

We become hoarse crying out for our rights, but we have forgotten our responsibilities to ourselves and to concerns that link us to our destiny. We are accustomed to passing the guilt and responsibility on to others. We do not realize that in almost five centuries at a university such as San Marcos, hardly a discovery of scientific importance was made, and not one original idea was advanced

40

in the humanities. Nothing and nobody except ourselves would prevent an Edison, Bell, Freud, Kant, Einstein, or Heidegger from flourishing in Lima, Havana, Caracas, or Mexico City. Latin American societies do not encourage new ideas. We are unconcerned with the task of changing the world in which we live. We do not allow for our own creativity. It would be wrong to suggest that we live in backward societies that despise changes, since we are so pleased to notice them when they occur. We are simply reluctant to initiate those changes on our own. We have not understood that it is audacity and innovation that determine the course of history, not the other way around. We have not understood that it has been five centuries since the object of our civilization has been changed. That is why we have become marginal nations.

Indigenous Problems of Latin America

The real issue is the policies of the Latin American countries themselves. I agree that the problems of Latin America are primarily indigenous.

Jeffrey Wallin, *The Center Magazine*, January/February 1987.

No doubt the radical will find another example of imperialism's evil in these words. He thinks that subjection is not only the commercial rape by the powerful, but a dreadful intangible influence. Our poor revolutionaries have never gone more than skin-deep in their analysis of social evils. They stir up bloody revolutions in order to change unjust situations. They do not understand that in these modern times the most profound revolutions take place not in the barracks or in the mountains, but in the laboratories and in the offices of the most daring intelligentsia. Radical transformation of the roots of our societies will not be brought about solely through changes in property distribution, through the violent removal of the powerful elite, or by drastic constitutional modifications. Radical change will not come about without progress in science and technology, aided by the new perceptions of progressive humanists. The contours of all societies and the directions in which they move are dictated by creative world centers, not by ideological barricades. This is true of Castro's Cuba as well as of Pinochet's Chile.

Preaching Against Foreign Influence

Certain nationalists raise their voices in support of the traditional heritage of Hispanic-American countries. Anyone who preaches against foreigners or things foreign can find an audience to listen and to applaud his ravings. A more serious look into the problem suggests the opposite approach: open the borders wide to foreign influences in a conscious way. Although the concept of nationhood is strongly entrenched in our beliefs, it has practically lost all significance. Imitation of North America is symptomatic of a world phenomenon that will be difficult to change in the near future. It is useless to rant against blue jeans or rock music because these are only the cosmetic touches of a larger transcultural inventory including antibiotics, television, the jet, and even abstract ideological debate. We are also not untouched by the counterculture, by the antipsychiatry and ecology movements, and by almost all points of view that might encourage our intellect. Reality is terrible, but we cannot ignore it. Our brain, our society's brain, stays outside our borders and—even if it upsets us—there is no way of dispensing with this organ.

The reasonable approach is to humbly accept a model of society that is not going to be generated by us; the process of conformity is irreversible. There is no way of getting off the wagon or of isolating ourselves to avoid the pull from creative centers. Global and instantaneous communications, among other things, have established an interdependence that converts self-sufficiency into an absurd fantasy.

How Do We Become Integrated?

It is impossible to swim against the tide. The reasonable approach is not to break the ties that link us with our "brain." We should try to become part of that brain by taking on some of its creative work. Some may consider this point of view as a "surrender" or as "traitorous"; they should consider that the alternative is worse: to remain in tow by creative centers without even symbolic rebellion or the least bit of spiritual autonomy. Each time these words are calmly heard, it becomes more important to shake off the old restrictions. Each time, it is more essential to understand that nationalism is no longer possible. Words such as *country* and *nation* have lost all meaning except for their old emotional charge. If we could accept that humanity is progressing to a point of uniform convergence, charted by the country that is leading the world, we could play a stronger role in this progress. If we could be in on the final stretch, we would regain our self-respect. There is no other route that will enable us to contribute to our own destiny.

This requires an intense, painful, and collective exercise in humility. We must begin by defining what we are and how we should change in order to join the mainstream. It is wrong, for example, to maintain that our economic and intellectual collapse is the result of decaying social and political structures. No doubt these factors have contributed, but the root of the problem is in our own idiosyncrasies and, to a lesser extent, in our perceptions of history. Latin Americans and their leaders have not considered that the idea of progress and the desire for innovation have determined the course of recent history. We belong to another tradition, the Hispanic or Hispanic-Roman, which thinks of society as immutable. It has a slow vegetable growth which unfolds in a fixed pattern and relegates creativity to an ornamental level. Yesterday, our society gloriously produced Cervantes, Goya, and Valazquez, and today it gives us Vargas Llosa, Garcia Márquez, and Octavio Paz. Seldom do we produce cultural products of worth outside of artistic realms.

Criticizing US of No Help

Self-criticism is a rare commodity in Latin America. Most Latin American intellectuals are inclined to blame the United States for Latin America's shortcomings. This is true of the writers—Gabriel Garcia Marquez, Miguel Asturias, Pablo Neruda, for example—and of the economists, Raul Prebisch and the ECLA school foremost among them.

Self-criticism is *over*-developed in U.S. intellectual circles, with the result that U.S. intellectuals are telling Latin American intellectuals just what they want to hear: that Latin America would be a wonderful place if only it could break out of the clutches of the Yankee devil. The two tendencies reinforce each other, erode the quality of scholarship both in the U.S. and in Latin America, and lead those Latin American intellectuals and politicians who want to do something about Latin America's condition down a dead-end street.

Lawrence E. Harrison, *Catholicism in Crisis*, September 1984.

Living in a static society, we have developed a restricted social outlook. On the periphery of the world it is not necessary to be disciplined, methodical, curious, or constant. If the objectives of our lives were to transform substance or ideas, to question the world in which we live, and to deny it by acts of intellectual rebellion, we would have no choice but to alter our temperaments and to transform our social values. It is a dangerous blunder to keep repeating that the success of countries such as the United States is due to the exploitation of Third World countries or to good fortune in the distribution of natural resources. Each day more experts are convinced that the key element in the development of wealth is "human capital." In 1945, Japan was destroyed, and its people were hungry. Forty years later, it is one of the most prosperous, productive centers of the world. Japan has thoroughly used its immense human capital. What is behind the Japanese—or Swiss, Swedish, German, Korean, English, Singaporean, American, Dutch, or Norwegian—miracle? What is behind the miracle of each society that has risen spectacularly in the last few centuries? It is simple: a temperament adapted to pursued objectives and the use of valuable human capital. If we cannot change our objectives because they have been determined outside of our borders, then we must change our idiosyncrasies in order to substantially improve our human capital. . . .

No Solution Available

Modifying our values to create opportunities for success cannot happen spontaneously and without a plan. We must accept two fundamental hypotheses: First, the causes of our relative backwardness and social and economic failures are to be found within ourselves. Second, it is possible, through an intensive and extensive learning process, to add to our social outlook those values that will determine the success of the civilization in which we live. Any sensible person interested in exercising power in a constructive way realizes that conventional prescriptions have lost ground in the effort to end backwardness, poverty, and inequality in Latin America. This applies to supporters of both the Right and the Left. Who could seriously propose that agrarian reform, economic planning, decentralization, nationalization, or forced industrialization could gain new support from modern citizens? We have been left without a solution because we have credited our misfortunes to external circumstances. Now we know that the sources of our misfortunes are to be found in ourselves, a fact Latin Americans must accept with all its consequences. We are faced with the inevitable decision about how to change ourselves. There is not a trace of utopianism in my proposals. They contain crude realism and coherent logic. . . .

No matter how much our workers and managers are inspired to work more and to work harder, we cannot hope to compete unless we change our fundamental attitudes. We are unable to compete with people who have instilled in their value systems a passion for excellence and a pride in workmanship. These are variables that economic models ignore because they are not easily measured. These are factors that determine the failure of theories when they are put into practice. If today's Chilean or Argentinian industries cannot compete with those of the United States, Japan, Korea, or Taiwan, it is—among other reasons—because the attitudes of men involved in the design, production, and marketing processes are totally different. These differences translate into distinct levels of cost and quality, a situation that cannot be remedied by laws of the market, as optimistically prescribed by proponents of free commerce.

We are condemned to live within the same system and pursue the same objectives as other Western countries. We can only advance toward the vanguard if we emulate the attitudes of those who lead. It is indispensable to reform all our educational efforts to disseminate social virtues and to change aspects of our character that relegate us to oppression and backwardness. This is not a short-term project, but a profound ideological revolution that could steadily improve our repertoire of social virtues over several generations. We can improve to the point of working within the social and economic model that history permits. . . .

The Task of the United States

I have proposed an extensive effort in humility and understanding on the part of Latin America. For this effort not to be futile, a concession from the United States is necessary: a change of attitude toward us. The United States proclaims itself the head of the Western world, but it does not realize its responsibilities outside of the maintenance of military alliances, the transference of marketable technology, or the contribution of capital. The political leaders of the United States, especially those in Congress, usually ignore what happens in Latin America with an attitude bordering on disdain. Jose Martí, who lived a great deal of his adult life in the United States, referred to it as "the mixed-up and brutal North that despises us." Sharing the New World does not necessarily generate affective ties or even curiosity about a neighbor. Hardly a handful of lawmakers in the United States would know the current political parties of Venezuela or Argentina. The United States only notices Latin America when it thunders from the Left, a fact that inevitably creates resentment.

Latin America increasingly adopts the American way of life while surrendering its own spiritual autonomy. An uncomfortable sensation of strangeness arises, a sensation made worse by the near-total indifference of the United States to Latin American countries and governments. No one can seriously believe that we form part of a common perimeter of civilization just because we imitate the United States. We follow the United States like mice following the Pied Piper, without knowing the route but believing it is ours. We are neither consulted nor invited, and sometimes we are not even informed. I am not just referring to political relations, but to all activities that our societies have in common. The United States maintains the fiction that it is the head of the Western world, but there is not a real neck joining that head to Latin America. There are hardly any channels of communication. . . .

The US Role

Some years ago, during the hopeful period of John F. Kennedy, it appeared that the two great cultures of America might begin to come closer together. This turned out to be a useless alliance for progress. Several billion dollars evaporated without bringing about the desired closeness between the two worlds. Today the

United States contemplates with desperation its failure to stop Salvadorian guerillas. Despite its power and the weight of certain arguments, Washington cannot gain the support of Latin American countries for their own defense. Even though this war is being fought on Latin American soil, it is perceived as a responsibility of the United States. If the United States is the unconsulted guardian of our daily activity, it is also responsible for our political destiny. If Latin American countries have no foreign policy, it is because the defenseless character of dependent societies prevents the development of long-term objectives and strategies. If they are not active as agents of history, there is no reason to expect that they will act on foreign policy.

Latin America's Role

The United States should understand that Latin America needs to play a role in the emerging global civilization. The United States should encourage this by gradually inviting Latin Americans to cooperate in the active and creative tasks of development. Not only because of the serious ethical responsibility that the "head" of any organism has toward its "body," but because if Latin America's political and social degradation is allowed to continue, the United States will have to face a growing number of hostile countries. Those countries would hate the power that did not summon them for the tasks of civilization and that systematically chose to ignore them.

"Latin America now desperately needs a new major transfer of capital from the industrialized nations of the world."

More US Aid Is Needed To Help Latin America

Carl J. Migdail

In the late 1950s, the US initiated the Alliance for Progess, an expensive and comprehensive program to aid development in Latin America. Because poverty and underdevelopment persisted in spite of the Alliance, many critics cite it as an example of the ineffectiveness of US aid. In the following viewpoint, Carl J. Migdail, a retired Latin American correspondent for *U.S. News & World Report*, argues the opposite. He believes that the Alliance for Progress did make definite improvements in Latin America and that a new injection of US aid is the key to improving current conditions.

As you read, consider the following questions:

1. What does the author claim was good about the Alliance for Progress?
2. Which country does Migdail believe must lead a new Alliance for Progress?

Carl J. Migdail, "Today's Reality," *Americas*, March /April 1986. Reprinted from *Americas*, a bimonthly magazine published by the Organization of American States in English and Spanish.

People usually turn away quickly and coldly when, in answer to their specific questions after I return from a journalistic swing through Central or South America, I describe what I have seen. The reality of Latin America today, and its gloomy implications for the future, make them uneasy. The inescapable truth, though, which should not be avoided, is that unless major political changes take place in our Hemisphere, the future of Latin America is very bleak indeed.

When I first started work in Latin America—in 1951 for the United Press in Mexico City—the outlook for our region was vastly different. Everywhere there was hope that the future would be better. Problems were huge and seemingly limitless—outmoded and inefficient political, social and economic systems, lack of capital and modern technology, ignorance, disease and hunger. But World War II was over, and a new world was being built that also would include Latin America.

In 1955, when I became Chief of Press at the Organization of American States in Washington, D.C., I discovered the existence of another major positive ingredient that seemed to assure Latin America a gloriously optimistic future—hemispheric solidarity, the conviction that Latin America and the United States, working together through the OAS, could wipe out underdevelopment in every country in the Hemisphere. As the period of the late 1950's and early 1960's now fades from memory, what was accomplished then should not be either underestimated or forgotten.

US Aid and Latin American Development

Collective responsibility for hemispheric development was institutionalized and implemented in 1958 with then Brazilian President Juscelino Kubitschek's call for an "Operation Pan America." The key idea: underdevelopment everywhere in Latin America was a problem of common concern. Then in quick succession came new programs to complete coordination for hemispheric development, such as the Act of Bogatá in 1960 and the Alliance for Progress in 1961. Everybody could feel the accelerating pace of Latin American development and movement toward possible economic integration. The Latin American Free Trade Association started, and Central America formed its common market.

The number of dictatorial regimes in the region began to dwindle as the new spirit of progress also kindled inevitable greater participation in governments by young, talented, civilian technicians. Stirred by its new conscience of joint responsibility for the individual welfare of all Americans, regardless of nationality, the governments of the OAS, in a precedent-shattering trend in the early 1960's, edged toward setting aside traditional straitjackets of national sovereignty to allow multilateral involvement in the observance of guarantees of human rights in each country of this

Hemisphere.

Then in only a few years came the disastrous disintegration of the idea of Western Hemisphere unity and collective responsibility for development, which has brought us today to a generalized feeling of hopelessness in Latin America. Survival, not progress, now has become the daily problem for most leaders of the region.

Aid Linked to Progress

We have taken great satisfaction in the remarkable trend toward democracy taking place in Latin America and the Caribbean. We have supported this trend, not only because it is in accord with our deepest values but also because we believe it is in our interest. We have found that we can have the most stable long-term relationships with countries where government is founded on the consent of the governed. . . .

Without adequate economic aid to assist several of these democratic countries to recover and realize the economic betterment of their people, the odds for sustaining democracy will become much less favorable. Moreover, we have an economic stake in the prosperity of our neighbors.

Elliott Abrams, speech before the Senate Foreign Relations Committee, March 25, 1987.

Many things contributed to the reversal of the tide of joint progress. Governments in Latin America mismanaged their economies. With progress came even more, not less, corruption in some countries. The United States, beset by its headaches in Vietnam, turned away from Latin America. With the triumph of Fidel Castro's revolution in 1959, Cuba offered the left in Latin America a faster and more radical approach than the evolutionary goals of the Alliance for Progress.

US Aid a Failure?

Now revisionists consider the Alliance for Progress a classic example of the failure of the United States and Latin America to act as international social engineers. After passing through inconclusive periods of low-profile policy toward Latin America, the United States is now anxious to avoid multilateral programs. Critics of the Alliance for Progress in Latin America and the United States do not ask, however, how much sooner the entire region would have arrived at today's dire condition of permanent economic and social crises if there had not been a massive, joint hemispheric effort at development 25 years ago.

A huge transfer of resources from north to south—Latin America's over $360 billion foreign debt—already has taken place, and conditions in most countries are worse than before. Mexicans, who are crushed by the burden of a $100 billion foreign debt, feel their country's recent spectacular oil boom hurt, not helped, them. Peru's dynamic new President, Alan García, knows that, under present conditions, there is little chance he can improve the substandard way of life of most of his countrymen. And when we discuss the condition of Latin America, the tendency is to shy away from even mentioning Bolivia, where officials have estimated the 1985 inflation rate at over 20,000 percent.

Joint Development a Necessity

Latin America now desperately needs a new major transfer of capital from the industrialized nations of the world. But this time those nations do not have the capital readily available for transfer, and they lack the political will to make the sacrifices needed to do so. In addition, even if billions of dollars in investment money once again flowed south, Latin America probably would mismanage and waste the new resources much as it did before.

This, unfortunately, is today's reality. There is also now a total lack of collective will for mutual development. The OAS has become a multilateral instrument trying to recuperate its mission. And this Hemisphere was left emotionally and politically divided after the South Atlantic conflict of 1982.

Without a firm, persistent political decision by the industrialized nations led by the United States to join Latin America in a new era of joint development, this unpleasant future seems inevitable: the industrialized nations, now entering a new period of technological breakthroughs based on computers and the use of robots in production, move way ahead. Most countries of Latin America remain in the present daily struggle to stay as they are or slip backward into increasing anarchy or senseless violence that can only aggravate national problems.

"I am convinced that it is the way Latin Americans see the world—their values and attitudes—that are the principal obstacle to progress in Latin America."

US Aid Will Not Help Latin America

Lawrence E. Harrison

Lawrence E. Harrison served in the US Agency for International Development (AID) for twenty years, during which time he directed aid programs in five Latin American countries. He is the author of a highly controversial book, *Under-Development Is a State of Mind: the Latin American Case*, in which he insists that Latin Americans are responsible for their country's economic stagnation and debt. In the following viewpoint, he explains this theory and concludes that Latin American countries must change their culture and attitudes to solve their economic troubles.

As you read, consider the following questions:

1. What differences does Harrison see between Latin American nations and the democratic nations of the US and Canada? Why are these differences significant?
2. On what does the author believe Latin America's progress depends?
3. The author argues that there are several Latin values and attitudes that must change for progress to occur. What are they?

Lawrence E. Harrison, "Latin America's Trouble Isn't Our Fault," *The Washington Post National Weekly Edition*, April 14, 1986. © The Washington Post. Reprinted with permission.

The 25th anniversary of President Kennedy's speech inaugurating the Alliance for Progress [occurred in March 1986]. The Alliance's vision for Latin America was a democratic, socially progressive, economically dynamic one, which would inoculate the area against the Castro infection. Conceived as a 10-year program, the Alliance was staggered by a spate of military takeovers in 1963 and 1964, by Kennedy's assassination and by the U.S. military intervention in the Dominican Republic in 1965. By the end of the '60s, it was essentially dead. Puerto Rican Operation Bootstrap architect Teodoro Moscoso, first U.S. coordinator of the Alliance, wrote its epitaph:

". . . just as no human being can save another who does not have the will to save himself, no country can save others no matter how good its intentions or how hard it tries. The Latin American countries have been too dependent on the United States, while the United States has been too nosey and eager to force down the throats of its southern neighbors its way of doing things."

The achievements of the Alliance were not insignificant, particularly in education and health, and also in economic growth, which approximated the 2.5 percent per capita annual Alliance target well into the '70s. The Alliance also reinforced the beleaguered democratic currents in Latin America that have led to the recent hopeful democratization trends. But authoritarian military governments dominated politics until recently, and the distribution of income, wealth and land in most countries continues to be skewed heavily toward the few who are rich and powerful.

Uncomfortable Questions

The success of the Marshall Plan was the measure of the shortfall of the Alliance. To understand this shortfall, one must ask several uncomfortable questions that derive from the vast differences in political, economic and social progress between Latin America on the one hand and the United States and Canada on the other:

• Why is the average North American 15 to 20 times better off economically than the average Latin American?

• Why are income, wealth and land far more equitably distributed in the United States and Canada than in Latin America?

• Why are proportionally so many more North Americans literate than Latin Americans?

• Why are democratic political institutions, due process and civilian control of the military so deeply rooted in the United States and Canada and so rare in Latin America?

• Why does the typical Latin American chief of state—and I hasten to acknowledge that there are exceptions—leave office vastly richer than when he entered?

Illustration by Craig MacIntosh

Craig MacIntosh. Reprinted by permission of the Star Tribune: Newspaper of the Twin Cities.

In the early '60s many of us explained these dramatic contrasts by U.S. neglect of Latin America; we prescribed a large dose of Yankee ingenuity and resources. Most Latin Americans endorsed this prescription, notwithstanding its strong implication of Latin American impotence, at least partly because it did not force Latin Americans to look inward for explanations of Latin America's condition.

Searching for External Causes

The search for external causes reached its pinnacle with the dependency theory vogue, which first appeared in the '60s and is still with us. It wasn't neglect by the United States; it was exploitation by the United States, which made itself rich by keeping Latin America poor. The United States allegedly bought Latin America's primary products cheaply while charging high prices for its manufactured exports. Meanwhile, U.S. investors were allegedly reaping unconscionable profits from their investments in Latin America.

Dependency theory is an intellectual construct that doesn't hold water and leads Latin America down a dead-end street. Some of the evidence that it is largely mythical:

• The United States, Canada and Australia all developed rapidly and democratically during the 19th century as exporters of primary products and recipients of large infusions of foreign investment. Today, the United States is the world's largest exporter of primary products.

• Foreign trade and foreign investment represent a small fraction of the U.S. economy, which may be the most self-sufficient in the world, at least among the advanced countries. The total effective demand of the five Central American countries for U.S. products approximates that of Springfield, Mass.

• Trade with and investment in Latin America represent a small fraction of the U.S. total worldwide. The bulk of both is with Western Europe, Canada and Japan. The United States trades more with and invests more in Canada than all of Latin America.

• There is evidence that Latin American countries with relatively more U.S. investment (Costa Rica, for example) have done better than those with relatively less (such as Nicaragua). There is also evidence that Latin American businessmen have taken substantially more out of their countries than have foreign businessmen, both in higher profit margins and capital flight.

Latin America's Vast Resources

Most people agree that Latin America's resource endowment is at least comparable to that of Canada and the United States. If dependency theory is largely a myth, how else can we explain the striking discrepancy in political, economic and social progress? What *really* explains why the Alliance for Progress foundered?

After 25 years of working on Latin America's development problems, I am convinced that it is the way Latin Americans see the world—their values and attitudes—that are the principal obstacle to progress in Latin America. Those values and attitudes derive from traditional Hispanic culture, which nurtures authoritarianism, an excessive individualism, mistrust, corruption and a fatalistic world view, all of which work against political pluralism and economic and social progress. That culture also attaches a low value to work, particularly among the elite, and discourages entrepreneurship, thus further braking economic growth. . . .

In this hemisphere it is the United States that has played the principal regional role in promoting democratic development, above all by its example but also by its policies, including the Alliance for Progress, the Carter administration's emphasis on human rights and the Reagan administration's current emphasis on democratic solutions.

Latin America Must Change

Latin America's future progress will depend importantly on its ability to see itself objectively; to suppress the tendency to seek foreign scapegoats; to work toward the kinds of cultural change that will improve the prospects for democratic progress; and to assume responsibility for its own future. Those kinds of values and attitudes could perpetuate the current wave of democratization.

But past performance suggests that there are strong cultural currents at work that threaten democratic continuity and economic dynamism. The fatal flaw of the Alliance for Progress was its failure to recognize the force of these currents. The promising crop of Latin American democrats now in power will inevitably get caught up in them.

Simply by surviving and turning over power to a freely elected successor—a process that a prominent Nicaraguan oppositionist asserts has never occurred from one party to another in Nicaragua—these leaders will have overcome long odds and contributed to changed expectations on the part of their countrymen. But even then, democracy and economic dynamism will be far from ensured. The demise of democracy in Chile and its interruption in Uruguay demonstrate how fragile pluralism is in Latin America, even in societies where it appears deeply rooted.

Enlightened Latin American leaders can make progress on such problems as literacy, health, economic policy and population growth. But they may be able to effect only small changes in the values and attitudes that are the principal obstacles to progress, many of which have endured for almost five centuries. The most important—and difficult—challenge to those committed to progress in Latin America is how to accelerate constructive cultural change.

Recognizing Ethnocentrism

Ethnocentrism is the attitude or tendency of people to view their own race, religion, culture, group, or nation as superior to others, and to judge others on that basis. An American, whose custom is to eat with a fork or spoon, would be making an ethnocentric statement when saying, "The Chinese custom of eating with chopsticks is stupid."

Ethnocentrism has promoted much misunderstanding and conflict. It emphasizes cultural and religious differences and the notion that one's national institutions or group customs are superior.

Ethnocentrism limits people's ability to be objective and to learn from others. Education in the truest sense stresses the similarities of the human condition throughout the world and the basic equality and dignity of all people.

Most of the following statements are taken from the viewpoints in this book. Some have other origins. Consider each statement carefully. *Mark E for any statement you think is ethnocentric. Mark N for any statement you think is not ethnocentric. Mark U if you are undecided about any statement.*

If you are doing this activity as a member of a class or group, compare your answers with those of other class or group members. Be able to defend your answers. You may discover that others will come to different conclusions than you. Listening to the reasons others present for their answers may give you valuable insights in recognizing ethnocentric statements.

E = ethnocentric
N = not ethnocentric
U = undecided

1. In Haiti, 87 percent of the children suffer malnutrition and 82 percent of the population is illiterate.

2. Because the miseries of traditional life are familiar, they are bearable to ordinary people who, growing up in the society, learn to cope.

3. The subordination of Latin America's strategic interests to those of the US is due to an imbalance in economic power.

4. Our lack of concern for Third World residents is quite proper because the lower orders feel no pain.

5. The US presence in the Caribbean and Central America is an effort to bring development to these backward lands.

6. The United States does not follow the lead of Europeans. Europe and the rest of the planet are yoked to the US.

7. The United States will not allow any constructive development in the nations under its domination.

8. We live in chaos and under dictatorships because the United States intervenes in our countries.

9. Hong Kong, Taiwan, and South Korea, poor countries of 30 years ago, are now prosperous nations.

10. Economic and social development cannot be the top priority for US security policy in Latin America.

11. Latin America has urban centers that were already established when Chicago was a prairie overrun by buffalo.

12. Latin America follows the United States like mice following the Pied Piper.

13. The United States must join Latin America in a new era of joint development.

14. The US has been too nosey and eager to force down the throats of its southern neighbors its way of doing things.

15. In this hemisphere, the United States has played the principal regional role in promoting democracy.

16. Latin American attitudes are the principal obstacle to progress.

Periodical Bibliography

The following periodical articles have been selected to supplement the diverse views expressed in this chapter.

Adolfo Gilly	"Central America and the Crisis of US Hegemony," *Contemporary Marxism*, Fall 1985.
Charles Krauthammer	"Guerrilla Warfare: Morality and the Reagan Doctrine," *Current*, February 1987.
Irving Kristol	"A Transatlantic 'Misunderstanding,'" *Encounter*, March 1985.
Warren L. McFerran	"Losing Latin America," *The New American*, June 8, 1987.
Jeff McMahan	"Turning the Tide," *Monthly Review*, January 1987.
Michael Novak	"The Missing Roots of Democracy," *Los Angeles Times*, April 3, 1987.
Ronald Reagan	"A Force for Freedom in the Caribbean," *Department of State Bulletin*, September 1984.
Ronald Reagan	"Central America and US Security," *Department of State Bulletin*, May 1986.
Andrew A. Reding	"Books on Latin America," *America*, March 28, 1987.
Viron P. Vaky	"Political Change in Latin America: A Foreign Policy Dilemma for the United States," *Journal of Inter-American Studies and World Affairs*, Summer 1986.

How Should the US Deal with Latin American Human Rights Conditions?

Chapter Preface

Promoting human rights in other countries has always been a stated goal of US foreign policy. This goal, however, is often in conflict with other stated goals, such as promoting democracy and stopping communism. These conflicting foreign policy concerns often place the US in the uncomfortable position of defending inconsistent policies in Latin America. For example, the US continues to aid friendly dictators like Augusto Pinochet in Chile in spite of widespread evidence that his government is directly responsible for politically-motivated torture and murder. Many US analysts believe this stance is fully justifiable: The US cannot afford to alienate these dictators because it is engaged in a global power contest with the Soviet Union. If economic and military support were withdrawn, these Latin American countries would turn to the Soviet Union to supply them, as Cuba did.

Critics of this position argue that by aligning with such unseemly characters, the US seeds hatred and poverty among the citizenry of these countries. When the dictator is overthrown, as Somoza was in Nicaragua, the populace does not forget that the US sponsored their oppression. The authors in this chapter debate what importance the US should place on promoting Latin American human rights.

"Abusive governments should be publicly condemned."

The US Should Apply Sanctions to Repressive Regimes

The Americas Watch Report on Human Rights and
US Policy in Latin America

Should the US take some type of action against repressive Latin American dictatorships? Many argue that the US has a moral obligation to condemn these regimes by applying trade and economic sanctions against them. In the following viewpoint, the Americas Watch Human Rights group argues that US pressure can do much to alleviate the torture and political oppression many Latin Americans experience. The Americas Watch has monitored human rights conditions in Latin America, and US policy toward them, since 1981.

As you read, consider the following questions:

1. How does the US "do harm" in Latin America, according to the authors?
2. What successes of US policy do the authors cite?
3. Both Ted Carpenter, author of the opposing viewpoint, and Americas Watch agree that current US human rights policy is ineffective. On what point do they disagree?

From WITH FRIENDS LIKE THESE: THE AMERICAS WATCH REPORT ON HUMAN RIGHTS AND U.S. POLICY IN LATIN AMERICA by Americas Watch. Reprinted by permission of Pantheon Books, a Division of Random House, Inc.

An ancient maxim of medical practice cautions: *Primum non nocere* (First do no harm). It is a maxim that is also relevant when recommending a policy to guide the United States in dealing with human rights practices in other countries.

The Reagan administration has done harm by its public praise for governments that systematically abuse human rights, as when its first secretary of state, Alexander Haig proclaimed "dramatic, dramatic reductions" in human rights abuses in Chile, Paraguay, Argentina, and Uruguay while they were still under brutal military rule; when Ambassador Jeane Kirkpatrick purported to see "elements of constitutionalism" in the military dictatorships in Chile, Argentina, and Uruguay; when Kirkpatrick praised the "moral quality" of the government of El Salvador at a time when its army and death squads were killing thousands; and when President Reagan asserted that then President Rios Montt of Guatemala was "totally dedicated to democracy" and that complaints of human rights abuses by the Rios Montt government were "a bum rap."

The Reagan administration has done harm by its public embrace of those responsible for gross abuses, as when Ambassador Kirkpatrick traveled to Chile to greet President Pinochet and announce a desire "to fully normalize our relations" and as when then President (General) Viola of Argentina, a principal author of the "dirty war," traveled to Washington to become one of the first foreign heads of state to be received officially in Washington by the Reagan administration; and when another Argentine general with blood on his hands, Leopoldo Galtieri (subsequently president; later imprisoned like Viola) was sponsored by the Defense Department on an official visit to the United States. . . .

The Reagan administration has done harm by systematically disregarding U.S. law and international law on human rights and, in the process, undermining efforts to protect human rights by establishing the rule of law.

How To Handle Abusive Governments

In part, a policy that promotes human rights involves doing the opposite of those things that do harm. Abusive governments should be publicly condemned. Public praise should go to those leaders who improve the protection of human rights, and the United States should distance itself from those responsible for abuses. Those who report on human rights abuses, often at great risk to themselves, should be honored. Blame ought to be placed squarely where it belongs, on those committing abuses. Demonstrating respect for both domestic and international law should be a constant concern.

The record of the Reagan administration in dealing with the death squad issue in El Salvador illustrates both the harm that can be done by U.S. policy and what can be accomplished when that policy shifts.

From its first days in office, the Reagan administration stoutly denied that the death squads were controlled by the security forces, attributing the murders they committed to "extremes of the right and the left." As late as August 1983, Elliott Abrams asserted, "The assumption that the death squads are active security forces remains to be proved. It might be right, though I suspect it probably isn't right." If anything, such assertions helped to embolden the death squads and, in the fall of 1983, their victims included well-known labor leaders and political figures, including an official of the Salvadoran Foreign Ministry judged to be insufficiently anti-Communist. The U.S. Congress became increasingly alarmed about the links between the armed forces and the death squads, which were widely publicized in the press, and pressure on the Reagan administration increased. Finally, on December 11, 1983, Vice President Bush visited El Salvador, and in a meeting with thirty-one top military commanders, he issued an ultimatum: The death squad activity must be curbed, or continued U.S. aid was in jeopardy. Death squad killings in the first half of 1984 dropped to less than a quarter of the number in the first half of 1983. By mid-1984, the number of such killings

"ALAS, POOR FERDINAND—I KNEW HIM WELL.....ALAS, POOR BABY DOC... ...ALAS, POOR SHAH...ALAS, POOR SOMOZA...ALAS, POOR...."

Doug Marlette, *The Charlotte Observer.* Reprinted with permission.

each month was less than 10 percent of what it had been a year earlier.

The decline in death squad killings shows that money talks. This was also demonstrated in the May 1984 trial and sentencing of five Salvadoran national guardsmen convicted of murdering four U.S. churchwomen. For three years, the churchwomen's case had hung in limbo. Finally, wearying of the State Department's promises of "progress" on the case, the U.S. Congress enacted legislation that withheld $19 million in military aid pending a trial and verdict in the case. Faced with the loss of a significant portion of their military assistance, the Salvadoran military authorities allowed the trial to go forward.

Given the demonstrated effect that withholding—or seriously threatening to withhold—military aid has had on the Salvadoran armed forces, it is tragic that the Reagan administration has not employed the same strategy to end more pervasive atrocities: army and air force killings of civilian noncombatants in guerrilla-controlled zones. One would think that the United States would have an even better chance to end human rights violations committed by uniformed military personnel than by shadowy auxiliary gunmen. In fact, the United States has trained an entire generation of young officers and outfitted them with everything from uniforms to 750-pound bombs. Yet targeted bombings of homes, schools, crops, and civilians themselves; ground attacks against defenseless women, children, and old people; and rape, torture, and execution of captured guerrilla soldiers and civilians happen so frequently that these acts may be considered the Salvadoran armed forces' policy. It may be that the United States has not used its influence, financial and otherwise, to end such indiscriminate killings because it considers that these are necessary to win the war. Yet among those committed to that end, there are some who consider indiscriminate attacks to be counterproductive. . . .

A Meaningful Policy

For a human rights policy to be meaningful, it should be pursued even when other interests, or perceived interests, suffer as a consequence. Yet there are limits, of course. International law permits the restriction of certain rights in times of national emergency to the extent strictly required by the emergency; domestic law in the United States permits the restriction of even the rights to speak and assemble in circumstances of clear and present danger. By the same token, efforts to promote human rights internationally may be suspended to the extent necessary to preserve the national security of the United States in circumstances of great danger. The damage to a general effort to promote human rights need not be severe—so long as it is explicitly acknowledged that efforts to promote human rights are being suspended and for what reasons.

Acknowledgment permits debate over whether the circumstances are so threatening to national security as to warrant the suspension of efforts to promote human rights. On the other hand, failure to acknowledge that this is what is being done puts an administration in a position where it falsely claims to be maintaining an effort to promote human rights and to be accomplishing that end through the selfsame policy being implemented to pursue national security interests. This is the position into which the Reagan administration has put itself in the case of El Salvador. The contradiction is unfortunate from several standpoints.

Enemies of Freedom

The enemy of freedom is dictatorship, left or right. I believe that. Where we have the power to change it, we should. Where we do not have that power, we should draw a moral and judgmental political line between us and the tyrants, making this plain to oppressor and oppressed.

A. M. Rosenthal, *The New York Times Magazine*, March 23, 1986.

It is unfortunate because it limits the opportunity of Americans to debate forthrightly whether their national security interests are so vitally affected by the war in El Salvador as to warrant suspension of efforts to promote human rights. It is unfortunate because it requires the administration to misrepresent events in El Salvador in an effort to argue that its policies are in fact promoting human rights. This is what prompts officials to attack the motives and methods of human rights organizations with a gloomier view of the situation.

It is also unfortunate because, in the process of misrepresenting developments, the administration places itself in a position where, to save its face, it cannot take the positive actions within its power. . . .

Admitting Human Rights Abuses

The Reagan administration would have done far less damage to human rights in El Salvador if it frankly acknowledged all abuses but claimed that U.S. security interests were so overriding as to justify extensive military assistance to the Salvadoran armed forces despite their abuses. Most likely, it did not take this course because it feared it might lose the debate that would have ensued. . . .

At times when governments themselves undertake efforts to promote human rights, the United States should provide support, both through symbolic diplomatic gestures and materially.

When confronted with unprecedented slaughter in Uganda in 1978, the U.S. Congress enacted legislation banning the import of Ugandan products to the United States and the export of U.S. goods to Uganda. The loss of an important market for Ugandan coffee as well as much-needed U.S.-manufactured items contributed to the undermining of President Idi Amin, who was overthrown a year later. . . .

Though drastic economic measures can be justified on human rights grounds in circumstances such as those in Guatemala, military intervention is quite another thing. Though exceptions might be warranted when crimes against humanity are committed on the scale of Nazi Germany or Cambodia under the Khmer Rouge, the rule should be that military invasion, either directly or by proxy, should not be undertaken to promote human rights. For one thing, it is likely that military intervention will worsen the human rights situation, as has happened in Nicaragua where measures restricting human rights are justified by the government because of the emergency resulting from the U.S.-sponsored invasion, and where the *contras* themselves have committed many serious abuses. For another, as is also exemplified by Nicaragua, the actual reasons for the invasion are likely to be rooted in political and geopolitical considerations. The use, or abuse, of a human rights rationale to justify military intervention can only degrade the human rights cause.

If the first rule in promoting human rights is to avoid doing harm, the second rule is that human rights should be promoted for their own sake, not as part of an effort to achieve some other end. It is the failure to distinguish between the other interests of the United States and concern for human rights that so frequently leads us into doing harm.

"Cordial diplomatic and economic relations should be encouraged with all governments that are willing to reciprocate, be they democratic, authoritarian, royalist, or Marxist."

The US Should Not Restrict Foreign Relations with Repressive Regimes

Ted Galen Carpenter

Ted Galen Carpenter is a foreign policy analyst at the Cato Institute, a conservative think tank focusing on economic issues. In the following viewpoint, Carpenter describes the huge inconsistencies in US human rights policies in the last three decades. He argues that the US should maintain diplomatic and trade relations with all Third World countries, no matter how oppressive their governments might be.

As you read, consider the following questions:

1. What are the US government's justifications for its current policy, and how does Carpenter criticize them?
2. Why does the author insist that the US will benefit from maintaining trade relations with repressive regimes?
3. What problems does the author claim "benign detachment" by the US would resolve?

Ted Galen Carpenter, "The United States and Third World Dictatorships: A Case for Benign Detachment," *CATO Institute Policy Analysis*, No. 58, August 15, 1985. Reprinted with permission.

It is a central dilemma of contemporary American foreign policy that the world's leading capitalist democracy must confront an environment in which a majority of nations are neither capitalist nor democratic. U.S. leaders have rarely exhibited ingenuity or grace in handling this delicate and often frustrating situation.

The current turmoil in Central America is illustrative of a larger problem. American officials assert that this vital region is under assault from doctrinaire communist revolutionaries trained, funded, and controlled by the Soviet Union. Danger to the well-being of the United States is immediate and serious, administration spokesmen argue, and it is imperative that the Marxist-Leninist tide be prevented from engulfing Central America. Accomplishing this objective requires a confrontational posture toward the communist beachhead (Nicaragua) combined with massive support for all "friendly" regimes, ranging from democratic Costa Rica to autocratic Guatemala. Washington's Central American policy displays in microcosm most of the faulty assumptions underlying America's approach to the entire Third World.

Siege Mentality

The current strategy of the United States betrays a virtual siege mentality. It was not always thus. Throughout the nineteenth century U.S. policymakers exuded confidence that the rest of the world would emulate America's political and economic system, seeing the United States as a "beacon on the hill" guiding humanity to a better future. As late as the 1940s, most Americans and their political representatives still believed that democracy would triumph as a universal system. . . .

The actual results were acutely disappointing. No wave of new democracies occurred in this "Third World"; instead, decolonization produced a plethora of dictatorships, some of which appeared distressingly friendly to Moscow. This development was especially disturbing to Washington since it took place at a time when America's cold war confrontation with the USSR was at its most virulent. The nature and magnitude of that struggle caused American leaders to view the Third World primarily as another arena in the conflict. Consequently, the proliferation of left-wing revolutionary movements and governments seemed to undermine America's own security and well-being.

Washington's response to this adversity has been a particularly simplistic and unfortunate one. American leaders increasingly regarded any anticommunist regime, however repressive and undemocratic it might be at home, as an "ally," a "force for stability," and even a "friend." At the same time, they viewed leftist governments—even those elected under democratic procedures—as little more than Soviet surrogates, or at least targets of opportunity for communist machinations. . . .

It is reprehensible for a government that preaches the virtues of noninterference in the internal affairs of other nations to have amassed such a record of interference. The level of shame mounts when American meddling undermines a sister democracy and helps install a repressive autocracy. Yet in Iran, Guatemala, Zaire, and Chile that was precisely what happened. Post-Mossadegh Iran endured the shah's corrupt authoritarianism for 25 years before desperately embracing the fanaticism of the Ayatollah Khomeini. Guatemala after Arbenz has witnessed a dreary succession of military dictatorships, each one rivaling its predecessor in brutality. The ouster of Patrice Lumumba facilitated the rise to power of Mobutu Sese Seko (nee Joseph Mobutu) in Zaire. Mobutu's regime is regarded as one of the most corrupt and repressive on any continent.

Recognizing Realities

The decision about just when and how to withdraw support from a dictatorship is excruciatingly difficult. There are no rules, no laws; choices must be made case by case with subtlety, sophistication and patience. Differences of degree as well as kind must be recognized. It is not enough to put governments into two files, democratic and undemocratic. There are regimes that are improving and regimes that are deteriorating. There are sound and unsound democracies, tolerable and intolerable dictatorships, more or less repression.

Henry Grunwald, *Time*, May 12, 1986.

Perhaps Chile is the saddest case of all. Although deified by Western liberals, Salvador Allende had his unsavory qualities. His enthusiasm for Marxist economic bromides pushed his nation to the brink of disaster. He also exhibited a nasty authoritarian streak of his own, including an intolerance of political critics. Nevertheless, his actions remained (although sometimes just barely) within constitutional bounds. Moreover, he was the last in an unbroken series of democratically elected rulers stretching back more than four decades—an impressive record in Latin America. The Pinochet dictatorship that replaced Allende nearly 12 years ago is conspicuous for its brutal and systematic violation of individual liberties. Yet Henry Kissinger can assert that the "change in government in Chile was on balance favorable—even from the point of view of human rights." Such a view reflects either willful blindness or an astounding cynicism.

Those individuals who justify America's existing policy toward the Third World cite strategic, economic, and ideological considerations. On the strategic level, they argue that the United States must prevent geographically important regions from falling under the sway of regimes subservient to the Soviet Union. Otherwise, a shift in the balance of global military power could jeopardize American security interests, perhaps even imperil the nation's continued existence. Economically, the United States must maintain access to vital supplies of raw materials and keep markets open for American products and investments. It is not possible, this argument holds, for an economy based upon free enterprise to endure if the world is dominated by state-run Marxist systems. Finally, beyond questions of strategic and economic self-interest, the United States must thwart communist expansionism in the Third World to ensure that America and its democratic allies do not become islands in a global sea of hostile, totalitarian dictatorships.

All these arguments possess a certain facile appeal, but they hold up only if one accepts some very dubious conceptions of America's strategic, economic, and ideological interests. Moreover, proponents have often employed these arguments as transparent rationalizations for questionable foreign policy initiatives. . . .

Security Considerations?

One can and should question whether the United States actually has strategic interests, vital or otherwise, in areas thousands of miles removed from its own shores. Moreover, Washington's current approach assumes that the presence of authoritarian Third World allies somehow enhances America's own security. It is a curious belief. How a plethora of small, often militarily insignificant nations, governed by unpopular and unstable regimes, could augment U.S. strength in a showdown with the Soviet Union is a mystery. One could make a more plausible argument that attempts to prop up tottering allies *weaken* America's security. These efforts drain U.S. financial resources and stretch defense forces dangerously thin. Worst of all is the risk that a crumbling Third World ally could become an arena for ill-advised American military adventures. As we saw in Vietnam, the entrance to such quagmires is easier to find than the exit. . . .

The Economic Dimension

The economic thesis for current U.S. foreign policy is no more persuasive than the strategic rationale. Assumptions that rightist governments serve as pliant instruments of American economic objectives or that left-wing regimes become commercial adversaries cannot be sustained as a general rule. It is true that countries ruled by right-wing autocrats tend to be friendlier arenas for U.S. investment, but the price in bureaucratic restrictions and "commissions" (i.e., bribes) to key officials is often very high. Moreover, governments of whatever ideological stripe usually operate according to principles of economic self-interest, which may or may not correspond to American desires. . . .

Rather than adopting economic sanctions as a device for political intimidation, the United States should relish the prospect of promoting commercial connections to the greatest extent possible. Nothing would more readily provide evidence to left-wing leaders that a system based on private property and incentives is vastly superior to the lumbering inefficiencies of Marxist central planning. On those rare occasions when the United States has pursued a conciliatory rather than a truculent and confrontational approach, the results have been gratifying. The Marxist regime in Mozambique, for instance, first looked to the Soviet bloc for economic as well as ideological guidance, only to confront arrogant Russian imperialism and a recipe for economic disaster. The disillusioned leadership now has begun to turn away from the USSR and open its country to Western trade and investment, a process that is likely to accelerate in the coming years.

Withdrawing Support May Not Work

Americans sometimes think that it is enough to express disapproval of a regime and to withdraw economic support. Both gestures make us feel better, but they do not necessarily work.

Henry Grunwald, *Time*, May 12, 1986.

The most misguided justification for America's attachment to right-wing Third World states lies in the realm of politics and ideology. Proponents assume an underlying ideological affinity between authoritarian systems and Western democracies. They insist that while rightist regimes may be repressive, such governments are natural U.S. allies in the struggle against world communism. Conversely, revolutionary leftist movements are "totalitarian" in origin and constitute accretions to the power of that global menace. . . .

An Alternative: Benign Detachment

A new policy must eschew inconsistent moral posturing as well as amoral geopolitics. The most constructive alternative would stress "benign detachment" toward *all* Third World dictatorships, whatever their ideological orientation.

The concept of benign detachment is grounded in the indisputable reality that, for the foreseeable future, the United States will confront a Third World environment in which a majority of nations are undemocratic. It would unquestionably prove easier to function in a community of capitalist democracies, but we do not have that luxury. Democracy and capitalism may emerge as powerful doctrines throughout the Third World, but such a transformation would be long-term, reflecting indigenous historical experiences. We certainly cannot hasten that process by abandoning our own ideals and embracing reactionary autocrats. In the interim, the United States must learn to coexist with a variety of dictatorships. Benign detachment represents the most productive and least intrusive method of achieving that objective.

This approach would reject the simplistic categorization of right-wing regimes as friends and Marxist governments as enemies. It would require redefining America's national interests in a more circumspect manner. No longer should Washington conclude that the survival of a reactionary dictatorship, no matter how repressive, corrupt, and unstable it might be, somehow enhances the security of the United States. A policy of benign detachment would likewise repudiate the notion that there is an underlying kinship between rightist autocracies and Western democracies. Right-wing dictatorships are just as alien to our values as their left-wing counterparts.

America's primary objective should be a more restrained and even-handed policy toward repressive Third World regimes. Cordial diplomatic and economic relations should be encouraged with *all* governments that are willing to reciprocate, be they democratic, authoritarian, royalist, or Marxist. This would require normalizing diplomatic and commercial relations with such states as Cuba, Nicaragua, and Vietnam while curtailing aid to so-called allies. . . .

The Case for Non-Involvement

An even-handed policy should avoid involvement in Third World quarrels not directly pertinent to America's own security requirements, however crucial they might seem to the immediate participants. The United States has no holy writ to destabilize the governments of Cuba or Nicaragua because it finds them repugnant, nor to preserve autocratic systems in South Korea or Zaire because it considers them congenial. By the same token, America has not been anointed to overthow the Pinochet regime in Chile or reform the South African government, even though zealous liberals might think such actions would promote human progress.

A policy of benign detachment is not isolationist—at least insofar as that term is used to describe a xenophobic, "storm shelter" approach to world affairs. Quite the contrary, it adopts a tolerant and optimistic outlook, seeing Third World states not merely as pawns in America's cold war with the Soviet Union, but as unique and diverse entities. Extensive economic relations are not merely acceptable, they are essential to enhancing the ultimate appeal of capitalism and democracy. There is even room for American mediation efforts to help resolve internecine or regional conflicts, provided that all parties to a dispute desire such assistance and our role harbors no danger of political or military entanglements. The United States need not practice a surly isolation. America can be an active participant in Third World affairs, but the nature of such interaction must be limited, consistent, and nonintrusive.

A policy of benign detachment would bring numerous benefits to the United States. No longer would America be perceived as the patron of repressive, decaying dictatorships, or as the principal obstacle to indigenous change in the Third World. Our current policy tragically identifies the United States and—even worse—its capitalist democratic system with the most reactionary elements around the globe. This foolish posture enables the Soviet Union to pose as the champion of both democracy and Third World nationalism. It is time that America recaptured that moral high ground. If the United States allowed the people of Third World nations to work out their own destinies instead of trying to enlist them as unwilling combatants in the cold war, Russia's hypocritical, grasping imperialism would soon stand exposed. Moscow, not Washington, might well become the principal target of nationalistic wrath throughout Asia, Africa, and Latin America. Moreover, the inherent inequities and inefficiencies of Marxist economics would soon become evident to all but the most rabid ideologues.

An End to the Hypocrisy

Equally important, a conciliatory noninterventionist posture toward the Third World would reduce the risk of U.S. military involvement in complex quarrels generally not relevant to American security. Savings in terms of both dollars and lives could be enormous. Our policy threatens to foment a plethora of "brush fire" conflicts with all the attendant expense, bitterness, and divisiveness that characterized the Vietnam war.

Finally, and not the least important, reducing our Third World commitments would put an end to the hypocrisy that has pervaded U.S. relations with countries in the Third World. It is debilitating for a society that honors democracy and fundamental human rights to embrace regimes that scorn both values. A nation that believes in human liberty has no need for, and should not want, "friends" who routinely practice the worst forms of repression. A policy of detachment would restore a badly needed sense of honor and consistency to American foreign policy.

"Denying the people of Chile international financial resources would deepen the country's problems, exacerbate social and political tensions and weaken . . . Chilean society."

US Aid Must Continue In Spite of Chile's Human Rights Violations

Elliott Abrams

Since 1973, Chileans have been living under the repressive and brutal dictatorship of Augusto Pinochet. Many have argued that the US government's continued relationship with Pinochet is the only thing that keeps the dictator in power. Others believe denying Pinochet's regime US aid would only cause the collapse of Chile's economy and make continued violence inevitable. In the following viewpoint, Elliott Abrams, the US Assistant Secretary for Inter-American Affairs, takes the latter view. Abrams argues that while the US is concerned about Pinochet's human rights violations, denying US aid would not bring about a positive change.

As you read, consider the following questions:

1. Why does Abrams believe it is impossible for the US to help bring democracy to Chile?
2. Why does Abrams believe the situation in Chile is changing for the better?

Elliott Abrams, "U.S. Support for Transition to Democracy in Chile," *Department of State Bulletin*, March 1986.

74

It is a pleasure and a privilege for me to appear before you in response to your invitation to discuss U.S. policy toward Chile as it applies to U.S. voters in international financial institutions regarding loans to Chile.

I would like to say a little about the policy framework in which we operate when considering these issues for Chile.

US Policy

U.S. Government policy toward Chile is straightforward and unequivocal: We support a transition to democracy. This reflects our strong preference for democratic governments in general and the centrality of democracy and economic development to our policy in Latin America. We believe that the most effective means to pursue many varied interests in Chile—including regional security, curbing narcotics trafficking, promoting trade and cooperation on international issues, and fostering human rights—is to encourage the restoration of democracy. We believe this can happen on terms that are worked out by Chileans themselves, and which are satisfactory to the large majority of Chileans who want a stable democratic society, where human rights are protected.

We would like to see Chile participate very soon in the surge toward democracy which has been sweeping the hemisphere. We also know that we cannot impose on Chileans when and how this will occur. But we can help them to make it happen sooner by implementing a prudent foreign policy which actively pursues all possible ways of encouraging dialogue and moderation, which at the same time avoids actions on our part that exacerbate tensions in Chile.

While the vast majority of Chileans want to return to democratic government, there is considerable difference of opinion within Chile over the timing and procedure concerning a transition to democracy. . . .

Democracy and Human Rights

I have emphasized our support for democracy because this is central to the decisions we make on specific issues concerning Chile. Other important elements include our general concern for eliminating human rights abuses wherever they occur, and our desire to support sound economic policies which promote economic growth, take into account market realities, and encourage responsible management of debt. Precisely because full respect for human rights is not apparent in Chile, efforts to encourage a transition to democracy take on greater importance. We believe the best guarantee that human rights will be carefully protected is provided by the establishment of representative and responsive democratic institutions.

The human rights situation in Chile still causes serious concern, although certain positive changes have occurred since June [1985],

75

when a state of siege was lifted, leaving in effect less severe restrictions on constitutional protections under a state of emergency. The differences are particularly noteworthy in areas of freedom of expression and judicial review of government actions. . . .

Lifting the state of siege also restored judicial review of certain executive actions under the transitory provisions of the 1980 constitution. Furthermore, Chilean courts have demonstrated some independence and diligence by investigating several important cases of human rights violations potentially involving members of the security forces. As a result of a court investigation into a number of kidnappings and the murder of three members of the Chilean Communist Party, a judge ordered the detention of seven *carabineros*, including two colonels. This prosecution provoked a sweeping shakeup in this police organization and the resignation of the *carabinero* commander, also a junta member. Such investigations suggest that over time Chile's judicial system could bring about significant improvements in the human rights situation provided the courts are permitted to operate independently and exercise full authority. . . .

US Encouragement Can Work for Chile

The U.S. can and should seek to encourage Chile's government actively to restore democracy, but it should not take action that could be counterproductive to that goal. . . . For all its problems and for all the justifiable criticism of the Pinochet regime, the fact is that Chile is moving steadily if slowly toward democratic government and the improvements in human rights conditions that are sure to follow.

Esther Wilson Hannon, The Heritage Foundation *Backgrounder*, November 18, 1986.

Implementation of these recommendations could produce a positive impact on other elements in the human rights situation that cause serious concern. Although judicial review of government actions is greater now, the government retains the ability to act in certain matters without judicial review, and has continued a policy of sending some of its critics and opponents into internal exile by administrative decree. While we welcomed the decision of the Chilean Government to allow 500 more Chilean exiles to return, we hope the government will work to resolve the situations of the several thousand Chileans who are still barred from returning. The media has been allowed greater freedom of action but political freedoms and civil liberties are severely limited under the states of exception that remain in force. The government has promulgated one of the political transition laws provided for by the 1980 constitution, regarding an electoral tribunal, but no progress has occurred toward legalizing political parties, passing an electoral law or reestablishment of electoral registers.

Extremist Violence Continues

Violence from many sources continues to plague Chile. Antigovernment terrorism continued even under the state of siege. Court cases such as that affecting the *carabineros* represent an advance but are also evidence of the persistence of abuses by security forces. The frequency of terrorism and other violent acts has made progress on all human rights issues much more difficult.

Incidents of violence have occurred in conjunction with antigovernment protests, in which circumstances are often unclear and responsibility for specific acts difficult to determine. Hundreds of people have been detained, although in most cases only briefly, in connection with political protests. . . .

Reliable reports of torture and mistreatment of those detained by the authorities continue to be received by human rights organizations. Since June [1985] there has been an increase in charges by human rights groups and government opponents of temporary kidnappings, beatings, and torture by unidentified persons. Churches have been bombed or attacked with gunfire, priests and lay workers physically threatened or attacked. Responsibility for these attacks and threats is difficult to place, but some appear to be the work of a rightwing terrorist group called Chilean Anti-Communist Action. Human rights groups charge that Chilean intelligence or security forces are involved. Identification and swift prosecution of those responsible is the most effective answer to such allegations. . . .

IFI Loans to Chile

We take human rights considerations into account in determining how the U.S. votes on loans by international financial institutions (IFIs) to a given country. Our standard practice is to consider each proposed IFI bank loan for Chile or any other country on a case-by-case basis. We then determine the U.S. position on the basis of all relevant factors, including economic, human rights, and statutory criteria. Interagency review mechanisms exist to ensure that both human rights and economic policy considerations are carefully factored in during the decisionmaking process. An interagency working group on human rights and foreign assistance, cochaired by the Human Rights and Humanitarian Affairs Bureau and the Economic and Business Affairs Bureau at the State Department, meets regularly to review all upcoming loans in the IFIs. To consider financial and economic policy factors, the Treasury Department chairs a comparable interagency working group on multilateral assistance.

During the Reagan Administration the United States has generally, but not always, voted in favor of IFI loans to Chile. For example, in December 1983 the U.S. executive director in the Inter-American Development Bank (IDB) opposed a loan for mining investment in Chile on the basis that the mining firms could have borne the debt service costs instead of receiving an equity infusion from the government. We abstained on three loans to Chile following a careful review of all relevant considerations, including the restrictions in effect at that time under the state of siege.

Chile's Solid Economy

Our judgment on Chile's economic policies is that, considered in isolation of human rights concerns, they provide a strong basis for voting in favor of most IFI loans for Chile. The economic management team of the Government of Chile has a solid free market orientation and is considered by international financial institutions to be highly skilled. . . .

There are certainly real possibilities for a peaceful democratic outcome in Chile. The Administration will continue to provide every encouragement to those Chileans truly committed to democracy and help to strengthen, not weaken, their position with respect to other elements in the society. We will continue to advocate dialogue between the government and democratic opposition.

Elliott Abrams, *Department of State Bulletin*, October 1986.

On June 18, [1985], after the Chilean Government has lifted the state of siege restrictions, the U.S. executive director at the World Bank voted in favor of a $55 million investment loan for a methanol project in which the U.S. firm Signal Corporation is participating. Since then, again following the careful interagency review I have described, the U.S. executive directors in the IDB and the World Bank have voted in favor of other loans to Chile including a $250 million World Bank structural adjustment loan key to Chile's economic recovery efforts. We will decide future votes also on a case-by-case basis, using the aforementioned review mechanisms and criteria.

Chile's Economic Situation

IFI loans are important to Chile, where the economic situation remains precarious. Since 1970 Chile has suffered the worst decline in its terms of trade of any country in Latin America. With the worldwide drop in commodity prices, Chile's export earnings have fallen dramatically. In 1984 Chile's export earnings were over $1 billion below where they had been in 1980.

The economy's overwhelming dependence on copper, compounded by one of the region's highest per capita levels of external debt, has not allowed Chile to benefit as much as might be expected from its generally good performance in applying responsible stabilization policies, an area in which Chile has one of the best records in the hemisphere. In 1982 and 1983 the Chilean economy declined by a cumulative 15%. Despite expansion of 6% in 1983, unemployment remains high, at about 14%, with another 9% of the workforce dependent for survival on low-wage government make-work programs.

A $2 billion financial adjustment program negotiated with commercial banks, the IMF [International Monetary Fund] and the World Bank, in conjunction with a restructuring of foreign debt with private banks and some official creditors, may produce a modest growth that could ease some of the pain of necessary economic adjustment. Presently foreign banks are providing final commitments for $785 million in new commercial bank credits in 1985-1986, which complement a separate $300 million commercial bank loan partially guaranteed by the World Bank. An IMF agreement provides 750 million special drawing rights, and helps to assure foreign lenders that Chile will continue to follow rational macroeconomic policies to allow orderly servicing of a foreign debt of nearly $19 billion.

The World Bank structural adjustment loan provides another means of monitoring Chilean economic performance over the next few years, further improving the prospects for continued sound economic policy and greater economic improvement. The Chilean Government's free-market oriented policies have helped eliminate some of the traditional rigidities in the Chilean economy and have helped to establish a base for effective implementation of this loan.

In light of the precarious economic situation in Chile and the additional suffering that another downturn would impose on the Chilean people, we believe it is important to continue to support Chilean economic policies that seek continued adjustment in conjunction with growth of the private sector and responsible debt management.

Bringing about changes for the better in Chile's human rights performance is central to our policy toward Chile. Under present circumstances, denying the people of Chile international financial resources would deepen the country's problems, exacerbate social and political tensions, and weaken the process of reconciliation being actively promoted by the Catholic Church and other responsible sectors of Chilean society. We believe that it is important for those favoring Chile's return to democracy to encourage this fragile process of national reconciliation to take root. That will require moderation and flexibility on the part of those concerned, including Chile's friends abroad. Our actions are most helpful to the degree that we support the flexible resolution of the deep-seated differences in Chile, without reinforcing the positions of those who argue that differences are irreconcilable, or without in turn contributing to creation of new divisions.

"If the United States wants to help democratization in Chile, it clearly will have to go beyond words and begin to use the economic power."

US Economic Pressure Is Needed To Protest Chile's Human Rights Violations

Pamela Constable and Arturo Valenzuela

Pamela Constable is the Latin American correspondent for the *Boston Globe*. Arturo Valenzuela is a professor of political science and director of the Council on Latin American Studies at Duke University. In the following viewpoint, the authors argue that the US must not allow Pinochet to continue in power, and should use whatever non-military means possible to help end his government.

As you read, consider the following questions:

1. According to the authors, what three factors keep Pinochet in office?
2. Why must the US help oust Pinochet, according to the authors?

Pamela Constable and Arturo Valenzuela, "Is Chile Next?" Reprinted with permission from FOREIGN POLICY 63 (Summer 1986). Copyright 1986 by the Carnegie Endowment for International Peace.

As a tide of democratic change sweeps Latin America, the dictatorship of General Augusto Pinochet in Chile has become a conspicuous and perplexing anomaly. Since 1980, military governments in 10 Latin American countries—Argentina, Bolivia, Brazil, Ecuador, El Salvador, Guatemala, Honduras, Panama, Peru, and Uruguay—have given way to some form of civilian rule. Today, Chile is the sole regional state with any democratic roots that is bucking the tide. Pinochet continues to keep company only with General Alfredo Stroessner, the Paraguayan strong man whose backward country has known only harsh rule and civil strife since colonial days.

The downfall of two authoritarian rulers, Jean-Claude Duvalier of Haiti and Ferdinand Marcos of the Philippines, has focused new attention on Chile, where Pinochet has rebuffed virtually all demands for change since seizing power in the 1973 coup that toppled elected socialist President Salvador Allende Gossens. As in Haiti and the Philippines, the Chilean regime has faced a national ground swell of opposition. Indeed, whereas for years the Duvalier and Marcos political machines dominated their weak competitors, Pinochet's opponents have long been organized in a wide spectrum of established political parties. But thus far the general has frustrated at every turn even this sophisticated opposition. . . .

Inside Pressure Mounting

In justifying his continued rule, Pinochet often invokes the specter of socialist "chaos" that preceded the 1973 coup, explaining in October 1985 Chile must pass through a "dictatorship of democracy" before the state can be trusted to civilian stewards. Chilean officials also insist that they are only following the constitutional transition to democracy and thus cannot understand all the fuss. . . .

If the United States wants to help democratization in Chile, it clearly will have to go beyond words and begin to use the economic power it has employed to press left-wing Nicaragua and, to a lesser extent, South Africa. But, as they consider these measures, U.S. policymakers will need to understand why the aging Pinochet clings to power and what has enabled him to do so almost alone among neighboring tyrants. Why has Chile, with an educated citizenry and a long history of stable civilian rule, failed to rebuild its democratic institutions? Can Pinochet be persuaded to step down? Is there a chance for bloodless exile, like that of Duvalier and Marcos, or could Chile become another Nicaragua?

One way Pinochet has differed from other regional dictators is in his personal dominance over the armed forces. From the first days after the coup, the general began putting his stamp on the new regime, which soon became an extension of one man's rule. Most Chileans thought that the military would remain in power only briefly, but Pinochet already was planning an indefinite stay. . . .

Economic Policies a Success

Economic success also helped Pinochet consolidate his power. Until 1981, the neoconservative theories he embraced seemed to be working miracles. Encouraged to borrow overseas, businesses flooded Santiago with consumer imports, while government economists promised that lower tariffs, reduced social spending, and tight monetary controls would lead to greater industrial efficiency and to recovery. Although many firms failed to survive the competition, most business leaders adapted to partnership with the military. As for the poor, who bore the brunt of these policies, their leadership had been so decimated that protest was unthinkable. At the height of the boom, voters approved the new constitution in balloting that, while highly manipulated, reflected strong support for Pinochet.

Pressuring Chile Would Not Harm US

By adopting a policy toward Chile that neglects consideration of human rights, the United States is siding with the repressive policies of the Pinochet government against moderate political forces; it is also siding with one faction of the government against other factions that have advocated further liberalization. . . .

A U.S. policy of pressuring the Chilean government to liberalize would not conflict with the need to coordinate U.S. policy in concert with its neighbors. The Pinochet regime has few defenders on the continent, even among military regimes, which are critical of the excessive personalization of military rule. Pinochet has not been visited by any foreign head of state during his long tenure in office, and his hosts in Brazil and Argentina deliberately downplayed his visit to those countries. Pinochet's position of tacit support for Britain in the Falklands/Malvinas dispute only contributed to his isolation on the continent. Finally, most neighboring countries, including Argentina, Brazil and Uruguay, are now joining Peru and Bolivia in a transition process back to democratic rule which will leave Chile as one of the few military regimes on the continent.

Arturo Valenzuela and Robert Kaufman, *From Gunboats to Diplomacy,* 1984.

As a new decade dawned, attitudes began to shift. National numbness to repression gave way to a more deeply rooted democratic instinct. Political parties quietly began to rebuild and plan for a return to civilian control. Most important, the regime's economic model collapsed. In 1982, Chile's growth rate fell 14 per cent and unemployment reached almost 30 per cent. Since then, the economy has recuperated only slightly, while repayment of its $20 billion foreign debt has consumed most export revenues. Rigidly applied monetary and free-market policies have left Chile vulnerable to international recession and dropped per capita consumption in 1985 to a level lower than that of 1962. . . .

A Lesser Evil

Aside from his determination to remain in power, three factors keep Pinochet in office: the obedience of the armed forces, the grudging support of business, and the debilitating divisions still crippling the opposition. Underlying all three factors is a phenomenon that sets Chile apart from its neighbors: the strength of a Marxist Left that managed to win power through the ballot box. For many Chileans, the fear that this could happen again still makes Pinochet seem a lesser evil. . . .

During the early Reagan years, the only strong U.S. opposition to Pinochet came from Congress, where concern had been high since the coup and the 1976 assassination of Orlando Letelier, a former Allende minister, in Washington. Beginning in 1975, the regime's brutality inspired legislation barring U.S. bilateral assistance to countries with severe human rights problems and prohibiting U.S. support for many IFI loans to such states.

By late in Reagan's first term, however, events began to persuade the State Department that its sanguine view of Pinochet was wrong and that its reliance on quiet diplomacy to speed change had failed. As unrest grew, Pinochet only became tougher: first the canceled transition talks, then the state of siege, then the rejection of the National Accord. U.S. officials also realized that, instead of quashing left-wing influence, Pinochet was bolstering the appeal of radical groups by refusing to deal with moderate opponents. And Chile began to stand out as an embarrassing exception to the Latin American democratization—a trend for which Washington hoped to share credit. Finally, to be credible in its campaign against leftist regimes like Nicaragua's, the administration evidently decided that it had better start prodding right-wing rulers as well.

Condemning Pinochet

This shift in policy was first tested in spring 1985 in a series of visits to Santiago by high-level officials, followed by a series of diplomatic changes. First, Elliott Abrams, a former head of the State Department's Bureau of Human Rights and Humanitarian Affairs, was named assistant secretary of state for inter-American affairs. He replaced Langhorne Motley, another political appointee, who had fumbled by declaring in Santiago that Chile's future was "in good hands." Then Theberge was replaced by Barnes, a veteran diplomat who enraged Pinochet by meeting with opposition leaders, appearing at a candle-lit human rights ceremony, and making it clear that the administration wanted swifter change.

ROTHCO

Sacramento Bee

'SOMEDAY YOU'LL GO TOO FAR, GENERAL, AND I'LL HAVE TO VOTE AGAINST YOUR WORLD BANK LOAN!'

In March 1986, the United States went even further. After 6 years of voting against or abstaining on U.N. resolutions condemning human rights violations in Chile, U.S. representatives took the lead in drafting a new resolution that strongly criticized Pinochet and called for a return to democracy. At the same time, in a move aimed partly at Pinochet, Reagan announced that he would support "human rights and oppose tyranny in whatever form, whether of the left or the right."

Yet the administration continues to send ambivalent cues to Pinochet. Part of the reason is its refusal to accept the historical legitimacy of Marxist parties in Chilean politics. When criticizing Pinochet's resistance to change, U.S. officials often admonish the

Left and the quarrelsome opposition in the next breath, thus helping Pinochet discredit moderate opponents. The United States has pushed the opposition to exclude the Communists from participation in a future democracy. Also, U.S. officials give credence to the 1980 Constitution, despite widespread Chilean opposition.

A second administration mistake has been to underestimate Washington's potential for pressuring the Chilean military. Thus its diplomatic aims have been muddied by a friendly Pentagon approach to its Chilean counterparts. Defense officials regularly include Chile in regional exercises and request training and aid funds from Congress. Currently, the United States is expanding a space program landing strip on Chilean-owned Easter Island. Defense officials argue that such ties are the most effective way to press for reforms, yet they have failed to use them for that purpose. In a widely publicized Santiago ceremony in October 1985, U.S. Army Lieutenant General Robert Schweitzer, president of the Inter-American Defense Board, praised Pinochet for "liberating" Chile from the "double scourge of terrorism and communism," adding that "we can understand the difficulties your Excellency is encountering in guiding your great nation's transition toward democracy." The Pentagon is in a unique position to press the military to distance itself from Pinochet. Unless it uses those links to push for change, however, it boosts Pinochet's claim that he still has important friends in Washington.

Inconsistent Policies for Aid

Most important, since 1980, U.S. officials have voted for $2.2 billion in multilateral loans to Chile, although the International Financial Institutions Act of 1977 currently bars U.S. support for most such loans to countries with "a pattern of gross . . . human rights violations." In a September 1985 report, the Organization of American States found torture a "deliberate and systematic" practice in Chile. During the state of siege, lifted only in June 1985, Washington abstained on several loan votes, but by the year's end it had voted affirmatively on $900 million in new loans.

U.S. officials such as Abrams have told Congress that poor Chileans would suffer more from sanctions than the regime and that a blanket cutoff would rob the United States of what little leverage it has retained after the Carter administration's ban on aid. The first argument makes little sense, since many multilateral loans fund public works projects or provide balance-of-payment supports. The second underestimates the value of U.S. influence in Santiago.

Pinochet, too, has shown himself sensitive to American criticism and pressure. Usually, his reaction takes the form of indignant bluster. Yet on the one occasion when substantive pressure was threatened—the 1985 multilateral loan abstentions—the dictator quickly lifted the state of siege.

Pinochet is more vulnerable to economic sanctions than at any time since the coup. The bankruptcy of many businesses has made it impossible for the country to meet interest payments on its foreign debt without credit from the IFIs. As long as such aid continues, the business elite remains reluctant to break with the regime. If the United States uses this opportunity to apply pressure, however, it can help boost conservative support for the opposition and push Pinochet to accept the National Accord. The United States merely needs to threaten to oppose loans on a selective basis. Moreover, in pursuing economic sanctions, the administration need not fear facing significant opposition from the U.S. business community, which has made relatively small investments in Chile since Allende's fall.

Concrete US Actions

U.S. interests are best served by an early return to democracy in Chile. While maintaining correct diplomatic relations with the Pinochet government, the United States should make it clear that it is unhappy with the prolongation of arbitrary rule. This means, of course, that the Reagan administration should refuse to certify that Chile has made progress on human rights and should threaten to rescind its decision to renew economic and military aid and government-backed credits. Because of the vulnerability of the Chilean economy, the United States should also insist that it will vote against Chilean aid by multilateral agencies and that it is prepared to consider a policy of discouraging loans to Chile by private banks unless the military government gives genuine proof of its willingness to respect political and human rights.

Arturo Valenzuela and Robert Kaufman, *From Gunboats to Diplomacy*, 1984.

If Washington is serious in its new vow to oppose tyrannies of both left and right, it must use every available nonmilitary tool to strengthen the democratic opposition in Chile. The United States alone cannot force Pinochet out of office, but its potential for influence with the military and business sectors can help speed the return to democracy. The longer Pinochet remains, the dimmer glows the hope that Chileans can regain peacefully stewardship of one of the West's oldest democracies.

"Politically motivated deaths [in Guatemala] have dropped steadily."

US Involvement Has Improved Guatemala's Human Rights Situation

United States Bureau of Inter-American Affairs

In spite of many critics' assertions that the US has an inconsistent and even harmful human rights policy, the US maintains that it is attempting to build democracy and human rights in every Latin American country it maintains relations with. In the following viewpoint, published by the Bureau of Inter-American Affairs, this stance is supported. The brief argues that elections in Guatemala prove that US involvement is improving the situation there.

As you read, consider the following questions:

1. What steps has the Cerezo government taken to improve human rights, according to the author?
2. What evidence does the Bureau give to support its conclusion that human rights are improving?
3. What, does the Bureau say, will the US continue to do?

United States Department of State, Bureau of Inter-American Affairs, "Guatemala's Transition Toward Democracy," November 1986.

Central America's most recent transition from military to civilian rule took place on January 14, 1986, with the inauguration of Vinicio Cerezo as President of the Republic. Cerezo, the candidate of the Christian Democratic Party, is the first civilian to be elected president of Guatemala since 1966.

The transition was exemplary: three free and competitive elections between July 1984 and December 1985 led to the writing of a new constitution and the election of Cerezo. Receiving more than 1 million votes in a runoff for the presidency, Cerezo obtained two-thirds of the votes against a civilian candidate representing the center-right.

In leading Central America's newest democracy, President Cerezo and his government must now overcome a legacy of decades of officially condoned violence and guerrilla insurgency, socioeconomic ills, and estrangement from the international community.

A Tragic History

From the 1944 ouster of strongman General Jorge Ubico and the 1944-54 decade of "social revolution" to the military governments and organized guerrilla warfare that lasted from the 1960s through the first half of the 1980s, Guatemalan life has been marked by violence against both individuals (assassinations, kidnapings, and intimidation) and society (military coups, electoral fraud, and a bloody insurgency). Major sectors of society—the military, business, political parties, labor, and Indian communities—fragmented into mutually antagonistic forces. Major social problems—skewed income and land distribution, disparities in the quality of life between Indian and non-Indian, and growing numbers of landless and jobless—have increased the intensity and human costs of the conflicts.

National Reconciliation

One of President Cerezo's fundamental concerns is to bring the Guatemalan nation back together after years of guerrilla war and polarizing violence. One of the last acts of the military government was a general amnesty for acts of political violence, including guerrilla activities, that took place between March 1982 and January 1986. Shortly after taking office, Cerezo said he would be prepared to discuss the reincorporation of guerrillas into the political life of Guatemala. Some guerrillas are evidently willing to talk, but others continue to conduct armed attacks in parts of the highlands. . . .

Prospects for national reconciliation have been strengthened by improvements in the human rights situation and by the return from abroad of many Guatemalans who previously feared for their lives. The Social Democratic Party (PSD) competed openly in the elections, winning representation in the National Congress, currently led by the Christian Democratic Party of Guatemala (DCG). As in neighboring El Salvador, the political opening is producing a rejuvenation of labor and cooperative movements, the restoration of autonomy to university life, and renewed dialogue between the government and the private sector.

Human Rights

Politically motivated deaths have dropped steadily. U.S. Embassy reports show a decline in such deaths from an average of 350 per month in 1981, to under 50 in 1985, to fewer than 13 per month in the first 6 months of 1986. The number of disappearances has also dropped, from a high of 35 per month in 1984 to 8 per month during the first half of 1986. There is no indication that the Guatemalan Government is involved in current cases. In fact, there is no clearcut case of an individual being killed or kidnaped for political activities or beliefs. In his [1986] address to the UN General Assembly, President Cerezo stated that, under his government, "no party or popular organization can complain of repressive actions, disappearances, torture, or murder of any of its members." The OAS [Organization of American States] Human Rights Commission stated in its annual report that: "There is little doubt that during the first seven months of his [Cerezo's] administration there has been a perceptible change [*sensible cambio*] in the human rights situation."

Guatemala and Respect for Human Rights

We witnessed a free election in Guatemala as that country joined El Salvador in the strengthening of democratic institutions in Central America for which Presidents Cerezo and Duarte are to be congratulated. The measures they have taken have, indeed, served to restore respect for human rights in their countries. They have demonstrated that the democratic process and respect for human rights go hand in hand.

Richard Schifter, speech given on Human Rights Day, December 10, 1986.

Declines in politically related violence have not been matched by similar declines in common criminal violence. A monthly average of 150 criminally related murders, another 200 serious physical assaults and robberies, and 500 stolen cars make Guatemala one of the most violent societies in the world. Cerezo recognizes the importance of ending human rights abuses and criminal violence. The Constitution mandates the establishment of a human rights ombudsman, and the government is assigning a high priority to professionalizing the National Police. Investigative and protective capabilities are being strengthened to support the independent judicial process and to help establish confidence in the legal process after decades of extrajudicial violence. In June 1986, President Reagan forwarded to Congress a certification on human rights and political conditions in Guatemala that recognized improvement and enabled the United States to respond favorably to a written request from President Cerezo for nonlethal military assistance, the first U.S. military aid for Guatemala since 1977.

International Activity

In October 1986, President Cerezo received promises of $300 million or more in aid from Belgium, Spain, Germany, France, and Italy. The aid covered activities ranging from economic development to help for professionalizing the National Police. During this highly successful tour of Western Europe, and in prior visits to Mexico, Central America, Venezuela, and the United States, Cerezo found growing recognition of Guatemala's democratization process. Declaring himself a "fanatic of democracy," Cerezo advocates regular elections and has proposed the establishment of a directly elected Central American parliament. Guatemala is hosting several regional and international meetings, including functions related to the OAS, the European Community (EC), and the Contadora process, thus effectively ending Guatemala's international isolation.

Reactivation of the Guatemalan economy, which has suffered relatively little from guerrilla attacks and which has the strongest private sector in Central America, has become a top priority for the Cerezo government. In June 1986, Cerezo implemented an economic stabilization program developed through extensive dialogue with private sector representatives. Exchange rates were adjusted pending complete unification. Price stabilization measures were put into effect. Guatemala is discussing a stand-by program with the International Monetary Fund (IMF), which appears favorably impressed by Guatemala's economic stabilization efforts. After 5 years of economic stagnation, there is hope that inflation could slow in 1986, followed by positive economic growth in 1987. Although more time and additional measures are likely to be needed, the Cerezo government seems to be on the right track—and has the support of Guatemalan business and labor, of the international financial institutions, and of many foreign governments, including that of the United States.

Guatemala-US Relations

A strong, active, and democratic Guatemala improves democratic prospects throughout Central America. Secretary of State Shultz reported to the President in July 1986 that the success of the democratic transition in Guatemala demonstrates the importance of fully meeting the levels of U.S. assistance recommended by the Kissinger commission. . . .

The United States supported the transition from military to civilian government. Total U.S. assistance (development, financial, food, and military) rose from $32 million in fiscal year (FY) 1984 to $103 million in FY 1986. U.S. assistance has ranged from rural development projects in the Indian highlands, support to help offset trade imbalances, improving the electoral system, and modernizing and professionalizing the investigative capabilities of judicial institutions, to providing training and nonlethal equipment to the armed forces. This assistance is an important U.S. policy instrument to support democratic ideals and institutions in general and the civilian rule of President Cerezo in particular.

Guatemala's Revolution

Guatemala and El Salvador are both leaders in a revolution that is transforming the hemisphere. Latin America is conclusively demonstrating that the democratic form of government has universal meaning, that it is not just a luxury for wealthy industrial societies. On the contrary, democracy, by freeing untapped social energies and providing opportunities for their productive exercise, can serve as the foundation for material prosperity and social progress in our hemisphere.

George Shultz, speech before the General Assembly of the Organization of American States on November 11, 1986.

Guatemala is still struggling against violence, a lingering insurgent threat, socioeconomic ills, and institutional frailties. The United States will continue to support Guatemalan efforts to strengthen democratic institutions and the rule of law, to promote economic development and social progress, and to encourage the professionalization and responsible orientation of the armed forces and police. These are goals that unite the United States and Guatemala with each other and with other democratic nations.

"The intensity of repression will not depend on the personal wishes of the civilian sitting in the Presidential Palace. . . . The terror apparatus is in place."

Guatemala's Human Rights Conditions Are Not Improving

NISGUA (Network in Solidarity with the People of Guatemala)

NISGUA is a private organization whose purpose is to educate the North American people about the current political, military, economic, and human rights situations in Guatemala. In the following viewpoint, a representative of NISGUA argues that US assertions that Guatemalan conditions are improving are a lie. Guatemala has been ruled for so many years by brutal military dictatorships that it would be close to impossible, NISGUA argues, for a single civilian leader to have much impact on controlling the military.

As you read, consider the following questions:

1. What, according to NISGUA, does Cerezo's election represent?
2. Why does the author argue that repression is likely to continue?
3. Why are elections no guarantee of improvements in human rights, according to the author?

Network in Solidarity with the People of Guatemala, "Understanding Today's Guatemala," March 11, 1986. Reprinted with permission.

The bruised and battered body of Beatriz Eugenia Barrios was found two days after the December 8 [1985] Guatemalan presidential elections. Her hands were cut off. Written on a note placed on her body was the message, "More is to come."

Four armed men of the government security forces kidnapped Beatriz, a 26-year-old teacher and mother of two, the night before her scheduled flight to Canada. Canada had granted her refugee status after an earlier experience of kidnapping and torture at the hands of the security forces.

Coming so soon after the much heralded elections, her brutal murder was a blunt message to the newly elected Christian Democratic president, Vinicio Cerezo. According to many observers, her death carried the reminder: *though we transfer formal power, the Army wields real power.* Officials of the Christian Democrats acknowledged having "received" and understood the message during a visit to Washington, D.C.

The Reagan Administration has characterized the civilian elections as a fundamental and historic change in the bedrock of Army power in Guatemala. A Department of State briefing book triumphantly declares the elections to be "the final step in the reestablishment of democracy in Guatemala."

Is this a realistic description? How do we understand the recent elections? Will the election of a civilian president mean changes for the Guatemalan majority? Do the elections signify a fundamental shift of power away from the Army which has ruled the country—directly or indirectly—for over 30 years? Can the new administration bring about desperately needed broad-ranging social and economic reforms?

Can It Change?

The heart of the matter is this: has the Army changed from the one that killed Beatriz and over 50,000 others, and "disappeared" thousands of others in the last five years [1980-85] alone?

Guatemala, Central America's most populous country, elected a civilian president. As expected in Guatemala and abroad, Vinicio Cerezo of the Christian Democratic Party (CD) won the December 8, 1985 presidential run-off elections. He easily outdistanced Jorge Carpio Nicolle, candidate of the newly formed right-wing Union of the National Center. Cerezo becomes only the second civilian president since the U.S.-sponsored overthrow of the democratically elected Jacobo Arbenz government in 1954, an event which ushered in over 30 years of military-dominated rule.

Cerezo's election has raised hopes—both inside the country and internationally—that he can make changes in a country that various human rights organizations have described as "a nation of prisoners", "a country of widows and orphans", and a government both "bitter and cruel". Guatemala's new president has surprised many people with his regional diplomatic policies, especially his current opposition to U.S. efforts to isolate and topple the Nicaraguan government.

The elections, and Cerezo's victory, raise important questions about a key but often overlooked country in the Central American region. Some frequently asked questions are included below, followed by a discussion of the issues and facts surrounding the new Guatemalan government. . . .

Economic Assistance and Continuing Repression

The granting of economic assistance to Guatemala has depended in the past five years on evidence of fewer human rights violations and more satisfaction of humanitarian needs, and rightfully so. But economic assistance can only be effective if the government of Guatemala is willing to permit programs to achieve these goals. "Effectiveness" depends on the degree to which developmental assistance actually reaches the intended population. The United States has shown a willingness to accept a high degree of corruption, however unpalatable, on the grounds that the net effect of the economic assistance has been positive for its long-range interests.

This is no longer the case in Guatemala. Providing funds for huge infrastucture projects allows national resources to be diverted to military endeavors so that economic assistance becomes, in effect, indirect military assistance.

Even humanitarian programs, such as those set up after the 1976 earthquake, which are aimed at improving the quality of life for deprived groups are no longer effective. Any Guatemalan who is willing to participate in such projects runs the risk of assassination. In other words, because of the attitudes of the government and its supporters, providing even humanitarian assistance to Guatemala can lead to an increase in violence against the populace.

Robert H. Trudeau, *From Gunboats to Diplomacy*, 1984.

Will Cerezo bring to trial those responsible for past human rights abuses?

One crucial barometer of the degree of real power Cerezo holds is whether he chooses to bring to trial Army officers responsible for the deaths of more than 50,000 civilian non-combatants in the last five years and the kidnapping of thousands more. Unlike Argentina, where some senior military officers were tried for past human rights abuses, no one expects trials for Army officers or conclusive investigations into the whereabouts of the "disappeared" in Guatemala.

Days before Cerezo's inauguration the Army passed a governmental decree granting amnesty to anyone who committed human rights abuses after the March 1982 coup of General Rios Montt.

No one expects Cerezo to challenge the amnesty.

"We are not going to investigate the past. We would have to put the entire army in jail," Cerezo said. But the problem is not the mere lack of prison space. Luis Martinez Mont, party secretary of the Christian Democrats, declared, "Don't even mention Argentina around here. This is not a defeated army like Argentina's. This is a victorious army. And you don't dare talk of bringing a victorious army to trial." Cerezo stated the obvious when he noted, "If I put the army officers on trial, I'd be committing suicide."

If Cerezo can't bring to trial Army officers for past abuses, can he at least stop future abuses?

Cerezo said his administration, "can and must put an immediate end to the kidnappings." To this end he has offered one clear policy proposal: "I will reorganize the police and disband the security forces most deeply involved in repression—especially the Department of Technical Investigations (DIT), which has acquired an unacceptable power of its own. It will not be a change of label but a real purge."

In fact on February 4, [1986], the new government picked up dozens of members of the DIT in a well-publicized arrest. Cerezo has gained a lot of political capital with this raid, but news accounts have overlooked important facts. The DIT is not an independent agency, rather it operates at the behest of Army intelligence, the G-2. Although members of the DIT have kidnapped and committed murder, it is the security forces of the G-2 that bear primary responsibility for urban repression. Equally important, the agents of the DIT are civilians, and the Army has little concern for these civilian underlings. The Army would not allow Cerezo to move against Army personnel in the G-2, the hub of the state repressive apparatus. Finally, the punishment for the crimes of the DIT members is expected to be light, mostly firings and perhaps a few isolated arrests and trials.

Limited Power To End Murder

The initials of the infamous death squad, the Secret Anti-Communist Army (ESA) have made their first appearance, on walls in the capital city, since the fall of General Lucas Garcia in 1982. This reappearance of an extreme right-wing death squad offers the new civilian government and the Army a convenient scapegoat for ongoing human rights abuses. However, the ESA is not an independent group, but operates under the authority of the Army G-2. Amnesty International documented this connection between the Army and the ESA in the late 1970s during the Lucas Garcia regime.

Cerezo's power to end the killings and "disappearances" will be limited. This is the case, not because he can't control the death squads, but because he can't control the Army and security apparatus in whatever form they operate. . . .

SYLVIA by Nicole Hollander. Reprinted with permission.

Why is it safe to predict that the repression will continue?

Regardless of his intentions, Cerezo's administration cannot stop the human rights abuses because he cannot break the "logic of repression." What Amnesty International called "a government program of political murder" is a calculated response by the Army to the depth of popular opposition to the status quo. Demands for higher wages or better living conditions have traditionally been met with selective killings and "disappearances" of union and community leaders. When the Army has suspected entire Indian communities of supporting the insurgency, wholesale massacres have resulted. The greater the challenge to the wealthy and the Army, the harsher the response.

Piero Gleijeses, a Guatemalan scholar, describes this logic: "Without social reforms in Guatemala, elections are a cruel joke, and repression will remain the only means of assuring peace. The intensity of repression will not depend on the personal wishes of the civilian sitting in the Presidential Palace, but on the degree of challenge from below felt by the country's real rulers. The terror apparatus is in place, and fully intact.''. . .

What will happen to the estimated 150,000 refugees living in Mexico?
Cerezo obviously wants them to return as a visible sign of normality in the country. The continued exile of the refugees serves as a constant international indictment of the Guatemalan government. At a minimum, Cerezo would have to guarantee their lives and safe return. This might be possible if the Army continues its present policy of placing a few hundred returned refugees into military-controlled villages.

Promises of safety aside, the economically devastated Indian highlands (where most of the refugees resided) can provide few opportunities to make a living. In some cases the refugees cannot return to their original homes because the Army has destroyed hundreds of villages. Already strapped by insufficient land and declining opportunities for seasonal labor on the large coffee and cotton plantations, Indian peasants are left with few options other than government food-for-work programs. Cerezo cannot provide adequate solutions for the exiled Guatemalans. . . .

Conclusion

The elections and the accompanying political opening (primarily restricted to the cities) are key components of the Army's long-term strategy to maintain domination over Guatemalan society. Although the Army knew it was necessary to open up some political space to legitimize the new civilian administration, it wants to ensure that popular organizations like unions, peasant groups, student and teacher associations, and Christian organizations do not gather too much steam and become a threat to the stability and viability of the regime. Hence, the political opening must be carefully controlled. . . .

The Reagan Administration has used the elections to step up U.S. aid to Guatemala. The U.S. approved $104 million in aid for fiscal year 1986. Reagan has requested $144 million in military and economic aid for fiscal year 1987. Clearly, U.S. aid needs to be conditioned on the existence of democracy in Guatemala and not just a reward for staging an election.

In Guatemala, elections do not provide a sufficient condition for democracy to flourish. For Guatemala to be democratic certain minimum conditions must be met, among them: an end to the killings and disappearances; the freedom to organize and freedom of expression; an end to discrimination, cultural oppression and the disenfranchisement of the Indian majority; and a reorientation of the economy so that it serves the needs of the poor majority and not the desires of the wealthy.

Ranking Foreign Policy Concerns

This activity will allow you to explore the values you consider important in making foreign policy decisions. While your answers may differ from those of other readers, these disagreements simply mirror the reality of international relations. In studying world politics you will discover that countries, depending on their location, military strength, and economic power, have different priorities for their foreign policies. Consider the difference in foreign policy concerns between Nicaragua, a small, poor nation facing armed opposition at home, and the US, a wealthy nation which is fighting no wars. Since Nicaragua is bordered by hostile Honduras and is fighting a civil war, its priorities must be to defend the government from violent overthrow. The US, on the other hand, can concentrate on foreign policy matters such as human rights because it borders two friendly nations and faces little threat of external attack.

© Huck/Rothco

The authors in this chapter debate US priorities concerning human rights in Latin America. Some analysts believe, as the cartoon illustrates, that America unjustly supports military dictators who violate their people's human rights. Others argue that US aid cannot be predicated on human rights, but on whether or not a government supports American economic and military policies.

Part I

Step 1. The class should break into groups of four to six students. Each group should rank the foreign policy concerns listed below as though the group represents the president of the United States. Use the number 1 to designate the most important concern, the number 2 for the second most important concern, and so on.

_____ promoting democracy

_____ protecting national security

_____ supporting governments friendly to your country

_____ promoting friendship between countries

_____ protecting human rights

_____ fighting communism

_____ ending dictatorships

_____ providing military aid to friendly nations

_____ initiating trade with other countries

_____ promoting your nation's political ideology

Part II

Step 1. Working within the same group, rank the foreign policy concerns as though the group represents the leadership of Nicaragua.

Step 2. After your group has agreed on the rankings from both perspectives, compare your answers with those of other groups in a classwide discussion.

Step 3. The entire class should discuss the following questions:
1. How important was supporting human rights from the US perspective?
2. How important was supporting human rights from the Latin American dictator's perspective?
3. How do you explain the difference?
4. How would your priorities change if you were the democratically-elected leader of a stable Latin American country?

Periodical Bibliography

The following periodical articles have been selected to supplement the diverse views expressed in this chapter.

Elliott Abrams — "An End to Tyranny in Latin America," *Department of State Bulletin*, March 1986.

Elliott Abrams — "The Myopia of Human Rights Activists," *The New York Times*, August 10, 1984.

Gordon L. Bowen — "How Things Are Getting Better in Guatemala," *Commonweal*, October 18, 1985.

John Dinges and Saul Landau — "Derailing Pinochet," *The Nation*, March 7, 1987.

Harold Evans — "Getting Away with Murder," *U.S. News & World Report*, March 23, 1987.

Mark Falcoff — "The Coming Crisis in Chile," *Policy Review*, Fall 1985.

Forbes — "The U.S. View from Guatemala City, an interview with Ambassador Piedra," May 18, 1987.

Tim Frasca — "Chile: The Danger of 'Stroessnerization,'" *AfricAsia*, March 1987. Available from AfricAsia, 13, rue d'Uzes, 75002, Paris, France.

Tim Frasca — "Chile: Pinochet Isolated, Opposition Divided," *AfricAsia*, November 1986.

Piero Gleijeses — "The Guatemalan Silence," *The New Republic*, June 10, 1985.

Paul L. Goepfert — "Democratic Opening," *The Progressive*, November 1985.

Isebill V. Gruhn — "The Nature of Human Rights," *Social Education*, September 1985.

Philip Jacobsen — "Chile: For or Against Pinochet?" *World Press Review*, November 1986.

Beatriz Manz — "A Guatemalan Dies, and What It Means," *The New York Times*, July 14, 1986.

Thomas Molnar — "Notes on Chile," *The World & I*, May 1987.

The New Republic — "Democrats and Comandantes," July 28, 1986.

James Painter | "Guatemala in Civilian Garb," *Third World Quarterly,* July 1986.

Mario Payeras | "The Guatemalan Army and US Policy in Central America," *Monthly Review,* March 1986.

Mark Rabine | "Guatemala's 'Redemocratization,'" *Contemporary Marxism,* 14.

Reason | "Should It Stay or Should It Go: The Reagan Doctrine: An interview with Laurence W. Beilenson, Jack Wheeler, Ted Galen Carpenter, and Christopher Layne, with Robert W. Poole," June 1987.

Pat Robertson | "Dictatorships and Single Standards," *Policy Review,* Winter 1987.

Tina Rosenberg | "The Moral Limits of Self-Interests," *The Atlantic Monthly,* December 1986.

George Shultz | "Promoting Inter-American Cooperation," *Department of State Bulletin,* January 1987.

Robert Joe Stout | "The Happy Birds Move On," *The Christian Century,* March 4, 1987.

Clark Taylor | "Guatemala: The Trouble with Elections," *Radical America,* vol. 19, no. 5.

Lester C. Thurow | "Who Said Military Dictatorships Are Good for the Economy," *Technology Review,* November/December 1986.

William D. Zabel | "We Send Pinochet a Wrong Signal," *The New York Times,* November 28, 1986.

Are Latin American Revolutions a Threat to the US?

Chapter Preface

Controlling Latin American revolutions to make sure they do not result in Marxism is a major US foreign policy concern. The US government believes that these revolutions are exportable; that is, a pro-Marxist regime in Nicaragua would quickly lead to similar regimes in Honduras, Guatemala, El Salvador, and Mexico, resulting in an anti-US regime on its own border.

Critics state that this type of reasoning is nonsense. They argue that this view assumes that Central American nations have no free will. In actuality, these governments are independent nations and would not blindly succumb to Marxism. US officials counter that Cuba presently exports arms, personnel, and influence to Nicaragua and that Nicaragua is doing the same in Honduras. They argue further that behind all of these revolutionary efforts lies the military might of the Soviet Union whose ultimate aim is to destabilize the West. Whether or not US fears are realistic is a main topic of the viewpoints in this chapter.

"The common denominator of all Marxist-Leninist groups in Central America . . . has been their open, consistent, and deeply felt belief that the United States is their main enemy."

Revolutionary Movements Are a Direct Threat to the US

Michael S. Radu

Michael S. Radu is a research associate with the Foreign Policy Research Institute in Philadelphia and a Peace Fellow with the Hoover Institution, a research center devoted to the study of domestic and international affairs. Radu's writings include works on revolutionary movements in Latin America and Africa. In the following viewpoint, Radu criticizes US policymakers for their belief that Latin American revolutions stem from internal problems such as poverty and social injustice. Rather, he argues, these movements are guided and funded by the Soviet Union in order to engage the US in direct conflict with these countries.

As you read, consider the following questions:

1. The author believes the public holds certain inaccurate beliefs about Latin America. What are they?
2. What does the author contend is the ultimate effect of Soviet involvement in revolutionary movements?

Reprinted from THE RED ORCHESTRA: INSTRUMENTS OF SOVIET POLICY IN LATIN AMERICA AND THE CARIBBEAN, edited by Dennis L. Bark, with permission of the Hoover Institution Press. © 1986 by the Board of Trustees of the Leland Stanford Jr. University.

The presence of Soviet proxies in the western hemisphere—particularly since the Cuban Revolution and even more spectacularly since the late 1970s—has raised the prospect of communism in the Americas as a permanent and spreading phenomenon. The scholarly literature abounds with claims that the Americas are or should be insulated from the conflict between the superpowers. . . .

Here in a nutshell are the major reasons that Soviet proxy involvement and activities in Central America and the Caribbean are so seldom even mentioned—as well as the reasons why they are so successful in many respects. The premises of the liberal establishment and of much of the U.S. public concerning Central America and the Caribbean can be summarized as follows:

•The U.S. can and should avoid treating the region as an area of confrontation with the USSR, and it can do so by unilateral action.

•Change is inevitable and it inevitably involves a diminishing of U.S. influence and advantages for the USSR and Cuba. The latter two aspects need not be a security threat to the United States, albeit that the factors of such change are implicitly recognized as Marxist (why, otherwise, would they be hostile to the United States *and* to the advantage of the USSR and Cuba?). (The distance is short indeed from this view of change to the Marxist claim of representing progress and the inevitable course of history.)

•Revolutionary change in the short term is the only road to long-term stability, which is alleged to be the aim of undefined Latin Americans and the ideal goal of the United States. The logical convolution manifest here (that is, change now will be stability tomorrow) can only be explained by the apparent belief that change occurs inevitably in Central America because of the nature of the status quo (presumably "injustice, poverty, repression"). Ironically, if revolutionary change under the banner of the Leninist credo does occur in the region, history argues that it will indeed result in immutable stability—of the type existing today in the USSR, Cuba, and Eastern Europe. That the Latin Americans would like to seek such stability is far less certain if one refers to the majority of people in the area.

•In order to encourage change and ensure future stability, the United States should refrain from using force in Central America and the Caribbean. The implication, spelled out in the overwhelming majority of political statements, academic studies, and articles published in the last few years, is that the crisis in Central America today is not military in nature and therefore cannot and should not be met with military power or involvement by the United States. Conversely, because the crisis is not military in nature, it does not by itself represent a security threat to the United States—unless the latter transforms it into a military conflict by misguidedly projecting power into the region. . . .

The Soviet Proxy Network

The prevailing opinion on the nature of and solutions to the crisis in Central America can be abridged as follows: The crisis in Central America is revolutionary, spreading, and, sometimes but not always or permanently leftist; but it is grounded in native conditions and represents the wave of the future. The aims of the revolutionaries are nationalistic and center on economic and social progress. Unless the United States forces them into the arms of Cuba and the USSR by militarily intervening in the region—directly or by aiding local governments threatened by the revolutionary wind of change—they will not pose a threat to U.S. security or basic national interests.

Marxist Revolutions a Threat

What must be of concern to the United States, particularly in a region as close to us as Central America, is the replacement of a non-representative government by a dictatorship that is more efficient, more brutal, and, above all, more permanent. Revolutionary regimes that call themselves Marxist or communist and that follow the Bolshevik approach to power have two undesirable features: they are irreversible, and they want to expand their type of rule into neighboring countries—by force, if need be.

Fred Iklé, *Harper's*, June 1984.

It is only in light of these perceptions in the United States, and particularly in the U.S. media and Congress, that the *methods* of proxy employed by the USSR can be understood. Only a clear understanding of the roots and nature of the Central American and Caribbean revolutionary groups will permit an accurate assessment of the scope of the proxy network at Soviet disposal. And a realization that such proxy activities are based on a *network* of groups, individuals, interests, and governments is necessary to understand the effectiveness of (and difficulty of countering the) Soviet proxy involvement. Each of these elements reinforces the others, and none can be understood without clarifying its links to the other two. . . .

The Roots and Nature of the Revolutionary Groups

If there is a place in the world that consistently disproves the myth of the declining role and attraction of ideology, and of Marxism-Leninism in particular, it is Latin America and, to only a slightly lesser extent, the English-speaking Caribbean. In defining the role of Marxism in Latin America, Venezuelan writer Carlos Rangel correctly wrote that Marxism "offers a cosmic vision, and can therefore act as a unifying force. Moreover, its pole of attraction lies . . . in a power that is the very tangible, present-day rival of the United States: the Soviet Union . . . It has been amply proven that the failures of Marxism in no way lessen its seductive power." This would not be new were it not tied to the well-established fact that Latin America is also "the last region of the globe where educated people who have access to all necessary information continue (or claim to do so) to believe that everything unpleasant in Latin America is the result of external agents (North American imperialism or—the reverse of the same medal—the international communist conspiracy)."

Although anti-Americanism has been a general cultural trait of Latin American elites during the past century, Marxism-Leninism today serves as its reinforcement and means of effective articulation. The extraordinary scope of Marxism's attractiveness in Latin America explains the even wider scope of the communist proxy network on the continent. . . .

The US as Enemy

The common denominator of all Marxist-Leninist groups in Central America since their inception, and regardless of their feuds, has been their open, consistent, and deeply felt belief that the United States is their main enemy. As *the* enemy, the United States has played an essential role in unifying such competing elements as Trotskyites, Maoists, Castroites, and orthodox Marxists. The realization that the external support necessary to conquer power would come only from the USSR and its satellites was the necessary corollary of a rapidly spreading conviction among the revolutionaries in Central America that victory required a regional and ultimately global perspective that put aside doctrinal differences. These factors were clearly demonstrated in the cases of both Nicaragua and El Salvador.

The statements and actions of the Sandinist National Liberation Front (FSLN) in Nicaragua since it seized state power in July 1979 provide a perfect example of the natural linkage between anti-Americanism and pro-Soviet positions in a Marxist-Leninist political environment. Not only did the FSLN immediately introduce a new national anthem defining the *yanquis* as "enemies of mankind," but it also started building the largest military force in the history of Central America, under the pretext of a possible future conflict with the United States. At the same time, as a corollary of such attitudes and perceptions, Nicaragua openly supported the Soviet invasion of Afghanistan at the end of 1979, and a few months later the FSLN and the Soviet Communist Party signed a formal agreement on party-to-party relations. . . .

The leadership of the Farabundo Marti People's Liberation Forces (FPL—the oldest, once the largest, and now the second-largest guerrilla group in El Salvador) was equally clear in this respect: "The United States has never asked authorization to invade Latin America. It is time that our peoples tighten ranks against the *main enemy*. The revolution in Central America is one, is indivisible, and the Salvadoran [revolutionary] process cannot and should not deal in an isolated manner from, or on the fringes of, those [processes] taking place in Guatemala and Honduras'' (italics added). FPL leader ''Isabel'' went further, stating that ''this struggle advancing in the Isthmus, first and foremost as a result of the triumph of the Nicaraguan people, has transformed Central America into true revolutionary *foco*. It is because of this that our organization has as a fundamental point in its strategy the Central Americanization of the struggle.''. . .

" ... and our duty to all humankind is simple...!"

Ed Gamble. Reprinted with permission.

Factionalism in the guerrilla groups in Central America has long been interpreted as a serious obstacle to Soviet influence over them. Since the late 1970s, however, factions have become less significant and, to the extent that such differences persist, are additional assets in the Soviet proxy network.

Revolutionary violence has been the most important issue facing the Central American Marxists since the 1960s and the source of most debates, conflicts and clashes within the left. The Communist parties (CPs), for decades the only organized force of the Marxist left in Central America, were totally submissive, if minor, tools of the Soviet Union. Their cadres were trained in the USSR and the Soviet bloc, their leaders were selected on Moscow's orders, and their tactics and positions were decided, sometimes in minute detail, by the Kremlin. . . .

The members of the proxy network in Central America and the

Caribbean fluctuate in membership, differ over specific issues, and vary in their interconnections. Some members are temporary, some permanent; some are united by their strategic aims, some by immediate considerations or a vague community of perceived interests. Membership itself, and the role various members play at specific times, can be defined according to (1) ideology, (2) institutional nature, (3) location, (4) specific role, and (5) degree of autonomy from Soviet control.

Ideology. The members of the network may be roughly divided into Marxist-Leninists, radicals of various shades, socialists, social democrats, or just loosely defined "progressives"; the main distinction between the first type and all the others is in the Marxists' strategic aims and degree of attachment to the USSR and its manifest regional proxies. Thus, the Marxist-Leninists' specific and public aims are (1) the destruction of the free-market system and the democratic political process, or at least the chance of democracy in the region and (2) the elimination of all U.S. influence in any form. All these aims are identical to or at least closely connected to the USSR's global strategic goals. The radical, leftist, or simply anti-American members of the network are united in their mutual opposition to the governments targeted by the Marxist-Leninists and in their hostility to U.S. influence in the region. These members do not generally cooperate with the USSR, consciously act on Soviet advice, or try to promote Soviet aims.

Institutional nature. Network members may be nongovernmental institutions, national or international in character; subnational groups operating against or outside government policies; or governments.

Location. The network members may be national, regional, continental, or global (that is, outside the western hemisphere).

Specific role. The role played by a particular network member may be a strictly legitimizing one, that is, centered on propaganda, political and diplomatic, as well as moral support; or it may be financial and military support or direct involvement in Marxist-Leninist violent activities (whether in the region or outside it on behalf of regional actors). . . .

Global Aspects

One of the major characteristics of the network is its international nature, which often assumes a global aspect. Not only are all the political and diplomatic resources of a superpower deployed, but the resources of the global hostility toward democracy and free enterprise are equally well harnessed. Soviet proxies throughout the world (Ethiopia, Vietnam, Eastern Europe, Angola, Mozambique, and South Yemen) and Soviet allies or circumstantial allies (Libya, Syria, or such genuinely nonaligned but consistently anticapitalist and antidemocratic regimes as Algeria,

109

Iran, and Iraq) are all encouraged to become network members at a very low cost. They may even do so of their own volition, for reasons having infinitely more to do with anti-Americanism than with national interest.

To a large extent, Western governments and important parties or groups behave similarly for similar reasons, that is, anti-Americanism is the least costly and most spectacular way of underscoring national independence. This applies to Mexico and France but also to Latin American countries like Ecuador until recently and Argentina after the Falklands experience.

The global aspects of the network, particularly the role of radical and Marxist regimes in the Third World, play an essential role in transforming Central America and the Caribbean into a Soviet-oriented scene of struggle. Libya was the largest supplier of aid to the NJM regime in Grenada, and Iranian, Palestinian, and other radical Middle Eastern actors play a well-known and prominent role in training, financing, arming and politically supporting Central American Marxist-Leninists. These facts serve both to magnify Soviet ability to deny involvement in the region and to reduce Soviet costs for actual involvement. Central American Marxists are quite open in proclaiming their solidarity with anti-Western and, particularly, anti-American Third World actions, feelings, and policies. The effect is to paralyze the United States by forcing it to increase its spending of resources and political capital in the western hemisphere and to lower its commitments of resources for U.S. or Western involvement elsewhere in the Third World.

"It would in no sense be in their interest for Central American revolutionary governments to face the active hostility of the United States."

Revolutionary Movements Are Not a Threat to the US

Phillip Berryman

Phillip Berryman is a writer who began working in Central America in 1965 researching the role of the Catholic Church in Latin America. From 1976 to 1980 as a Central American representative for the American Friends Service Committee, he was in a position to observe the deepening crisis in the region. He returned to the US from Guatemala in 1980 and has since published numerous articles and two books on Latin America. In the following viewpoint, Berryman argues that the US government's insistence that Central American revolutionaries are Soviet proxies is nonsense.

As you read, consider the following questions:

1. Why, according to Berryman, do revolutions occur?
2. What does the author argue are revolutionaries' main concerns?
3. What should the US do when confronted with Latin American revolutions, according to Berryman?

The alternative to the present policies, which are aimed at militarily defeating revolutionary movements, must be the kind of political approach advocated by many governments. Implicit in such an approach is the possibility that leftist governments might emerge in Central America as they have in Africa—for example, internationally supervised elections in Rhodesia-Zimbabwe led to a Marxist government (which the conservative Thatcher government in Britain has successfully lived with).

Such a possibility represents the major stumbling block for the United States. Even congressional critics of administration policy hasten to insist that the advent of more leftist governments in Latin America would signify defeat for the United States.

The underlying question in considering negotiated approaches is whether revolutionary movements threaten U.S. security and are incompatible with U.S. interests.

Security Threats

The most persistent justification for U.S. policy in Central America has been that revolutionary governments or movements there jeopardize U.S. security. The assumption is that these movements are connected to the Soviet Union through Cuba and that their taking power must represent a victory for the USSR and a defeat for the United States.

Arguments along the following lines are often advanced:

> Nicaragua, backed by Cuba, is already supporting subversion in neighboring countries; other revolutionary governments would only extend subversion and widen the threat.
>
> Revolutionary governments in Central America linked to the Soviet Union and Cuba would force the United States for the first time to deploy defense forces to protect its southern flank, thus reducing its ability to project its power elsewhere in the world.
>
> U.S. sea lanes in the Caribbean and the Panama Canal would be made more vulnerable by additional revolutionary governments in the region. Even now, the USSR has a greater capacity to interdict U.S. shipping than did the Nazis.
>
> Communist takeovers will send a tidal wave of refugees to the United States, reaching perhaps into the millions, putting even greater pressure on U.S. jobs and communities.
>
> Finally, there is the question of credibility. If the United States cannot prevail in an area as close as Central America, its ability to influence events elsewhere in the world will be impaired.

The Nature of Revolution

The first point is perhaps the most crucial insofar as it involves the nature of revolution itself and how revolution occurs. Some use physical analogies—"dominoes," "cancer," "prairie fire'—that emphasize geographical contiguity. [Former] Secretary of State Haig spoke of a Soviet "hit list" as though the course of all revolu-

Tony Auth. © 1984, Washington Post Writers Group, reprinted with permission.

tions were determined from the Kremlin. Those who see revolution as the result of small conspiratorial groups assiduously trace connections to a world-wide terrorist network.

Revolution, however, does not occur as a result of the handiwork of a conspiratorial elite. Rather, it begins when social change—indeed, social breakdown—is affecting large numbers of people, so that they become committed to struggle, and when the power structure is weakened or delegitimized. (We are, of course, speaking of genuine revolutions and not barracks coups.) Revolutionary organizations have an undeniable role, but by themselves they cannot create revolutions. . . .

Revolutionary Movements Vary

Those who focus on the security threat tend to see revolutionaries as part of a monolithic global communist movement. In fact, however, revolutionary organizations vary greatly among themselves. Many, if not most, Marxists are independent of Moscow. The Central American revolutionaries are, by and large, Marxists but they do not link their fates to the Soviet Union. This is partly a result of their experience and partly a function of their nationalistic ideology. In other words, they want to be nonaligned.

The notion that revolutionary governments threaten U.S. security should be looked at with a sense of proportion and a degree of common sense. Clearly, an offensive Soviet deployment in the Western hemisphere—in Nicaragua for instance—would be a

113

dangerous escalation in an arms race that is already out of control. Even now, however, Soviet submarines are poised off U.S. shores with nuclear weapons able to reach their targets in minutes. Moreover, for a tiny Central American country to accept Soviet missiles would be suicidal, since it would immediately become a nuclear target. . . .

In reality, any military confrontation between the United States and the USSR, even if it began with conventional weapons, would be almost certain either to escalate rapidly or to move toward negotiations. Again, it would be suicidal for a tiny Central American country to make itself a target for the United States.

Those whose main focus is U.S. security argue that a Central American country might allow the USSR to install naval facilities that would enhance its Caribbean presence, but it is hard to see what that would add to what the USSR has had in Cuba for two decades.

Real US Concerns

Despite its inherent irrationality, the possibility that a revolutionary country might provide the Soviet Union with some offensive military capability, in return for military protection, economic aid, or trade, cannot be utterly excluded. After all, that is what Cuba did in the early 1960s. Preventing such an outcome should be an ultimate consideration for the United States. Hence, one aim of a negotiated approach should be to remove Central American conflicts from the arena of East-West confrontation.

Some here in the United States assert that Marxist governments in Central America will generate hordes, perhaps millions, of "feet people," refugees fleeing totalitarianism, and that they will head for the United States. First it should be noted that already an estimated 300,000 Salvadorans and Guatemalans have come to the United States—fleeing not Marxism, but the violence of their own governments.

Some Nicaraguans fled the Sandinista revolution either with Somoza or later. Most of those who arrived in the United States are not properly refugees but expatriates—they chose to leave Nicaragua because they anticipated that their standard of living could decline under the revolution. Some poor Nicaraguans also fled, particularly Miskito Indians who escaped to Honduras. Should a revolutionary government come to power in El Salvador, no doubt some people will flee, either because they believe their standard of living will fall or because they fear the consequences of their ties to the army or government. . . .

US Cannot Impose Its Will

The credibility argument—that is, that Central America is a test of U.S. resolve and power which has grave implications elsewhere—is dangerous and pernicious. Over the long run, neither of the superpowers can permanently impose its will on other nations. Security must be grounded not in military might but in respect for the rights of others, for self-determination, and for pluralism and diversity. American citizens should not be made to feel that their sense of self-worth depends on their government's ability to "prevail" in tiny countries almost a thousand miles from their border.

The Best Interest of Latin Americans

Instead of being filled with anti-Soviet paranoia, we need to be filled with pity for our neighbors. If fear of further Communist presence in the Western Hemisphere and self-interest (such as the protection of our "front or backyard" and economic interests) are what will determine US policies toward Latin America, then any policy adopted would not necessarily be in the "best" interest of all involved. Policies based on such motivations would only perpetuate the Latin American reality—political unrest due mainly to economic deterioration and unequal distribution of wealth. Only policies that address the root causes of this reality can be in the "best" interest of the people in Latin America.

Magdelena I. Garcia, *e/sa*, December 1983.

No one doubts that the United States is technologically capable of turning Central America into a smoking wasteland. What is really in question is whether it will have the wisdom to seek solutions that can end the causes of strife and rebellion. This sort of credibility has ramifications that go beyond Central America.

What Do the Revolutionaries Want?

According to a prevalent stereotype, those who lead revolutions are power-hungry, ruthless, even bloodthirsty people, whose aim is to take over their countries in order to establish totalitarian regimes subordinate to the imperial aims of the Soviet Union. In that view, revolutions are irrational, a collective plunge into the abyss. They can be "understood" only as pathology.

The starting point here, on the contrary, is that Central American revolutions make sense—at least to those who have taken part in them. In many ways, revolutionaries themselves are as rational as corporation executives. They carefully calculate and weigh various options as they pursue their ends with single-minded determination. If their proposals and the means by which they would carry them out are better understood, then it will be much clearer to what extent their aims may be compatible with U.S. interests.

Assuming that Central American revolutionary movements embody proposals for meeting the aspirations of the population (whether they will work is a separate question), we shall examine the outlines of what these proposals entail on the basis of Sandinista government programs, documents of the Salvadoran and Guatemalan revolutionary movements, and analyses by Central American social scientists.

An End to Violence

Out of a concern to address the political and economic issues, the number one aspiration of people in Central America might be overlooked: peace. The basic reason for violence in Central America today is resistance to change on the part of those holding economic and political power. Many Central Americans have joined the guerrillas out of what they see as a need for self-defense: for them the army is the aggressor.

Not only must the murders and massacres be ended, but people must feel that their lives are secure. Despite the undeniable military buildup in Nicaragua, most citizens see the Sandinista army and police not as a repressive force but as supportive of the revolution they are seeking to build. Their insecurity comes from the U.S.-backed *contras*. A first aspiration is peace and security.

A New Economic Model

All observers recognize that any solution in Central America must entail economic change. What the United States has proposed, however, is largely an infusion of aid in massive amounts. To the extent that there is any notion of a new approach to development, it is that Central America and Caribbean countries should encourage export industries, such as those in Puerto Rico or Taiwan. As in those countries, corporations would be attracted by the comparative advantage of cheap labor. However, because they are so keyed to the export market, such industries are not too dissimilar to the banana plantation of old. They do little for genuine internal development. Moreover, the world economy has room for only a few Taiwans and Puerto Ricos, and Central America's present instability will make outside investors wary for quite some time. . . .

Based on a growing body of research and analysis, Central American revolutionaries hope to foment a new kind of mixed economy with strong state participation that will reorient production toward meeting basic needs (especially food self-sufficiency) and at the same time lay the groundwork for further integrated development. . . .

Just as revolutionary movements acknowledge their need for civilian expertise and broad-based coalitions to carry out the reforms they envision, they are pragmatic enough to recognize that they are located in what the United States has long regarded as its backyard. Their economies are tied to those of the West.

116

The United States has been the largest market for the region's agroexports and the primary source of its imports. In many cases, it would be too costly to switch to other kinds of equipment or technology. Even if they should desire to diversify their economic relations, it would be in their interest to remain within the Western economic system.

Moreover, the Soviet Union is clearly not willing to offer Nicaragua or any other Central American nation the large amounts of aid it would need to break away from the Western economic system. The Soviet Union may strain to support Cuba, but there is little reason to believe it could adopt other such clients. . . .

Finally, it would in no sense be in their interest for Central American revolutionary governments to face the active hostility of the United States. The resources employed against the Sandinistas are a negligible part of the U.S. budget, and yet they force the Nicaraguan government and people to bring major development efforts to a standstill and to shift to a defense-and-survival economy.

To conclude the point: Central American revolutionary movements, should they take power, would have every reason to reach an accommodation with the United States. . . .

Revolutions and Hope

A final objection should be considered. Some might believe that an accommodation with revolutionary movements in Central America would encourage revolutionary movements in other Latin American countries where U.S. interests are much greater (such as Mexico, Brazil, and Chile). Although it is never stated, this fear may be the real bottom line in economic terms. The United States' investment in Central America is only a minuscule 2.5 percent of its total investment in Latin America. But just as the Chilean coup was a devastating reminder to many Latin Americans that basic change may take many years, even generations, the Nicaraguan revolution has energized many with a sense of hope. Its demonstration effect is real.

However, it is ethically repugnant to think that Central Americans should have to continue to die in large numbers simply to send a message about U.S. determination. Central America belongs to Central Americans—properly speaking, the United States cannot lose it at all. Revolutions can come only from within a people. An outside demonstration effect can at most help people overcome psychological barriers and enable them to believe that victory is possible, but it will not supply any of the basic conditions for revolution. If U.S. policymakers or local elites are concerned about further revolutions, the lesson of Central America should impel them to examine whether similar structural conditions exist elsewhere and whether people's basic aspirations are being frustrated in a similar manner.

"If the dominoes fall in Central America, there's going to be total chaos."

US Security Concerns Are Real

Mark Hendrickson interviewed by Robert James Bidinotto

In the following viewpoint, Mark Hendrickson contends that the US must be concerned about what happens in Central America because it will ultimately affect all of Latin America and the US as well. Communism is influencing the political direction of these countries, he believes, and the US must be willing to intervene to stop the inevitable crumbling of fragile democracies. Mark Hendrickson has lived and taught in Mexico and Colombia, and has earned his M.A. and Ph.D. degrees in economics. He is interviewed by Robert James Bidinotto for *On Principle*, a conservative newsletter.

As you read, consider the following questions:

1. What, according to Hendrickson, is the Soviet Union's global plan?
2. Why is Central America vital to US security, according to the author?
3. Why does the author believe that communism in Latin America cannot be tolerated?

Mark Hendrickson interviewed by Robert James Bidinotto, "Caribbean Communism and U.S. Security," *On Principle*, December 9, 1985. Reprinted with permission.

RJB: Why should ordinary Americans be concerned about the current political situation in Central America? Of what possible importance is it to us if poor Third World nations such as Nicaragua go communist?

MH: There are two basic reasons. First, we should be interested for reasons of national security. Second, I would cite the complex and large-scale economic relations that exist between people in this country and the people of Central America. But the most important issue is our national security.

The current problems started, of course, when Cuba became a Soviet satellite on January 1, 1959. That gave the Soviets a foothold in this hemisphere. But we have to take a totally global perspective on this.

People lose sight of the fact that the rulers of the Soviet Union have something of a master plan, a global vision—a set of goals and means for achieving those goals—that have remained essentially unchanged since Lenin was in power. That is the perverse genius of the Soviet system. Unlike Nazism (which became impotent with the passing of Hitler), Lenin and Stalin succeeded in forming a dictatorship by bureaucracy, which essentially plods along the charted path regardless of who the titular leader is. Lenin himself established and outlined the plan for encirclement and defeat of the United States, a plan that would culminate in a one-world communist state. He predicted that the nations of Eastern and Central Europe would fall to communism; then the masses of China; and little by little, the tentacles of the communist empire would stretch around the globe.

RJB: And now those tentacles have reached too close to home. . . .

Vital to US Security

MH: Right. Central America is vital to U.S. security. This is partly because about two-thirds of the petroleum products imported into the United States pass through the Caribbean Sea; and at least half of all our international trade passes through the Panama Canal. As for trade with the region itself, it's estimated that a half-million jobs have been lost in this country already due to the current chaos in Central America—which demonstrates our economic vulnerability to what happens there. Militarily, we have to realize that, unlike Cuba, which is an island, the Central American nations are connected to the United States by land— which poses the eventual prospect of land-based aggression against this country.

People who oppose any U.S. intervention in Central America are saying that they don't want "another Vietnam." Well, I hope we don't have another Vietnam, either. I hope we don't witness the total enslavement of the peace-loving peoples of Nicaragua by communists backed by the Soviet Union. I hope we don't see a repeat of the "dominoes falling" as occurred in Southeast Asia, where once South Vietnam fell, Laos and Cambodia were overrun and savaged. But currently, Soviet-backed guerilla groups, which have their headquarters in Managua, Nicaragua, are active in Guatemala, El Salvador, Costa Rica and Honduras.

I also hope the media don't succeed in portraying the communist Sandinistas as patriotic nationalists, as they did with Ho Chi Minh; or the *contras* as a bunch of corrupt bums instead of decent, peace-loving people, as they did to our South Vietnamese allies. Mostly, I hope we give the *contras* sufficient supplies to win their country back—and that we do so soon, to prevent communist advances that would necessitate deploying U.S. troops to Central America.

Deceptive Use of Surrogates

The Soviet Union's ability to act through others, particularly through personnel or organizations acting in the name of small developing countries, has given it a significant operational and propaganda advantage vis-a-vis the West. By disguising Soviet activities and increasing local impact, the use of countries like Grenada, Nicaragua, and even Cuba—all of which are so small as to seem incapable of threatening U.S. interests—seeks to lull Western public opinion against accepting the reality of the Soviet challenge.

James H. Michel, statement before the House Foreign Affairs Committee, February 28, 1985.

RJB: One of the suspects arrested in El Salvador for the murders of the four American soldiers in that sidewalk cafe, confessed that the group was trained in Cuba, Nicaragua and Eastern Europe. Which bears out your argument that the Cuban and Nicaraguan regimes are expansionist, and that their Kremlin puppeteers remain loyal to Lenin's doctrine of encirclement.

MH: Various defectors have shared the same information. In fact, so have the Sandinista *commandantes*, who openly proclaim their loyalty to Marxism-Leninism, and have said that theirs is a "revolution without borders." The most popular mistaken notion about the Nicaraguan situation is that it is purely an internal Nicaraguan issue. But the fact is that the Sandinistas are Marxist-Leninists, armed through and controlled by Cuba and the Soviet Union, and that all their top-level leaders have spent time in the Soviet Union to receive indoctrination. We must recognize that they are internationalist communists—not patriotic nationalists.

If the dominoes fall in Central America, there's going to be total chaos. Take Mexico, for example. You cannot underestimate the anti-Americanism there, the leftist ideology of the government and the seething poverty exacerbated by the corrupt government. Remember the phenomenon of the "boat people" coming out of Vietnam when the dominoes fell in Indochina? You'll see "foot people" by the millions coming to this country across our 2,000-mile southern border, and the possibility of guerrilla aggression and infiltration from the south.

Obviously, the Nicaraguans and Mexicans can't conquer the United States by themselves. But, acting in concert with the Soviet bloc, they *can* force us to pull our troops back from NATO, South Korea, etc., in order to defend our national borders. Now a *gradual*, evolutionary withdrawal from NATO might work. But to *suddenly* pull American troops home in an emergency to defend this country would create a power vacuum in Europe and elsewhere; and this would let the Soviets totally Finlandize Western Europe.

RJB: It would be Finlandized without a word or shot being exchanged, as everyone acknowledged the new imbalance of power. You'd immediately see kowtowing from the West to the East.

MH: And if the Soviets then decided to finish off South Africa, from which we receive so many of our strategic minerals, or to take control of the Middle East oil supplies, we would be able to do nothing except defend Fortress America. The rest of the world would be lost. To think that we could then go it alone—

RJB: That would mean the Finlandization of the United States.

MH: That's the final step. Lenin said that after the rest of the world came into the Soviet orbit, America would lose the will to resist and would fall into Soviet hands "like overripe fruit"—to quote his famous metaphor. So I think you cannot possibly overestimate the stakes that the United States has in the security of Central America.

The Monroe Doctrine

RJB: Are you calling for re-assertion of the Monroe Doctrine?

MH: The Monroe Doctrine held that we would stay out of European affairs, but that we would tolerate no European empire-building in this hemisphere. Unfortunately, we abrogated that doctrine ourselves when we let Woodrow Wilson take us into World War I on behalf of Britain against Germany. But yes, I think the Monroe Doctrine should be invoked. The Soviet Union, an Old World power, should be prevented from establishing client states in this hemisphere. In Grenada, we reversed the "Brezhnev Doctrine"—the idea that once a country came into the Soviet bloc, it had to remain permanently communist and pro-Soviet—and the Reagan administration was 100 percent right in taking that step.

RJB: Some argue that to accept laissez-faire economics implies support of a radically noninterventionist foreign policy. Do you buy the analogy?

MH: Not completely. To me, laissez-faire economics implies a

Dick Wright. Reprinted with permission.

basically noninterventionist foreign policy, but not absolute nonintervention. For instance, if the people of Nicaragua want, by democratic means, to socialize their economy—let them do it. It would be self-defeating: socialism doesn't work. (Ludwig von) Mises proved that in his book, *Socialism*; and since it was published in 1922, many Third World countries have experimented with socialism and they've all regretted it. But if the people of a nation want to shoot themselves in the foot, let them.

However, in Nicaragua and other similar cases it isn't simply an internal matter of one group of citizens engaged in a political power struggle with another group of citizens. There's a "third man in the ring." One group is being aided and abetted by the Soviet Union and its satellites to impose a dictatorship on the rest. In the process, they have amassed the largest military force in the history of Central America. Soviets, Cubans, East Germans, Bulgarians, North Koreans, PLO members—all are helping the Sandinistas build a war machine whose long-range purpose is to bring war to our doorstep—and beyond.

Now, in a remote part of the world, such as Afghanistan, our government should not intervene—although personally I am contributing money to the cause of the Afghan resistance, as I hope all freedom-loving people are doing. But in "our own backyard," as the cliche has it, our own security is at stake and—unless you are an anarchist—you must believe that our government should take actions, even pre-emptive actions, to protect the well-being of American citizens.

RJB: So the problem isn't that there's an anti-American regime in Managua, but that it's a Soviet-backed communist regime.

MH: Exactly. And most Americans aren't facing up to that. You know, it's curious. If someone's a Mormon, or a Hindu, or a Catholic, you'd expect him to act in certain ways. Why then don't we expect Marxist-Leninists to act like Marxist-Leninists? Their doctrine is like a religion; it has a very prescribed outline of strategy and tactics to further the communization of a country; and it is inherently expansionist and aggressive.

Since the McCarthy episode, it has become more of a stigma to be known as an *anti*-communist than a communist. Just consider what this implies. Communism is anti-freedom and totally depraved—totally at war with "bourgeois" ethical notions about individual rights. Anti-communists are generally pro-freedom, pro-individual rights. Thus, the "moderate," middle-of-the-road commentator who denounces "extremes" is in effect saying that a "reasonable" position is to be partly anti-freedom and depraved.

So, many people in this country have displayed a total unwillingness to take a sober, objective look around the world at what Marxist-Leninists have done—or even to refer to self-avowed Marxist-Leninists as "communists."

RJB: Why do you think that's so? How do you explain the deliberate evasion of these facts?

MH: Some of the reasons lie in human psychology, in the psychology of fear. Like children who believe that hiding under the bedcovers will save them from the bogeyman, many adults block out and deny the reality of communist ruthlessness and its goal of global conquest. They ignore the fact that communists despise "bourgeois" values—fair play, honesty, the desire for peace and so on—and reassure themselves that "they're just like we are." Also, people want to be liked; and when they see how anybody who takes a strong public stand against communism gets attacked and derided, that intimidates them.

In addition, leftist ideas are still considered intellectually fashionable in many quarters. Redistributionism remains the opiate of the intellectuals. We saw signs of this when the Carter State Department forced El Salvador to redistribute farmland and nationalize banks and export industries in 1979. Then, when Salvadoreans fought back against this tyranny, they were branded "right-wingers"; and every death in the civil strife that followed was blamed on them by journalists and human rights groups.

Double Standards of Liberals

RJB: I marvel at the double standard. Toward old-fashioned, authoritarian, military dictatorships liberals declare a "human rights policy"—South Africa is the present example. But regarding communist regimes, they suddenly declare the "right of national self-determination" and the sanctity of each nation's "internal affairs."

MH: Right! Another example of the double standard was the way in which many media commentators criticized the Reagan administration for failing to pressure the democratically-elected government in El Salvador to engage in dialogue with the communist guerrillas—while at the same time declaring that the president had no business urging the Sandinistas to negotiate with the *contras*. This, even though the Sandinistas, unlike the Salvadorean government, had *not* been democratically elected.

Soviet Influence a Threat

The policy interests of the United States in Latin America and the Caribbean are challenged not only by endemic political, social, economic, and security conditions but also by an active, sophisticated, and opportunistic Soviet effort to gain increased influence in the region.

James H. Michel, statement before the House Foreign Affairs Committee, February 28, 1985.

RJB: What is the answer or antidote to our present confusion?

MH: I think if free-market economics and the ethics of liberty were better understood, it would make a difference in popular attitudes. I think the death of philosophy is responsible—there's so much sloppy thinking going on.

Freedom doesn't come free. There's a tremendous price attached to it. And we've become so comfortable enjoying the fruits of liberty that we've stopped tending to the tree from which those fruits grow.

That's what we must begin to do.

"The United States' political and economic subjugation of Latin America has given rise to the emergence and perpetuation in power of regressive groups."

US Security Concerns Are Fabricated

Rafael Hernandez

Rafael Hernandez is a senior research fellow and director of the Departamento de Norte America at the Centro de Estudios sobre America in Havana, Cuba. He is also an associate professor at the Instituto Superior de Relaciones Internacionales in Havana and has written extensively on US-Latin American relations. In the following viewpoint, Hernandez criticizes the United States' claims about its security concerns in Latin America. He contends that the US is really reacting to its loss of influence there. He concludes by arguing that the US must cease its endless intervention or expect Latin Americans to forcefully resist.

As you read, consider the following questions:

1. From the context of this article, define the word hegemony. After reading the viewpoint, look the word up in the dictionary.
2. Why does the author argue that the limited Soviet military presence in the Caribbean is irrelevant to US security?
3. Does the author think the US can know what's best for Latin America? Why or why not?

This work appears as "COMMENT: The United States and Latin America: The Question of Security" by Rafael Hernandez in THE UNITED STATES AND LATIN AMERICA IN THE 1980s: CONTENDING PERSPECTIVES ON A DECADE OF CRISIS, Kevin J. Middlebrook and Carlos Rico, Editors. Published 1986 by the University of Pittsburgh Press. Used by permission of the publisher.

If something like the concept of "security" exists in the body of strategic doctrine that inspires different U.S. administrations, it corresponds only to a binary logic that merits serious consideration because of the United States' economic and military power. Thus one asks: Is it possible that the whole structure of hemispheric relations for a global power such as the United States can rest on something so imponderable as "the threat of Soviet attack against the Western Hemisphere"? Not even the Roman Empire, in a much less complex world, rested on such a simple notion. What is at issue is not the Soviet Union's potential military presence or its actual political activity in Latin America, but the United States' hegemonic dominance over the region. United States hegemony does not face a military threat from any quarter, but it *is* affected by internal social change in different Latin American countries. It is true that the United States faces a crisis of hegemony in Latin America, but this is the result of many diverse factors that do not stem from a confrontation with the Soviet Union and communism (as the binary logic of ideological discourse suggests). However, before turning to an examination of these factors, it is useful to evaluate in more detail the assumptions that underlie U.S. security policies toward Latin America.

US Influence Is Pervasive

The idea of an "external military presence in the Western Hemisphere" is an important example of the way in which ideological considerations color the U.S. debate on strategic issues. What is a "military presence" in the age of fourth-generation intercontinental ballistic missiles, submarine-launched ballistic missiles with a range of eight thousand kilometers, and antisatellite weapons in outer space? In *strategic terms*, the limited Soviet military presence in the Caribbean is irrelevant in this context, especially if one takes into account that there are many other available sites at sea or on other continents from which the Soviet Union can conduct a nuclear action. Moreover, U.S. military power in the Western Hemisphere (especially in the Caribbean Basin) is so overwhelming that it is unrealistic to discuss the two superpowers' military presence on this continent in the same terms. The "national security" imperative has led the United States to establish a massive military presence much closer to the Soviet Union's own frontiers (including U.S. military installations in Europe, the Middle East, and the Far East) in the "other" hemisphere. In short, the only ominous "hemispheric" presence in Latin America (including the threat posed by nuclear weapons) is that of the United States.

The "external" character of this perceived threat is also paradoxical, given that it includes Cuba and Nicaragua (although no longer Grenada, where in 1983 the "actual military presence" of the

United States replaced the "potential military presence" of the Soviet Union). In the terms of this peculiar U.S. geopolitical discourse, Cuban military advisors in Nicaragua constitute an "external military presence in the hemisphere," while the British fleet operating near the Malvinas Islands is a legitimate defender of their sovereignty and an ally both within and beyond the hemisphere. It is doubtful that even President James Monroe would have engaged in such a contradictory application of his own doctrine. What is certain is that Cuba's relations—and those of Peru, Argentina, and other nonsocialist countries in Latin America—with the Soviet Union do not convert these countries into an "external force" in the same part of the world in which they have forged their histories, in many cases beginning earlier than the founding of the United States. . . .

A More Dramatic Conflict Than Ever

The United States has consistently underlined in its relations with Latin America, particularly now under the Reagan administration, security and strategic factors; conversely, the Latin American countries, although not denying security and defense aspects, have stressed economic and social issues, while struggling for better terms in commercial, financial, and investment ties. The U.S. posture has always prevailed either because of the Latin American inability to respond with a common, unified position, or due to the fact that in moments of crisis, Washington's demand for hemispheric solidarity has been accompanied by a temporary concern with economic and social problems of the region, a preoccupation that ceases as soon as the security goal has been accomplished. At present, this basic difference of perspectives and interests in conflict between the United States and Latin America seems more dramatic than ever.

Heraldo Muñoz, *Latin American Views of U.S. Policy*, 1986.

The development of modern societies in Latin America (both in terms of the emergence of popular sectors and the configuration of their progressive, democratic leadership) has occurred in permanent counterpoint to different U.S. administrations. Vargas, Quadros, and Goulart in Brazil; Cárdenas in Mexico; Perón in Argentina; Velasco Alvarado in Peru; and Torrijos in Panama (to mention only those leaders who are deceased) all faced major challenges from the United States. On the other hand, the United States' political and economic subjugation of Latin America has given rise to the emergence and perpetuation in power of regressive groups (oligarchies and military cliques) that have no relation to the self-determination and sovereignty of nation-states. Examples include Pinochet in Chile, Castillo Armas in Guatemala,

Somoza in Nicaragua, Batista in Cuba, and numerous generals in Bolivia—to mention only the classic examples of U.S.-inspired "hemispheric community."

Thus the United States has not demonstrated historically that it is capable of determining what is in the best interests of Latin American countries. Nor have U.S. interventions to "correct" Latin American leaders promoted the stabilization and democratization of these societies. For precisely these reasons, the majority of Latin American governments opposed the recurrence of U.S. military intervention in the region (especially after the 1982 Malvinas conflict and the invasion of Grenada). Some countries (particularly Argentina, Guyana, Suriname, Trinidad and Tobago, and Nicaragua) have expressed concern regarding the possibility of U.S. military action against them. Indeed, a list of the United States' covert actions, indirect incursions, and direct military interventions in the hemisphere would include the majority of Latin American countries.

Exaggerations and Misinformation

The corollaries to this curious U.S. formulation of "external military presence in the Western Hemisphere" are also peculiar. First, despite the concern that is often raised regarding the specter of "another Cuba," it is clear that the only factor that actually restricts political options or radicalizes the political process in Latin American countries is U.S. hostility to change. Only through ignorance of actual circumstances could the United States have perceived "another Cuba" in Grenada. If another "American tragedy" is now developing in El Salvador, it will be part of the bitter harvest of U.S. policy rather than the result of the "export of Castroist-communist revolution." After all, what did the United States seek by opposing the Cuban revolution in 1959 and early 1960—acting against a popular movement that punished war criminals, promulgated a moderate agrarian reform, and diversified its foreign relations? . . .

A second corollary is that "the strategic importance of the Caribbean Basin" for the United States justifies its large-scale military presence in the area. It is frequently claimed that in the event of an all-out confrontation between the United States and the Soviet Union that escalates to the nuclear level, U.S. supply lines through the Caribbean could be interrupted, with severe economic consequences. This line of reasoning (which might be called "the Day-After syndrome") casts the United States as a defenseless nation at the mercy of a handful of wicked developing countries at the service of the Soviet Union. These countries ostensibly have the capability of closing the Caribbean Sea and the Panama Canal, thereby cutting off supplies and strangling the U.S. economy— *which has survived a Soviet nuclear attack*. The silliness of this scenario does not merit comment. . . .

U.S. hegemony in Latin America faces growing resistance. In contrast to what one might think, the United States' policy toward Cuba is not a special case in this regard. Rather, this case reveals better than any other example the challenges that confront U.S. hegemony in the region. This goes beyond the question of whether the ghost of communism haunts Latin America, or whether or the peoples of Latin America are rising up against the U.S. empire.

"HERE ARE SOME MORE STABILIZERS!"

Justus. Reprinted by permission of the Star Tribune: Newspaper of the Twin Cities.

It is *not only* a question of popular reaction, nor is it *just* communism. Any dispassionate observer of contemporary Latin America must recognize that diverse political leaders and ideologies not generally linked to insurrection and violence have been significantly affected by the lesson of Cuba over the last quarter-century. Cuba is an exemplary case of disruption in the hegemonic system. Cuba changed its relation to this system in extremis. But, at the same time, Cuba represents a limiting case in the crisis facing the United States' hegemonic assumption in the region. As such, Cuba has demonstrated the range of actions and reactions that a Latin American country puts into play when it deals with the U.S. government as a sovereign equal. Cuba has also shown how vulnerable the hegemonic system's own inelasticity makes it when a Latin American country attempts to achieve a degree of autonomy. Even though Latin American political leaders are far from ending general dependency relations with the United States on the basis of an independent national development project, Latin American leaders of the 1980s nonetheless have reassessed their relations with the U.S. government. They have identified their own interests and they have initiated a more diversified foreign policy as part of an effort to improve their international negotiating position.

Mistakes in Cuban Relations

The ineptitude with which the U.S. government has confronted Cuba reveals a bundle of mistaken ideas and erroneous perceptions that increasingly complicates U.S. relations with other Latin American countries. Moreover, the United States' current ties with Argentina, Brazil, Mexico, Colombia, and Venezuela (to cite only the principal cases) also show that it has failed to maintain healthy collaborative relations (in the broadest political sense) with governments in the region. Latin American leaders have come to see more and more that their own interests are not served by yielding to U.S. influence.

Given that the U.S. government has lacked the capacity to cooperate politically with most Latin American governments, and given that it has failed to foresee the direction of social change in the region (for example, in Nicaragua and Grenada in 1979), the United States' most pragmatic response would be to establish a policy of accommodation that would not exclude Latin American domestic processes of sociopolitical change from the western orbit. A policy of this kind would establish incentives to maintain Latin American states' prowestern alignment. Cases such as Grenada (not to mention countries in regions such as Africa) show that revolutionary governments are not so temperamental or antagonistic regarding prowestern ties as has sometimes been suggested. By casting all issues in terms of "national security" concerns, the U.S. government loses an opportunity to benefit from the practical importance of economic relations. . . .

The ties that most U.S. groups have to conservative forces in Latin America reveal both their bias and their lack of a minimum plan to encourage political openings (and resolve crises of political "closure") in the region. Throughout the twentieth century Latin American societies have moved toward an economic modernity with improved income distribution, a political modernity based on a new kind of democracy, and a social modernity that is more egalitarian and participatory. These changes surely cannot be consolidated within the existing parameters of Latin American capitalism, and it is even doubtful that they can be effected within the context of reformed capitalism. Very probably—and from the perspective that informs this comment, inevitably—this ultimate modernity is called socialism. If this is the case, how will those U.S. groups with ties to Latin America respond? What is the United States' *minimum plan* for a Latin America in transformation? This is the challenge that U.S. power-holders have confronted since the Eisenhower administration. The United States' response has frequently been characterized by simplification and the most absurd references to ideology, depicting the complexity of Latin American social processes as a movement from "West" to "East."

A New Sense of Reality

Even if all Latin Americans do not agree concerning the merits of socialism, they share a new sense of reality regarding their "hemispheric neighbor." The disenchanted realism of Latin American political leaders and popular movements cannot be easily addressed by liberal proposals informed by "good will." For their part, the U.S. government and U.S. power-holders are not inclined toward a "new deal" for Latin America. Their perception of recurrent hegemonic crises in the region is to see an opponent behind each democrat and a Marxist behind each opponent.

For this reason, it appears as if force might be the only effective means of guaranteeing dialogue with the United States. In order to be able to negotiate, one must hold a position of strength; the interlocutors are the belligerents. Thus Central America now offers a historic lesson to other Latin American countries, just as Cuba did earlier: only those who will fight for their rights can (and deserve to) enjoy them. The hegemonic system will give ground only if it is forced to do so by necessity. In more "businesslike" terms, a negotiator only accepts an agreement that offers less than ideal benefits if he is in danger of suffering greater losses. Will the United States suspend hegemonic operations before its Latin America stock is permanently devalued? Time is running out.

*"Cuba has played decisive roles in installing
pro-Soviet regimes in Angola, Ethiopia,
Grenada and Nicaragua."*

Cuba Is a Threat
to the US

Timothy Ashby

Timothy Ashby holds a Ph.D. in international relations from the
University of California, and specializes in the study of Latin
America and the Caribbean. He also serves as the co-chairman
of the Heritage Foundation's Working Group on Counter-Terrorism
and is the author of *The Bear in the Backyard: Moscow's Caribbean
Strategy.* A former resident of Grenada, he also served as a visiting
research scholar at the Hoover Institution at Stanford University.
In the following viewpoint, Ashby gives countless examples of
ways in which Cuba is undermining US influence in Latin America
and beyond. The US must take direct action against Cuba, he contends, in order to thwart Castro's tactics.

As you read, consider the following questions:

1. Why does Ashby think Castro is sometimes forced to back
   foreign policy decisions he does not like?
2. What actions does the author believe the US should take
   against Cuba?
3. Why does Ashby believe accommodation with Cuba is
   impossible? How does this view differ from that of
   Robbins, author of the opposing viewpoint?

Timothy Ashby, "A Nine-Point Strategy for Dealing with Castro," The Heritage
Foundation *Backgrounder*, November 21, 1985. Reprinted with permission.

When he became Ronald Reagan's first Secretary of State, Alexander Haig had tough words for Cuba. He declared that "the overwhelming economic strength and political influence of the United States, together with the reality of its military power, (should be brought) to bear on Cuba in order to treat the problem at its source." The "problem" to which Haig was referring was Cuba's support for violent revolution, terrorism, and the destabilization of regimes friendly to the U.S.

The Reagan Administration still has not crafted a policy to keep Cuba in check. Cuba remains one of the USSR's most valuable military assets, actively serving Soviet policy objectives around the world. With regular armed forces exceeding 225,000 personnel and a militia that numbers nearly a million, Cuba is a Latin American military power second only to Brazil. Cuba has played decisive roles in installing pro-Soviet regimes in Angola, Ethiopia, Grenada, and Nicaragua. Today, more than 50,000 regular Cuban troops are serving in at least sixteen countries on four continents. Accompanying them are an equal number of militarily trained "construction workers" and "internationalists.". . .

Besides the troops garrisoning Angola and Ethiopia, Castro's forces foment violent revolution in Central America. Cuba's connection with Colombia's drug dealers and underworld is now an established fact. Most recently, the Cuban dictator began working actively against U.S. attempts to resolve the Latin American debt crisis. It is thus clear that the Castro regime has changed little over the years.

So long as Castro remains steadfastly in the Soviet bloc and pursues his disruptive foreign policy, the U.S. must not fundamentally ease its policies toward Havana. If anything, it is time to follow Haig's advice and get tougher.

Exploiting Castro's Vulnerability

Due to serious economic and military problems, the Castro regime has become increasingly vulnerable. To exploit these difficulties, the U.S. should follow a nine-point blueprint, consisting of:

1) Aiding guerrilla forces fighting Cuban troops throughout the world;
2) Recruiting anti-communist surrogates to counter the Cubans when U.S. involvement is not feasible;
3) Assisting militarily counterinsurgency programs throughout the Caribbean Basin;
4) Marshalling economic and educational assistance to foster democracy in the Caribbean region;
5) Mounting a propaganda offensive in world and regional organizations to highlight Cuban violations of international law;

6) Encouraging Latin American democracies to participate in U.S. military exercises in the Caribbean;
7) Launching an ideological initiative, featuring Latin American democracies, to counter the Soviet-Cuban model of development;
8) Increasing cooperation between the U.S. and Latin American governments in eradicating the narcotics trade, in which Cuba is heavily involved;
9) Resurrecting the Central American Defense Council (CONDECA).

These measures should induce Castro to stop promoting revolution abroad and to ease internal repression. At that time—and only then—could Washington consider the U.S.-Cuban talks sought by Castro. . . .

Cuba's Strategic Importance to Moscow

Cuba provides the Soviet Union with a military and intelligence capacity in the Caribbean, an area vital to the U.S. economic lifeline. Caribbean maritime routes carry about 55 percent of U.S. petroleum imports and approximately 45 percent of all U.S. seaborne trade. Cuba is very close to the Gulf of Mexico, the straits of Florida, the Yucatan channel, and the Mona straits. In the event of a NATO-Warsaw Pact confrontation, more than half of U.S. sup-

This illustration depicts the number of Cuban military personnel in each of the countries shown.

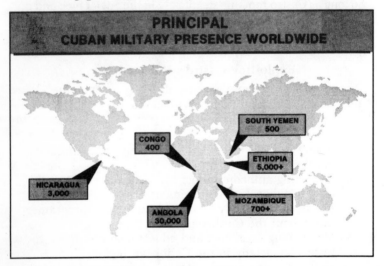

US Department of State

plies to NATO would depart from U.S. Gulf ports and pass by Cuba.

From Cuban bases, long-range Soviet warplanes, such as the Tu-95 Bear D and the Tu-142 Bear F reconnaissance aircraft, now regularly patrol the U.S. east coast and the Caribbean Basin. They spy on U.S. military installations and shadow U.S. carrier groups. Sensitive maritime and space communications and even private telephone conversations in the U.S. are monitored by the Soviet intelligence facility at Lourdes outside Havana. . . .

Cuba also serves as a weapons depot and conduit for Soviet-sponsored subversion and violent revolution in the Americas. Through Cuba, Moscow has provided financial and logistical support for thousands of communist guerrillas who are attacking Latin America's fragile young democracies. On the ideological front, Soviet propaganda is disseminated on Cuba's Isle of Youth, where each year over 20,000 students from Latin America, Asia, and Africa receive scholarships to study Marxist-Leninist revolution.

Cuba as a Proxy

Although Moscow and Havana have had their differences in the past 26 years, relations between the two dictatorships have remained close since 1968. Castro needs Soviet arms and financial support to stay in power and the Kremlin needs Cuba as a reliable surrogate and a huge military base a mere 90 miles from the U.S. mainland. There is, moreover, little that Castro could do to break his dependence on Moscow. Prior to 1968, Castro's grievous mismanagement of the Cuban economy and failed guerrilla expeditions in South America and the Caribbean had brought his regime to the brink of collapse. According to defectors, a secret agreement was signed with the Soviet Union in the spring of 1968 which effectively ceded sovereignty in exchange for Soviet economic aid.

The Soviet political and economic investment in Cuba reaped rich dividends during the 1975 Angolan venture. Nearly 18,000 Cuban troops were rushed to Angola on Soviet transport aircraft to assist the communist MPLA in winning control of the important southern African nation. Two years later, Castro dispatched 17,000 troops to Ethiopia where, under the command of Russian generals, they installed another Soviet satellite regime. Cubans are currently flying Mi-24 helicopter gunships in Nicaragua and supervising the construction of military bases and airfields.

It is said that Cuba is a small nation with a great power's foreign policy. Today there are an estimated 37,500 Cuban military personnel in Africa and at least 6,000 in Nicaragua. Cuban troops serve in Afghanistan, Iraq, Vietnam, Laos, Guyana, and South Yemen. In this hemisphere, Cuba has been linked to the terrorist activities of such Marxist guerrillas as the M-19 movement in Colombia, the Tupamaros in Uruguay, the Montoneros in Argentina, and Chile's Left Revolutionary Movement (M.I.R.). Over the past two decades, Cuba has provided logistical support, training and intelligence to revolutionary groups in every Western Hemisphere nation, including the United States. . . .

Cuban-Soviet Friction

Cuban dependence on the Soviet Union seems to have forced Castro into backing Soviet foreign policy positions that may be unpopular with the Cuban people. This probably also gets in the way of his attempts to play a leading role in the Third World. Cuban support for the Soviet invasion of Afghanistan, for example, tarnished his claim to leadership of the nonaligned movement and may have cost Cuba a much-desired United Nations Security Council seat in 1980. Going along with the Soviet boycott of the 1984 Olympics in Los Angeles denied Cuban athletes the opportunity to compete in such events as boxing and baseball, where they were virtually certain of winning medals. This would have earned Castro international prestige and fueled Cuban patriotism.

A Subversive Catalyst

Acting to fulfill his own revolutionary ambitions as well as being an agent of Soviet influence, Fidel Castro is working closely with subversive elements throughout Central America and the Caribbean. Castro's goal in the 1980s remains much as it was when he assumed power: to oppose the United States and create Marxist-Leninist regimes that mirror his own dictatorship.

U.S. Department of State, *The Soviet-Cuban Connection in Central America and the Caribbean*, March 1985.

Cuban subservience to Soviet interests also frustrates Castro's revolutionary aspirations in Latin America. Cuba at times views fomenting unrest in the region with greater urgency than does the Kremlin. There often have been intense polemics between the two countries over the pace and proper tools of revolution in Latin America. . . .

American Options

Washington should craft a graduated offensive strategy to exploit Cuba's growing weaknesses. For one thing, the U.S. should continue to warn Havana and Moscow that another Cuban-style, pro-Soviet, totalitarian dictatorship will not be tolerated in this hemisphere. For another, the U.S. should make it clear that the price of Cuban intervention in the Caribbean Basin would be very high; retaliatory measures against Cuban nationals involved in radical factions abroad or even Cuba itself should not be ruled out. . . .

Any U.S. attempts to normalize relations with Cuba while Fidel Castro remains in power are extremely unlikely to halt Cuban adventurism and temper Cuba's internal repression. Castro shows no sign of substantively changing his policy of exporting violent revolution and of actively serving Moscow's geopolitical interests; his hostility toward the U.S. has never abated.

Castro's activist policies are essential to his regime's survival, power, and ideology. There is no reason for him to bargain them away for U.S. economic concessions. They are the resource of Cuban leverage in dealing with Moscow, they hold promise for finding new allies that would reduce Cuba's isolation in the hemisphere, and they buttress his claim to a world leadership role. It is, moreover, unrealistic to assume that the Soviet Union simply would abandon the leverage and military gains it reaps because of Cuba as long as the Castro regime justifies its expense.

A normalization of relations between the U.S. and Cuba would strengthen Castro's hand domestically, add to his international prestige, and reduce his economic problems. The U.S would be seen as endorsing his radical policies. This would send a diplomatic message to Washington's Latin American allies to seek accommodation with communist Cuba. Rather than try to normalize ties with Havana, the U.S. should pursue the nine-point strategy and increase its efforts to check Cuban expansionist policies in this hemisphere and elsewhere.

"The United States has made policy in the hemisphere based on a distorted and highly exaggerated image of Cuba and the threat it poses to American interests."

Cuba Is Not a Threat to the US

Carla Anne Robbins

Carla Anne Robbins is a staff editor for *Business Week* where she writes frequently about the Caribbean. She holds a B.A. from Wellesley College and a Ph.D. from the University of California at Berkeley. In the following viewpoint, Robbins argues that the US government exaggerates the Cuban threat to the point that officials make counterproductive policies in responding to it.

As you read, consider the following questions:

1. Why does the US continue to exaggerate Cuban meddling in Central America, according to Robbins?
2. Does the author think that other countries agree with the US view of Cuba? Why or why not?
3. What does the author think are the underlying concerns which created the "Cuban threat"?

Carla Anne Robbins, *The Cuban Threat*. Copyright © 1983. Reprinted by permission of McGraw-Hill Book Company.

For two decades, American presidents have made policy in the hemisphere (and, to some extent, around the world) based on a set of faulty assumptions about Cuba and the threat it poses to American interests. These assumptions, which have achieved almost mythic status, have led each President to commit similar, costly mistakes: Kennedy's Bay of Pigs debacle, Johnson's invasion of the Dominican Republic, Nixon's covert backing of the Chilean coup, Ford's backing of UNITA and FNLA forces in Angola and *de facto* alliance with South Africa, the Carter resurrection of the Cold War in the Caribbean. In each instance, the United States allowed its faulty perception of Cuba to take precedence over the actual situation, overestimating the significance of the Cuban threat and overreacting in an attempt to contain the alleged threat. Each time, Washington's overreaction dealt a blow to the moderate forces at hand and severely strained America's alliances. . . .

What are the myths that have played such an important and destructive role in American policy making over the last two decades?

Myth 1: The Cubans Are Soviet Pawns

Of all the myths about Cuba, this one is the most prevalent. It is also the most difficult to explode because it is so basic to our perception of Cuba and because it is difficult to disprove methodologically. Without access to diplomatic cables and meetings between Moscow and Havana, it is hard to say where critical decisions are made and by whom. Furthermore, the logic of the "Cubans as pawns" argument is compelling. The Cubans depend economically and militarily on the Soviets for their survival, and the Cubans are staunch Soviet supporters in the international arena.

However, it must also be recognized that on numerous occasions in the past the Castro Government has acted independently of its Soviet backers, even in opposition to them: Cuba's public split with the Soviets in 1967 over the issue of armed struggle in Latin America is only the most dramatic example of numerous Cuban-Soviet disagreements over the past two decades of alliance. . . .

Myth 2: The Cubans Are Everywhere

According to this myth, Cuban agents are fomenting revolution all over the world. Anywhere the interests of the United States or its allies are in trouble, the Cubans are there. During the 1960s, there were almost daily reports of Cuba's subversive activities in Latin America. Havana was blamed for labor unrest in Argentina, student strikes in Colombia, nationalist riots in Panama, drug trafficking in Puerto Rico, and a civil war in the Dominican Republic.

The Cubans were even said to have trained the Black Panthers.

With time, each of these charges has been proved either vastly exaggeraged or completely untrue. Although Castro's revolution did inspire many Latin American radicals of the 1960s, Cuba's actual matériel and personnel commitments to the region were comparatively small. Throughout the 1960s, there were never more than a few hundred Cubans fighting in all of Latin America. . . .

Myth 3: The Cubans Are Always Subversive

According to this myth, a Cuban presence in any state leads inevitably to civil strife, the overthrow of legitimate regimes, and their replacement by Communist puppets. Even the most humane Cuban advisory mission is believed to be underlain with nefarious and subversive intentions. Cuban literacy teachers in Nicaragua are really indoctrinating Nicaraguan children in Communist propaganda. Cuban construction workers in Grenada are building an airport not, as they claim, to enhance tourism, but to give Moscow a new stage on the Latin American mainland. . . .

Cuba Is Not a Soviet Pawn

Although Cuba is closely allied with the Soviet Union, it is not a Soviet pawn. During the 1960s the USSR tried unsuccessfully to discourage Cuba's support for Latin guerrilla movements. In the 1970s Cuba changed that policy—which in any case had proved unsuccessful. Recognizing the change, almost all Latin nations have now restored diplomatic ties with Cuba; the continuing U.S. economic boycott, however, hinders Cuba from diversifying its trade.

American Friends Service Committee, *What Are We Afraid Of?*, 1986.

Today at least, a Cuban presence seems to be a stabilizing rather than a radicalizing force. In Nicaragua and Angola, the two states in which Havana apparently has the most influence, Cuban advisers have counseled moderation and caution both at home and abroad. Once again, when Washington gives aid to Nicaraguan exiles seeking to overthrow the Sandinista Government, it is Washington that is taking subversive actions against a legitimate government—primarily because of its alleged relationship with Cuba. Havana learned a long time ago that revolutions cannot be exported. It is time that Washington learned that lesson, too.

Myth 4: The Cubans Always Win

According to this myth, Cuba is a formidable enemy, able to use subversion as well as more traditional military means to impose its will and its chosen regimes on the countries of the Third World.

The revolutions in Angola, Ethiopia, and Nicaragua are thought to be prime examples of Cuba's near invincibility. A natural corollary is the belief that Cuba's invincibility can be contained only through the use of the most extreme, hard-line military policies.

The reality could not be farther from the myth. Throughout the 1960s, Havana's attempts to export revolution met one crushing defeat after the next. Cuba did not have much more success in the 1970s. The only successful revolutions that Havana thus far has managed to support were in Angola and Nicaragua. Two revolutions in twenty-two years is not a very impressive record. . . .

The primary source for the myth is the United States's inability to see the true causes of the revolutions in Angola, Nicaragua, and El Salvador. Because we believe the Cubans to be responsible for the upheavals in these countries, we also give them credit for the victories. The reality, however, is that the force behind these three rebellions was domestic circumstances: long histories of poverty, inequality, and government repression. Although Havana did help to speed the process by sending arms or troops or advisers, Havana did not create the revolutions or win them. The Angolan and Nicaraguan people staged and won their own revolutions. . . .

Myth 5: The Cubans Are International Outlaws

Those who believe this myth hold Cuba as beyond the diplomatic pale, much like Qadaffi's Libya or Uganda under Idi Amin. It is a country that is unresponsive to diplomatic convention or international law, one that can be dealt with only by force, not reason. This sort of insularity may have seemed true of Cuba during the mid to late 1960s, when U.S. hostilities forced the Castro Government into almost complete isolation in the hemisphere. Under repeated attack from the United States, forcibly excluded from the OAS, and unsure of its alliance with the Soviet Union (particularly after Khrushchev's betrayal during the missile crisis), it is not surprising that Havana was given to desperate words and defiant acts. . . .

Myth 6: The Cubans Are Inevitably Anti-United States

According to this myth, Cuba's hostility toward the United States is believed to be Havana's driving force. Whether Havana is shipping troops to Angola, arms to El Salvador, or advisers to Nicaragua, Havana can be counted on also to transfer its hostility to the United States. . . .

Despite their hostility to the United States, the Cubans have not advised their Third World allies to follow that route. The Cubans have urged the Sandinistas to maintain their economic and political ties with the West in general and the United States in particular. This is not to say that Havana has suddenly become pro-Washington. It has not. Rather, Cuba's repeated economic failures

141

and heavy dependence on the Soviet Union have made Havana realistic about the alternatives open to small states. These states, Havana is saying, cannot afford the luxury of opposing the United States.

Myth 7: Anyone Who Is Cuba's Enemy Is Our Friend

This is a myth that, over the years, has matched Washington with the strangest and most morally repugnant political bedfellows: the Somozas of Nicaragua, Trujillo of the Dominican Republic, Pinochet of Chile, and South Africa's apartheid regime. Alliances with the despots, simply because they too abhor the Cubans, contradict America's moral commitment to democracy and human rights and endanger our world standing. . . .

Myth 8: Anyone Who Is Cuba's Friend Is Our Enemy

This myth, the converse of the previous one, makes about as much sense. Why should Washington allow Havana to define who should be its friends or enemies and thus severely limit potential areas of influence? Change is a reality and a necessity in Central America today. The United States has a choice: It can either back change and progress or once again dig in its heels and resist for fear that change will lead to the creation of another Cuba. If the United States supports change and hopes to influence it in a positive, democratic, and pro-West direction, then ties to states like Nicaragua or Grenada, or even a left-wing El Salvador, must be maintained. In a head-to-head competition for influence with any of these states, there is little doubt that America's wealth and freedom can give the Cubans at least a run for their money. If Washington does not want Nicaragua, El Salvador, Honduras, or Guatemala to become other Cubas, then those lines of communication must be safeguarded, even if these states insist on communicating with Cuba as well.

Myth 9: The Cubans Never Change

This is the myth of the bad seed, the belief that ever since Cuba went Communist and embraced the Soviet bloc, it was irrevocably lost to all Western values, diplomatic influence, and positive change. There is much in this myth that recalls the old myth of Communist totalitarianism: Soviet Russia or Red China would never become less hostile or more responsible because any change would inevitably lead to the immediate collapse of their regimes. . . .

Cuba today does not resemble the Cuba of the missile crisis or the Tricontinental Congress any more than the United States is the same country that brought us the Bay of Pigs or the Vietnam War—one hopes. Each side must recognize the growth, maturity, and change of the other.

Myth 10: Everyone Agrees with Our View of the Cubans

This grand myth holds that all our allies share the same myths about Cuba. All see Cuba as a terrorist and an international pariah coldly subverting Third World regimes wherever it can, and refusing to discuss anything except in the language of force. There has never been such unanimity about Cuba, not even in the heyday of the OAS sanctions during the mid-1960s. It took the United States four years to get those sanctions passed by the OAS, with untold political pressures, and millions of dollars funneled into the Alliance for Progress and security assistance programs. Even then, Mexico, one of Washington's closest allies, still refused to break relations with Cuba. . . .

Cuba's Military Strength

Cuba has the largest and best-equipped armed forces of any Latin American nation except Brazil; Nicaragua's are insignificant by comparison. But Cuba's military strength does not provide a serious offensive capability, at least not one which could operate in the face of U.S. opposition, much less threaten the United States itself. Even if Soviet forces were involved, the United States would retain overwhelming military superiority in the region.

American Friends Service Committee, *What Are We Afraid Of?*, 1986.

For twenty years, the United States has made policy in the hemisphere based on a distorted and highly exaggerated image of Cuba and the threat it poses to American interests. To contain the Cuban threat, Washington landed marines in the Dominican Republic, gave covert and illegal backing to right-wing coups in Brazil and Chile, and consistently allied itself with right-wing regimes whose disregard for democratic practices and abuse of human rights is as inimical to American values as any of the abuses of Cuba's Castro Government. . . .

A New Policy Needed

It is time that the United States adopts a new policy for the hemisphere that is more consistent with U.S. ideals and interests. As a first step, the United States must stop overestimating the Cuban threat. American policy makers must recognize that except for the Cuban missile crisis, Cuba does not now and has never posed an objective threat to American power or security in the hemisphere. The few hundred guerrillas the Castro regime was able to muster and send to Latin America during the 1960s were not the cause of the region's instability. Nor has the limited amount of Cuban military aid sent to El Salvador, Honduras, and Guatemala been the cause of the instability in those countries. The escalating violence in Central America has indigenous causes:

poverty, inequality, and repression, too little land and too many people. . . .

The real threat from the Castro Government has been symbolic. It is a threat to our hegemony, to our ability to impose complete agreement in "our" hemisphere. It is not clear whether we ever really had such complete agreement, the pretensions of the Monroe Doctrine notwithstanding. Even before the Castro revolution, the United States faced opposition from left-leaning leaders like Guatemala's Arbenz and right-leaning leaders like Argentina's Juan Perón. Briefly during the 1960s the U.S. was able to command complete agreement, in reaction to the Cuban threat. But such agreement was costly in terms of progress and human rights in the hemisphere; and, inevitably, it was temporary. As Washington found out, it could no more agree with the right-wing reactionaries to the Cuban threat than it could agree with Cuba's followers.

The end of hegemony is a reality of the modern world and one the United States and the ex-colonial powers have had to learn to accept. More than any moral imperative, the U.S. must learn to accept opposition in the hemisphere because the costs of overreaction are so high. The Pinochets and the D'Aubuissons are no better allies and no more easily controlled than their left-wing opponents.

The real Cuban threat may be the reaction that forces the United States into untenable alliances with right-wing regimes, involves the United States in unpopular and often illegal overseas entanglements, alienates many of its citizens, and undercuts its prestige and influence abroad. The real Cuban threat may well come from within the United States.

Distinguishing Between Fact and Opinion

This activity is designed to help develop the critical thinking skill of distinguishing between fact and opinion. Consider the following statement as an example: "Cuba is only ninety miles away from the United States." This statement is a fact which would be impossible to deny. But consider this statement: "Cuba is a puppet of the Soviet Union." Characterizing Cuba's relationship with the Soviet Union as that of a puppet on a string would draw heavy criticism from the Cuban government and others who believe Cuba is an independent nation.

When investigating issues it is important to be able to distinguish between statements of fact and those of opinion.

The following statements are related to topics covered in this chapter. Consider each statement carefully. *Mark O for any statement you believe is an opinion or interpretation of facts. Mark F for any statement you believe is a fact. Mark U if you are uncertain.*

If you are doing this activity as a member of a class or group, compare your answers with those of other class or group members. Be able to defend your answers. You will discover that others come to different conclusions than you do. Listening to the reasons others present for their answers may give you valuable insights in distinguishing between fact and opinion.

O = *opinion*
F = *fact*
U = *uncertain*

145

1. About two-thirds of the petroleum products imported into the United States pass through the Caribbean Sea; at least half of our international trade passes through the Panama Canal.

2. The Cubans depend economically and militarily on the Soviets for their survival.

3. The common denominator of all Marxist-Leninist groups in Central America has been the deeply felt belief that the United States is their main enemy.

4. Many Latin American countries have experienced covert action, indirect incursion, or direct military intervention in their affairs by the United States.

5. Central American revolutionaries are, by and large, Marxists but they do not link their fates to the Soviet Union.

6. The Sandinistas are not patriotic nationalists but servants of the Soviet empire.

7. Cuba provides the Soviet Union with a military and intelligence capacity in the Caribbean.

8. With Soviet blessings, Havana is continuing Moscow's work and subverting other Third World states.

9. In order to encourage change and future stability, the United States should refrain from using force in Central America and the Caribbean.

10. Neither of the superpowers can permanently impose its will on other nations.

11. Communism is anti-freedom and totally depraved.

12. The Castro regime has one of the world's worst human rights records.

13. Cuban agents are fomenting revolution all over the world.

14. After more than half a century in power, the Somoza family was ousted during the 1979 Nicaraguan revolution.

15. Central American revolutions will continue to happen no matter what the United States does to stop them.

16. Latin American leaders have come to the conclusion that their own interests are not served by yielding to US influence.

Periodical Bibliography

The following periodical articles have been selected to supplement the diverse views expressed in this chapter.

Amitav Acharya	"The Reagan Doctrine and International Security," *Monthly Review*, March 1987.
Max Azlcri	"Cuba After 26 Years," *Contemporary Marxism*, 14.
Phillip Berryman	"Central America: A Commitment to Intervention," *Christianity & Crisis*, May 13, 1985.
Bureau of Inter-American Affairs	"Democracy in Latin America and the Caribbean: The Promise and the Challenge," *Department of State Bulletin*, March 1987.
Kurt Hyde	"Central America," *The New American*, January 5, 1987.
George Byram Lake	"Does Mexico Need a Revolution?" *National Review*, November 21, 1986.
Flora Lewis	"US-Cuba Cold Front," *The New York Times*, February 27, 1987.
Thomas G. Paterson	"Lost Opportunities," *The Nation*, March 7, 1987.
Hugh Thomas	"Too Kind to Castro," *The National Interest*, Spring 1987.

4 CHAPTER

What Form of Government Is Best for Latin America?

Chapter Preface

Political instability is virtually unknown to the US. Bordered by the ocean and by vast, impenetrable wilderness, the colonial US was nearly immune to penetration of its borders. If England had not been separated from the US by the Atlantic Ocean, American democracy might not have been shaped and maintained as easily. This is a primary distinction between the US and most of Latin America. Even though Latin American countries were established much earlier than the US, which might suggest more stability, most have had to deal with a legacy of foreign colonization, annexation, and destruction. In part because of this inheritance, Latin American governments have not had the luxury of developing lasting sovereign governments independent of foreign influence. As Carlos Fuentes, a well-known Latin American novelist, has remarked, "Latin America has had to do constant battle with the past. We did not acquire freedom of speech, freedom of belief, freedom of enterprise as our birthrights, as you [the US] did. We have had to fight desperately for them."

Carlos Fuentes and many other commentators believe the US hinders this "fight" for national sovereignty and independence. They point to US opposition to Marxist governments, its support of weak but friendly military dictators, and even its efforts to help Latin America economically as demonstrations of its reluctance to allow these countries to evolve at their own pace and in their own way. These people argue that the US has no right to dictate the course of Latin American affairs, and to try to do so is colonialism.

Others believe the US can and should use its considerable power to promote democratic trends and discourage communism. Latin American writer Mario Vargas Llosa, for one, believes the US is right to discourage Marxist regimes because they inevitably lead to oppression as exemplified by the governments of Cuba and Nicaragua. The authors in this chapter present their views on what role, if any, the US should have in Latin American countries' struggle for sovereignty.

"For the first time, democracy . . . [is] being established in our countries, with clear popular support and with an equally clear rejection of Marxist revolution or military support."

Democracy Is the Best Form of Government for Latin America

Mario Vargas Llosa

Mario Vargas Llosa is a Peruvian novelist and social commentator. In the following viewpoint, Llosa contends that democracy is being accepted as the preferred form of government in many Latin American countries. He argues that it is the best form of government for Latin America because it is the most representative of the people and allows for political change.

As you read, consider the following questions:

1. Why does the author believe the people of Latin America are turning toward democracy?
2. How does Llosa say industrialized nations should help Latin America?
3. Why does the author believe the greatest struggle for Latin Americans will be against themselves?

From a speech given by Mario Vargas Llosa to the Trilateral Commission. Reprinted with permission.

I represent no government and no institution. I am an independent writer convinced that the reforms Latin America requires to achieve development and social justice must be carried out within the framework of the rule of law and freedom and that only democracy can guarantee these things.

Seen this way, the Latin America of today justifies our cautious optimism. Never before in the history of our nations—that is, since we became independent from Spain and Portugal—has our part of the world had as many governments created by free (more or less) elections. Put another way, never before have there been so few authoritarian regimes as there are at present. Bloody tyrannies in Argentina and Uruguay have yielded to civilian government—the same is true in Brazil—as has the shameful anachronism until recently embodied by "Baby Doc" Duvalier, former "perpetual president" of Haiti.

Countries where, until 25 years ago, no elected president could finish out his term—Venezuela and the Dominican Republic, for example—are today models of pluralism, where antagonistic political parties are voted in and out of power and where the extreme right and the extreme left receive fewer and fewer votes in each succeeding election. Even in Central America, traditionally the most politically oppressed region, we have begun to see military regimes resign themselves—not always willingly, of course—to holding elections and yielding power to civilian leaders.

The Myth of Armed Revolution

But it isn't only military dictatorships that have diminished in number—to the point that the regimes of Gens. Alfredo Stroessner in Paraguay and Augusto Pinochet in Chile are now among the few surviving examples. The Cuban model of violent revolution is also less popular, especially compared with what it was just a few years ago, when Latin American guerrilla groups operating in a dozen countries were trying to turn Che Guevara's maxim, "Create in our continent, two, three Vietnams," into a reality. There are exceptions, of course: El Salvador, although even there guerrilla activities have lessened; Peru, where the apocalyptic fanaticism of the Shining Path continues to destroy lives and property even though it does not at this point constitute a real threat to the government; and Colombia, where political violence is often mixed up with the purely criminal violence of drug traffic. In the rest of Latin America the myth of armed revolution as a cure-all for our problems has ceased to convince the people.

But it would be unjust to celebrate this process in statistical terms. Of much greater importance is the way democratization is taking place. If we compare it, for example, with the period following World War II, when a democratic wave ran through the continent, we see that the current situation is not the result of external pressures or the work of local elites. This time, the decisive—in many cases the only—reason why governments based on legality, freedom and popular consent have replaced the arbitrary exercise of force or personal power has been the humble, nameless men and women, the usually poor, impoverished, often illiterate, people of our countries. It's true that in nations like Haiti and El Salvador it was essential for the United States to withdraw support or exert pressure to bring about the change, but even in these cases that external pressure would have come to nothing without the people. In the case of El Salvador, I can personally attest to the courage and self-sacrifice of the ordinary Salvadoran in the electoral campaign of 1984, turning out to vote in the face of intimidation and bullets.

Latin American Democracy

And how fares human rights on this day? Well, there are many encouraging signs. . . .

Our optimism today flows from renewed confidence in our principles and from the trend of history which is now clearly on the side of the free. Since the beginning of the decade, we have witnessed one of the greatest expansions of democracy on record. Latin America, once the bastion of the *caudillo*, the Latin strongman, is now, for the most part, democratic territory. Ninety percent of the people live in countries that have returned, or are in the process of returning, to democratic rule. . . .

Indeed, we have learned through painful experiences that respect for human rights is essential to peace and, ultimately, to our own freedom. A government which does not respect the rights of its own people and laws is unlikely to respect those of its neighbors. In this century, democratic governments have not started wars.

Ronald Reagan, speech given on Human Rights Day, December 10, 1986.

This fact seems extraordinarily important. For the first time, democracy or incipient democratic forms of government are being established in our countries, with clear popular support and with an equally clear rejection of Marxist revolution or military dictatorship. Today anti-democratic alternatives are running against the will of the people, supported only by economic or intellectual elites. In my own country, Peru, extremists tried to sabotage the 1985 elections by unleashing a terror campaign to keep people away from the polls; but only 7% of the registered voters stayed home, a real record compared with voter apathy in the more advanced democracies.

It would be naive to think that the ordinary men and women of Latin America have chosen democracy because of some ideological or intellectual conversion. What has spurred huge numbers of people to turn to this option has been the terrible violence—of which they have been the victims. This violence, the result of intolerance, fanaticism and dogma, has been practiced both by revolutionary terrorists and political or military counterterrorists. It littered our continent with the dead, the tortured, the kidnaped, the disappeared—and these people, in vast majority, have been the poor. Ordinary people have opted for democracy to find an escape from this nightmare reality of civil war, terror, indiscriminate repression, torture. People decided to support that system which, intuitively and instinctively, they thought would be able to defend human rights best—or oppress them least.

This undocumented fact of Latin American life—a democratizing process that originates in the people themselves—has presented us with a unique opportunity. We now have the chance to eliminate forever the vicious cycle of revolutions and military coups, to fight for development by linking our destiny with something we have always, in fact, been a part of: the liberal, democratic West.

Fragile Democracies

Naturally, this will not be easy. The democratization of Latin America, even with its new unprecedented base in our societies, is very fragile. To maintain and extend this popular base, governments will have to prove to their citizens that democracy means not only the end of political brutality but concrete progress in areas such as public health and education, where so much remains to be done. But, given the economic crisis Latin America is suffering today, those governments have virtually no alternative but to deceive the citizens—especially the poor—demanding ever greater sacrifices.

I am not one who believes that the problem of foreign debt should be met with demagogic gestures or a declaration of war against the international financial system. If such a war were to break out, Western banks might be affected, but our countries would be even worse off because one of the first victims of hostilities would be the democratic system.

The industrialized nations—their governments and banks—should face up to this matter realistically. They must understand what will happen if they demand that our democracies pay the service on their debts by implementing policies that have an exaggeratedly high social cost. We have already seen explosions of rage and despair in the Dominican Republic, Mexico and Brazil when the fabric of society is stretched too thin. The result could be the collapse of democracy and the return of dictatorships.

A realistic and ethically sound approach by creditors would demand that each debtor nation pay what it can without placing the stability of the system in jeopardy. At the same time, creditors should provide both the stimulus and the aid necessary to reactivate the economies of the debtor nations.

I am not trying to insinuate that the future of our democracies depends on you North Americans. We and we alone are responsible for our future. Moreover, I am convinced—although I'm not sure whether to to be happy or sad about it—that when a Latin American nation chooses democracy it not only chooses freedom and the rule of law but the most extreme form of independence as well. This is because no other type of government receives less support from the West—or seems to have less "sex appeal" as far as the West's communications media and intellectual elites are concerned—than those regimes in the Third World that try to live by the ideals of freedom and pluralism which are the West's greatest contribution to the world. On the contrary, when it doesn't inspire indifference, that struggle for democracy in the poor countries usually inspires skepticism and disdain from those who should be its most enthusiastic supporters. But perhaps this isn't such a bad thing after all. Because if we Latin Americans do win the battle for freedom we can say we won it ourselves—against our enemies and despite our friends.

Rejecting Political Violence

I am quite optimistic about the political future for democracy in Latin America because I am convinced that our poor, our peasants, our workers, our *lumpen* proletariat are ultimately in favor of consensus—of a state where diversity is accepted, where no one is persecuted, imprisoned, exiled or executed because of his ideas. And I think the poor in Latin America have reached this conviction not through an ideological process, but through daily experience with the results of intolerance. They have been victims of the intolerance of both extremes, oppressed by right-wing dictatorships, but also by left-wing fanatics who place bombs and kill people in order to reach "total justice." Each time the poor have a chance to manifest their choices, they come out in favor of moderate regimes, in favor of regimes in which they perceive instinctively the possibility that political violence will be rejected.

Mario Vargas Llosa, *The Wall Street Journal*, April 10, 1987.

If we want democracy to take hold, our most urgent task is to widen it, give it substance and truth. Democracy is fragile because in so many countries it is superficial, a mere political framework in which institutions and political parties go about their business in traditionally arbitrary, bully-like ways.

Differences in degrees of democracy vary from country to country; it is impossible to generalize. An abyss separates Costa Rica's exemplary democracy from, for example, Mexico's doubtful one-party democracy with its institutionalized corruption, or Panama's democracy, where civilian authorities govern but the National Guard rules. In Venezuela and the Dominican Republic, democratic tendencies have permeated the armed forces as well as the extreme right and left, drawing these elements into the political process. In Guatemala, Uruguay and Ecuador, by contrast, the military still exercises a kind of guardianship or an aloof autonomy that limits the actions of the civilian government.

The separation of powers is in many cases a myth, like equality of opportunity. The fact that huge sectors of the economy are nationalized—and almost always deficit-producing—is a constant source of inflation, corruption and discrimination. And democratic governments are neither more nor less to blame than dictatorships for promoting demagogic nationalism, the major obstacle to regional integration and the reason for the senseless waste of money in weapons purchases. Freedom of the press usually degenerates into irresponsible defamation, the right to criticize into libel and insult.

I could go on and on with the catalogue of deficiencies, but what really matters is that our democracies not only survive but that they also criticize themselves and better themselves. Otherwise they will perish. No democracy is born perfect or ever gets to be perfect. Democracy's superiority over authoritarian regimes is that, unlike them, it is perfectible. And unlike dictatorships which simply weaken if they try to reform, democracies get stronger—they can change and regenerate.

Perhaps our hardest struggle will be against ourselves. Centuries of intolerance, of absolute truths, of despotic governments weigh us down. The tradition of absolute power began with our pre-Columbian empires. The tradition that "might makes right," brought by the Spanish and Portuguese explorers, was continued by our own *caudillos* and oligarchies, often with the blessing or direct intervention of foreign powers.

The belief that violence is the answer is not new, much less revolutionary, in Latin America—contrary to our messianic ideologues. What is truly original, truly revolutionary for Latin America is the other option. The one that gives a long overdue lesson to Latin America's privileged classes—for whom military dictatorships represent a guarantee of order—and to intellectual elites, who keep the myth of Marxist revolution alive even after history has shown its promises to be a lie.

The other option is the one the innumerable victims and the poor have spontaneously chosen and are defending. After traveling the hard road of suffering violence, these people have reached the conclusion that all other systems are worse; they cling to the democratic alternative as if it were a life-preserver in a storm.

"Marxism provides a developed economic system which contains within it values essential to human liberation."

Marxism Is the Best Form of Government for Latin America

Fred J. Currier

The debate over what form of government would be best for Latin America is one of the most basic and influential surrounding these countries. The fact that Latin Americans are plagued with extreme political and social inequity, government corruption, and frightening levels of violence all lead commentators to argue for various political and economic solutions. In the following viewpoint, Fred J. Currier, a member of the history department at Villanova University, argues that Marxism is a form of government that would solve the collective political and economic problems in Latin America.

As you read, consider the following questions:

1. Why does Currier argue that Cuba provides a positive example for the rest of Latin America?
2. Why does the author believe Marxism is a moral improvement over capitalism?
3. Why is Marxism necessary, according to the author?

Fred J. Currier, "Liberation Theology and Marxist Economics," *The Monthly Review*, January 1987. Copyright © 1987 by Monthly Review Inc. Reprinted by permission of Monthly Review Foundation.

It is the argument here that Marxism alone offers a world economic picture of both development and dependence, and their interrelationships during an imperialist era, and thus Marxism-Leninism is essential as a foundation. . . .

Marxism and the Peasant

Marxism recognized that the self-supporting peasant was neither free nor secure. "His livelihood is more uncertain than that of the proletarian," Engels wrote. Capitalism, with the domination of exchange values on the marketplace, spelt the inevitable doom of the small peasant. Engels hoped that socialism would facilitate the transition toward social agriculture: "When we are in possession of state power we shall not even think of forcibly expropriating the small peasants. . . . Our task relative to the small peasant consists, in the first place, in effecting a transition of his private enterprise and private possession to co-operative ones, not forcibly but by dint of example and the proffer of social assistance for this purpose." What the peasants need to be shown is that by pooling their land and working it communally, part of their labor will be rendered unnecessary. "It is precisely this saving of labor that represents one of the main advantages of large-scale farming," and so the problem is to provide more land for the peasants to work or to provide them the opportunity of engaging in industry as supplementary to their work, and as far as possible this other work should be for their own use:

> The main point is and will be to make the peasants understand that we can save their houses and fields for them only by transforming them into co-operative property operated co-operatively. It is precisely the individual farming conditioned by individual ownership that drives the peasants to their doom . . . by capitalist large-scale production.

Marxist Practice in Cuba and Nicaragua

It is in this rescue of the peasants from poverty and their salvation as a class that the Cuban Revolution has been most dramatically successful—and the Nicaraguan Revolution provisionally so. No single event is more critical for Latin America than the Cuban Revolution, which since 1959 has been reconstructing Cuban society. Philip Foner, who has visited Cuba many times since the revolution in order to carry out his notable research (which began before the revolution) offers an authentic judgment: "I have traveled the length and breadth of the island over and over. I have been able to witness how small, underdeveloped Cuba eliminated hunger, illiteracy, and unemployment, how it provided education, medical facilities and adequate housing for great masses of its population, and how it effectively eliminated racism from its society." Through improvement of the health and education of its people, Cuba has accomplished substantial economic development during the past fifteen years. Even more important than sheer growth, Cuba's path toward development has been marked by concentration on equitable income distribution: "The degree of equality of income distribution was never sacrificed for growth."

Cuba has been successful in eliminating unemployment as a major source of poverty—almost a miracle in the context of Caribbean countries. While construction of new industry has played a part, the most substantial restructuring of the economy has touched the land and the peasants. An economy heavily dependent on sugar was the legacy of colonialism, and despite the radical transformation of society, the Cuban economy still depends on sugar as the major export, providing the bulk of its foreign exchange. But what Cuba has done is to reclaim its land for the people who do the work and to use the capital gained from sugar export for social welfare. . . .

The Sane Alternative

Capitalism faces a future of inevitable economic decline. This poses grave dangers, but it may also offer the hope of a far better future— depending upon what workers do, or fail to do, as the economy falls into deeper and deeper crises.

The sane alternative, the hope for a better future, is socialism. That alternative depends upon workers organizing on both the economic and political fields, to create a new social system based on social ownership and democratic workers' control of the industries.

The People, March 28, 1987.

Once a nationalist regime had come to power—one committed to national development, not dependent on foreign capitalist interests—there were inescapable demands to be fulfilled. The main thing that stood in the way of a socially just use of the land was the monopolization of much of the land by foreign corporations. Though it meant tangling with the United States, the revolutionary Cuban government began to nationalize Cuba's resources on the premise that these belonged to the workers. Land reform was extensive, with more than half of all Cuban land nationalized. Not all of the land was collectivized, however, for Cuba continued to experiment with small family farms. By the end of the 1960s, cane collectives and people's farms comprised about 38 percent of the total farm area. The rest of the expropriated land was distributed among small farmers, leaving a total of 62 percent of the farmland still privately operated. On the basis of these changes, Cuba has rescued its rural population from unemployment and destitution. . . .

Viewing the third world as a whole, two characteristics seem to define it. First, its society is composed of a substantial number of peasants, in many countries as much as 75 percent of the total population. Second, its economy can be described as underdeveloped—that is, incapable of employing a large number of workers and incapable of utilizing national resources to end the poverty of a majority of people. Since the third world comprises predominantly peasant societies, the unemployed are generally peasants who have little or no land; necessarily, then, the basic resource that is misused, in terms of the needs of impoverished peasants, is the land. . . .

It was natural to turn to Marxism, which depicted a global struggle, with the third world acting as proletarian nations serving the wealthy capitalist nations. Marxism offered an attractive instrument of comprehensive analysis of political, social, and economic structures and a praxis for changing the world. . . .

Marxism an Economic Key

Marxism provides an economic key—and, as it turns out, a moral principle, too—which explains the unequal exchange by which workers produce capital for owners of land or industry, and whole nations whose land and industry are foreign-owned produce capital for advanced industrial nations. It is through extraction of surplus value that unequal class relations are given their structural continuity. As long as private property is the basis for profit, as long as capitalism continues, inequality is assured. . . .

The Roots of Exploitation

Exploitation is ultimately rooted in the production process whereby society works for the primary benefit of those who in their control over production constitute a class of capitalists. From the standpoint of Latin America and all the third world, subject during this imperialist era to the economic and political domination of developed capitalist countries, the exploitation of workers can only worsen because the proletarianization of society worldwide must result from the increase of capital. For those controlling the capital, residing in Europe and the United States, the colonies or later dependent states were converted into sources of surplus value by the use of their land, mineral resources, and cheap labor. Capital begets proletariat, as Marx and Engels pointed out in *The Communist Manifesto*, and proletariat can only work when it enriches capitalists. This poses sharply the limitation of the capitalist system during this stage of third world revolution. Capitalism cannot operate from criteria of social justice, full employment, or equality. . . .

From the standpoint of the landless peasants, the land must be liberated with all its resources so that every person will have the opportunity to work, and so he who works will surely eat. From the standpoint of the urban worker, the means of production must be liberated so that no longer will surplus value belong to a ruling class either domestic or foreign. For liberation to become reality, an economic system must be created in which no class has the right to exploit another. . . .

Human Rights and Economics

Marxism provides a developed economic system which contains within it values essential to human liberation: the end of class exploitation, social ownership of their resources by underdeveloped nations, control of capital for socially just investments, and the expansion of human rights to include economic opportunity.

3

"Ours . . . is a more just society and we believe in it."

Communism Has Aided Human Rights in Cuba

Fidel Castro

Fidel Castro became president and premier of Cuba in 1959, after the fall of the dictator Fulgencio Batista. The Castro administration's avowed allegiance to Marxism-Leninism and its close relationship with the Soviet Union have resulted in various US actions. These include a failed attempt to overthrow Castro (commonly known as the Bay of Pigs), and an embargo of all trade with Cuba. While many officials in the US argue that Castro's regime has vastly improved the living conditions in that country, others, including every US president since Kennedy, argue that it is an oppressive and dictatorial society. In the following viewpoint, taken from a transcript of the MacNeil/Lehrer Newshour, Castro defends his administration, arguing that it tolerates differing political and religious beliefs.

As you read, consider the following questions:

1. Who are Cuba's political prisoners, according to the author?
2. How does Castro defend the "censorship" of the press?
3. What reasons does Castro give to defend his belief that his society is better than that of the US?

Fidel Castro interviewed by Robert MacNeil for the "MacNeil-Lehrer NewsHour." Reprinted by permission of MacNeil/Lehrer Productions.

[MacNeil: *White House spokesman Larry Speakes said that one of the obstacles the Reagan administration sees to improved relations with Castro is what Speakes called violations of human rights in Cuba. I asked Castro about that.]*

Castro: What are the violations of human rights in Cuba? Tell me. Which ones? Invent one. Do we have disappeared people here? Look, if the United States—

MacNeil: Well, let me give you an example of what he said. For instance, human rights organizations, like Amnesty International, estimate that you have up to 1,000 political prisoners still in your jails. Do you have political prisoners still in jail in Cuba?

Castro: Yes, we have them. We have a few hundred political prisoners. Is that a violation of human rights?

MacNeil: In democracies it is considered a violation of human rights to imprison somebody for his political beliefs.

Castro: I will give you an example. In Spain there are many Basque nationalists in prison. They're not political prisoners? What are they? Because you also have to analyze what is a political prisoner and what is not a political prisoner. Now then, those who committed crimes during Batista's time, did we have the right to put them on trial or not? Okay. Those who invaded Cuba through Playa Girón. Did we have the right to try them or not? Those who became CIA agents, those who placed bombs, those who brought about the deaths of peasants, workers, teachers. Do we have the right to bring them to trial or not? Those who, in agreement with a foreign power like the United States and backed by the United States and inspired by the United States, conspired in our country and who struggle and fight against our people in this revolution—because this revolution is not of a minority; this is a revolution of the overwhelming majority of people. What are these people? What are they? Political prisoners? Those who have infiltrated through our coasts, those who have been trained by the CIA to kill, to place bombs: Do we have the right to bring them to trial or not? Are they political prisoners? They're something more than political prisoners. They're traitors to the homeland.

No Political Prisoners

MacNeil: Is there anybody in jail simply because of his political beliefs—because he dissents from you politically?

Castro: No one is in prison because of either their political or religious beliefs.

MacNeil: After Jesse Jackson came here last summer you released twenty-six political prisoners. Are you going to release more of the kind you were describing a moment ago?

Castro: Of course we would not be willing to release them. It's a bit under 200, actually, in that situation. These are people who are potentially dangerous. We are not going to release them and send them to the United States for them to organize plans against Cuba, or for them to go to Nicaragua or Honduras or Central America as mercenaries, or to go to any country to prepare attacks so that when I visit these countries they organize a true human hunt, as they have done on other occasions. That's the psychology instilled in them by the CIA and the U.S. authorities.

A Revolution in Human Rights

For a week now I've been stewing over the question of human rights and Cuba. How to convince a U.S. reader, bombarded with lies about this country, that my experience tells me the Cuban revolution is at its very heart a revolution in human rights. . . .

The longer one stays in Cuba, the more one is taken aback by how deep the country's revolution in human rights goes. No neutral observer has come and gone from Cuba without expressing surprise at the depth and breadth of workingclass support for the revolutionary process.

The more I've looked into the matter the more convinced I've become that at its roots lies the basic human right to raise a family without constant economic and other anxieties. For everyone's children to get enough to eat and an equal shake in life.

Marc Frank, *People's Daily World*, March 31, 1987.

MacNeil: The other human rights question that is raised by the United States is that you don't have a free press. Your revolution is now twenty-six years old, it's very stable. In your recent speeches you've told of how successful it is. Why wouldn't you feel confident about allowing the press to have a full expression of ideas and discussion and opposition?

Castro: Well, you are right. We do not have a press system like that of the United States. In the United States there is private property over the mass media. The mass media belong to private enterprises. They are the ones who say the last word. Here there is no private property over the mass media. There is social property. And it has been, is, and will be at the service of the revolution. Here we do not have any multiparty system either, nor do we need it. The political level of our people, the information level of our people, is much greater. In surveys that have been made in the United States an astonishing high number of people do not know where Nicaragua is, where the countries of Latin America are. They don't know what countries are in Africa, what countries are in Asia. There is an incredible, astonishing ignorance. That does not happen here. Your system might be wonderful, but at least the results of ours are undoubtedly better.

MacNeil: May I raise a point? Your system, which you say works very well, it does presuppose that the leadership of the country, you, are always right, that you are infallible. Is that not so?

Castro: No, it does not presuppose that, because we are not as dogmatic as the church, although we have been dogmatic, and we have never preached a personality cult. You will not see a statue of me anywhere, nor a school with my name, nor a street, nor a little town, nor any type of personality cult because we have not taught our people to believe, but to think, to reason out. We have a people who think, not a people who believe, but rather who reason out, who think. And they might either agree or disagree with me. In general the overwhelming majority have agreed. Why? Because we have always been honest; we have always told them the truth. The people know that the government has never told them a lie. And I ask you to go to the world, tour the world, and go to the United States and ask if they can say what I can say, that I have never told a lie to the people. And these are the reasons why there is confidence. Not because I have become a statue or an idol but rather simply because of the fact that they trust me. And I have very, very few prerogatives in this country. I do not appoint ministers or vice-ministers or directors of ministries or ambassadors. I don't appoint anybody, and that's the way it is. We have a system, a system for the selection of cadre based on their capacity, etc. I have less power, 100 times less power than the president of the United States, who can even declare war and nuclear war.

The US Has Fewer Human Rights

MacNeil: But doesn't the system mean that the revolution is always right?

Castro: You, when you had your independence war you did not even free the slaves and yet you said you were a democratic country. For 150 years, you did not even allow the Black man to be part of a baseball team or a basketball team, to enter a club, to go to a white children's school. And you said it was a democracy. None of those things exists here—neither racial discrimination nor discrimination due to sex. It is the most fair, egalitarian society there has ever been in this hemisphere. So we consider it to be superior to yours. But you believe that yours is the best without any discussion whatsoever. Although there might be multimillionaires and people barefoot begging in the streets, without any homes, people unemployed. And you believe it's perfect, because you *believe* things.

I don't think that type of society is perfect, really, I think that ours is better. We have defended it better. It is a more just society and we believe in it. Now, we make mistakes, but whenever we make a mistake we have the courage to explain it. We have the courage to admit it, to recognize it, acknowledge it, to criticize it. I believe that very few—that there are probably few people like the leaders of a revolution who are able to acknowledge their mistakes. And I first of all acknowledge it before myself because first of all I am more critical with myself than with anybody else. But I'm critical before my people, critical before the world, the U.S., everybody. Far from—but don't worry. If this analysis had not been correct, the revolution would not be in power. The revolution would not be in power.

A Positive Force

The Cuban variant of socialism has been the impetus for many positive changes in the lives of the Cuban people. Cubans now have an adequate diet. They enjoy full employment. Education is available to all. Cultural activities are accessible to the people. There is a low incidence of crime. The streets of Cuban cities are safe. (The contrast with U.S. cities is striking!)

Clyde R. Appleton, *The Churchman*, May 1986.

MacNeil: How do you measure that? How do you, as the leader of this country, know that for sure when you don't have the vehicles for public expression and open discussion of issues that the democracies have, for example? How do you know that the people feel that way?

Castro: We have a party with almost half a million members. They're everywhere, in every factory. We know more than the United States about the things that happen there.

We Know How the People Think

MacNeil: But isn't the dynamic of a one-party state that the instruction and information goes downwards, and if people disagree with it, they don't dare say so? And so dissent which may exist doesn't come back up the system.

Castro: Actually, we know what there is, and we know the way our people think much better than what the president of the United States knows about the way the U.S. people think. You should have no doubt about that whatsoever. We have many ways of knowing this. Facts prove it. Let's suppose that people might not agree with the revolution. How could we have millions of people organized to defend the country? Could we have a non-people? Tell the South Africans, your South African friends, to give the weapons to the Blacks in South Africa. Tell your friend Pinochet to give the weapons to the people of Chile. Tell your friends in Paraguay to give the weapons to the masses, to the people. Tell many of the friends that you have in the world—you speak of democracy. The first and most important form of democracy is for the citizens to feel part of power and part of the state. And how do we prove this? We have an armed people, men and women, millions of people. If they were not in agreement they could solve things rapidly. We would not be able to stay in power for twenty-four minutes. Do you want more proof of that?. . .

MacNeil: Tell me an example of a mistake you feel you made and admitted.

Castro: In politics we have committed few mistakes, fortunately. We have been quite wise. In the decisions we have made in the economic field we made mistakes, and these were mistakes that resulted from our ignorance, because in general revolutionaries have ideas, very noble ideas: to have education, to have health for all, to have work, to have jobs, to have development. That is, very noble ideas, but very general.

MacNeil: You said in your speech to the National Assembly, we do not become capitalists. Do you begin to lean a little to capitalism?

Castro: No. To the contrary, to the contrary. Every day— mentally, spiritually, philosophically—I'm more convinced about the advantages of the socialist system over capitalism, more convinced about the fact that capitalism has no future. Well, I say no future on the long-term basis. I am not saying that capitalism will disappear in ten years. But the present capitalist system is no longer the capitalist system of the past century. . . .

Revolutionary Disappointments

MacNeil: Let me ask you to turn your mind back. You said many times and in some of your speeches recently that your revolution, by your definitions, has many successes—in medical care, in literacy, in infant mortality. By those definitions your revolution is a success. In what way does it disappoint you?

Castro: Do you ask if I feel any frustration? No. I have no frustration. I feel no frustration whatsoever. I can tell you this directly. We have done more than what we dreamed of doing. Many of the things we're doing now—we had some general ideas but not as precise and complete as we have now. I can tell you that reality has surpassed our dreams in what we have done. And we're not speaking about the future. It is not the same as it was at the beginning when we spoke of our good intentions; but rather we now speak with a revolution that is twenty-six years old. And it has certain advantages. I'm not speaking of things that we are intending to do but rather of things that have been done.

"Today . . . hundreds of political prisoners are naked, sleeping on the floors of cells whose windows and doors have been sealed."

Communism Has Destroyed Human Rights in Cuba

Armando Valladares

For over 25 years, the US government has argued that the government of Fidel Castro is responsible for hundreds of political assassinations and other human rights violations, including inhumane political prisons. Others in the US have argued this is pure propaganda. In the following viewpoint, Armando Valladares, a political prisoner in Cuba for twenty-two years, supports the US government's beliefs. While his account is entirely personal, many in the US have cited his experience as evidence of the appalling human rights situation in Castro's Cuba. Valladares claims he was imprisoned and forced to endure horrible humiliations simply for disagreeing with the Castro regime.

As you read, consider the following questions:

1. Why does the author say he was taken prisoner?
2. Of what crime is Valladares accused? Do you believe this accusation is adequately proved?
3. After reading Valladares and Castro, who do you find more convincing? Why?

This is my personal account of the twenty-two years I spent in the political prisons of Cuba, solely for having espoused and expressed principles distinct from those of the regime of Fidel Castro.

In my country there is a fact which not even the most fervent defenders of the Cuban Revolution can deny—a dictatorship has existed there for more than a quarter of a century. And no dictatorship can remain in power for so long without violating human rights, without persecutions, without political prisoners, without political prisons.

In Cuba at this very moment there are more than two hundred penal installations, ranging from maximum-security prisons to concentration camps to so-called farms and "open fronts," where prisoners do forced labor. In every one of these two hundred or so prisons there is material for dozens of books, which means that these pages are the merest sketch of the terrible reality of Cuban prisons.

Castro and Stalin

Someday, when the history of all of them is known in detail, mankind will feel the revulsion it felt when the crimes of Stalin were brought to light.

In its latest reports, Amnesty International has denounced the executions of dozens of political opponents of the regime, the physical mistreatment and abuse, the beatings. And when it appealed to the Cuban government to abolish the death penalty, the Vice-President of Cuba, Carlos Rafael Rodríguez, who had been a minister in the Batista government as well, answered that the death penalty was necessary in Cuba. Rodríguez was also quoted in an interview published in Madrid's *Diario 16* on October 10, 1983, as saying, in answer to the interviewer's question whether groups struggling for labor-union freedom and for human rights existed in Cuba, that indeed people holding such idyllic ideas as the freedom to organize into labor unions and the protection of human rights did exist, but that he predicted a future of ridicule for them.

For me, this represents the long night I have left behind me, but for the thousands of my countrymen still held in the jails, for my comrades, some of whom have already spent twenty-five years in prison, it represents daily reality. They have been held longer than any other political prisoners in Latin America, perhaps in the world. The violence, repression, and beatings, the torture, the lack of mail, news, and visits, and the solitary confinement are facts of life for them. Today, at this very moment, hundreds of political prisoners are naked, sleeping on the floors of cells whose windows and doors have been sealed. They never see the light of day, or for that matter artificial light. They are denied medical care and visits, and all because they refused to enter the Political Rehabilitation Program. . . .

My eyes flew open. The cold muzzle of a machine gun held to my temple had shocked me awake. I was confused and frightened. Three armed men were standing around my bed, and one of them was shoving my head into the pillow with his machine gun.

"Where's the pistol?"

As the man with the machine gun kept my head immobile, another slid his hand under it to check for that purely imaginary pistol I was supposed to be armed with. Then the oldest of them, a thin man with graying hair, spoke to me again. He brusquely told me to get dressed, I had to go with them.

Cuba Is a Totalitarian State

Cuba is the Western Hemisphere's paramount totalitarian state, the fiefdom of one of the world's longest lasting dictators. It is a country which seeks to repress all forms of independent expression, a country in which the population is intimidated not only by an all-powerful secret police apparatus, but one in which average citizens are called upon to spy on their neighbors. It is a country in which the slightest, most innocent expression of disapproval of the government can have seriously adverse consequences, such as a reduction in rations or the loss of the educational opportunities for one's children. What we see in Cuba at present, we fear, is the scenario of a fast-approaching future of Nicaragua, where the Sandinista regime has destroyed the democratic promises of the revolution, turning the country from one despotism to another.

Richard Schifter, speech given on Human Rights Day, December 10, 1986.

These were agents of Castro's Political Police. I was to learn later that the older man, the one doing the talking, had been an agent in the Batista regime as well. There was a fourth agent in the living room keeping watch on my mother and sister.

I hadn't heard them come in. When they knocked at the front door, it was my mother who had gone to open it. I was in a deep sleep in the last bedroom down the hall, with blankets piled on me to keep out the cold. . . .

Searching the House

When I had gotten my clothes on, they began the search of the house. The search was thorough, painstaking, long. They spent almost four hours going through everything. There was not one inch of the house they didn't go over with a fine-tooth comb. They opened jars and bottles, they went through the books page by page, they emptied toothpaste tubes, they looked at the motor of the refrigerator, at the mattresses. . . .

At that time I had a good job in the Caja Postal de Ahorros, which might be termed the Postal Savings Bank, an office attached to the Ministry of Communications in the Revolutionary Government. I had received several promotions, thanks largely to the fact that I was a university student. Some of the people I worked with there, I knew, were out to get me.

A few weeks before, one of the directors, a man I had developed a close friendship with, called me in to warn me that the Political Police had been around asking questions about me. I had had some friction in the office because I had frequently spoken out against Communism as a political system because it went against my religious beliefs and some of my more idealistic notions of the world. . . .

Labeled an Anti-Communist

It wasn't surprising, then, that I had been marked as an anti-Communist. One of my last outbursts was brought on by a slogan which was being spread throughout the country by the government propaganda apparatus. By that time Castro was accused of being a Communist, so they circulated the slogan "If Fidel is a Communist, then put me on the list. *He's* got the right idea." This slogan was printed on decals and bumper stickers and on little tin plaques to be displayed on the doors of private homes; it was published daily in the newspapers; it was blazoned on posters pasted up on the walls of schools, police stations, factories, shops, and government offices. The purpose of all this was quite clear and simple: Castro was presented to the country as a messiah, a savior, the man who would return the country to freedom, prosperity, happiness. Castro could never be linked to anything evil, to anything bad at all. Whatever Castro was, or might be, was good by definition. Therefore, if he was a Communist, then put me on the list. . . .

We went out into the street. It was four o'clock in the morning; the night was very cold and there was a stiff wind blowing in from the bay. They put me into a gray Volkswagen and an agent sat on either side of me. They handcuffed me. Another car joined us at the corner. Not one word was spoken, though from time to time the radio crackled out a message incomprehensible to me. One of the transmissions was for the car I was in. The driver picked up the receiver and responded with a short phrase—a coded countersign, I assume. . . .

Counterrevolutionary

I was called out and taken to the second floor, the records office. They took my fingerprints and photographed me with a sign that read "COUNTERREVOLUTIONARY."

That same afternoon I was subjected to my first interrogation. It was held in a small office before a one-way mirror of dark-green glass. A group of agents were waiting for me, but only one officer was sitting down, and he was the one who spoke to me. He told me they knew about everything; they knew I was a counterrevolutionary, an enemy of the Revolution. He said they were going to see to it, too, that I was punished for that. I told him in return that I hadn't committed any crime whatsoever, that they had searched my house from top to bottom and seen for themselves that there was nothing in my possession which could make them even remotely consider me a traitor or an enemy of the Revolution.

Torture in Cuba's Prisons

Torture and mistreatment of political prisoners is widespread. In April 1986, a dozen former prisoners testified before an international panel in Paris about examples of torture and inhuman treatment. Ana Lazara Rodriguez cited cases of guards throwing women down stairs and kicking them in the breasts and stomachs.

Father Miguel Angel Loredo, a Franciscan priest falsely accused of giving refuge to a political escapee, served 10 years in various labor camps, including the Isle of Pines, where guards beat him until he was unconscious. He says: "I was forced to labor in the stone quarries. While working under the Cuban sun for 12 hours at a stretch I lost consciousness four times. We were forced to work naked, without even shoes on. On one occasion I was suffering from phlebitis and had a 105 degree fever, but I still had to work. I lost so much weight that I could circle my arm with my thumb and little finger. For a long time I used to celebrate Mass secretly, but sporadically. In lieu of a chalice, I used a blood-stained metal plate that had belonged to a comrade. He was killed for having refused to eat grass like an animal."

Will the world continue to look away from human rights violations in Cuba—or will it finally apply to the Castro regime the same standards it uses in discussing South Africa and Chile and Taiwan and South Korea?

Allan C. Brownfeld, *Manchester Union Leader*, April 14, 1987.

"But we know about the remarks you've made in your office—we know you've been attacking the Revolution."

I defended myself. I said that I had not attacked the Revolution as an institution.

"But you *have* attacked Communism."

I didn't deny that. I couldn't, nor did I want to.

"Yes, that's true," I said. "I think that Communism is a worse dictatorship than the one we Cubans have just overthrown. And if Communist rule is established in Cuba, then Cuba will be just like Russia, going from czarism to the dictatorship of the proletariat."

"We didn't fight this revolution for just more of the same privilege and exploitation. Yankee imperialist exploitation is finished in Cuba, and we're not going to allow people like you, in the service of capitalist interests, to interrupt the march of revolutionary progress."

That, then, was my first interrogation. It hardly lasted ten minutes. . . .

The next day I went through my second interrogation. Each day they would give us the official newspaper, the daily *Revolucion*, which was calling us terrorists. In the interrogation I protested against that. The officer told me they were sure that I was an enemy of the people.

"You studied in a school run by priests," he said to me.

"Yes, in Escolapius. What difference does that make?"

"A big difference. Priests are counterrevolutionary, and the fact that you went to that school is one more piece of evidence against you."

"But Fidel Castro studied in a school taught by Jesuits. He went to Belén."

"Yes, but Fidel is a revolutionary. You, on the other hand, are a counterrevolutionary, tied to priests and capitalists, and so we are going to sentence you to jail."

"There isn't a shred of evidence against me. You have discovered nothing that incriminates me in any way."

A Potential Enemy

"It's true—we have no proof, or rather no concrete proof, against you. But we do have the conviction that you are a potential enemy of the Revolution. For us, that is enough." . . .

The next morning very early I was taken to my last interrogation. It almost had the flavor of a farewell.

"We know that you have connections to elements that are conspiring against the State, that you are friendly with some of them. If you cooperate with us, we can give you your freedom and send you back to your job."

"I don't know any of those people. I don't have any contact with conspirators."

"This is the last chance you have to get yourself out of this."

"I don't know anything. You people can't send me to jail, you can't find me guilty, because I haven't done *anything*. There's no proof against me. You have no evidence to show."

"Our conviction is enough for us. We know that you are a potential enemy of the Revolution. Look!" And he tossed several afternoon newspapers at me. In big letters on the front pages was written "FIRING SQUAD FOR TERRORISTS."

"They want an example made of you, so . . . ." He left the threat hanging in the air. . . .

Thirteen days had passed since the morning I had been taken from my home and carried to the Ministry to be asked a few questions. In that short time, the Political Police had prepared the whole case. Of course, in twelve or thirteen days it was physically impossible to conduct an investigation, but that's the way the trials were. I was not allowed to talk privately with the lawyer defending me, nor did they allow him access to the list of charges.

In the second courtroom we found a wooden platform with a long table set up on it. At the table the members of the tribunal were sitting talking among themselves, laughing, and smoking cigars, which they held on one side of their mouths, chomping on them in Pancho Villa style. They all wore military uniforms. This, then, was one of those typical tribunals, made up of anybody at hand. This one was composed of laborers and campesinos. At the start of the trial, the president of the tribunal, Mario Taglé, put his feet up on the table, crossed one boot over the other, and leaned back in his chair and opened a comic book. From time to time he turned to the men on each side of him and showed them some tidbit that had struck him as particularly funny. They'd all laugh. And the sad truth was that paying any attention to the proceedings, even out of courtesy, was utterly unnecessary, and they knew it. The sentences had already been decided on and written out at Political Police Headquarters. Say what one would, do what one would, the sentence was not to be changed. . . .

Injustice

But neither then nor later—because for twenty years I kept asking—could any of the authorities tell me where I had committed an act of public destruction. Such a crime, one would think, is concrete, visible, palpable. I asked the prosecuting lawyer where—in which factory, in what business, on what date—I was supposed to have caused this damage. He was unable to answer, because I had, of course, never done anything of the kind. It was like a murder trial in which the district attorney, asked who has been killed, says he doesn't know; and asked about the corpse, says there is no corpse. Imagine killing a figment of someone's imagination.

No tribunal in a more rightist regime could have found me guilty. There was not one witness to accuse me, there was no one to identify me, there was not a single piece of evidence against me. I was found guilty, simply out of the mistaken "conviction" held by the Political Police.

173

"We expect you [the United States] to support
us in the same way that President Reagan
supports democratic forces in the Philippines."

The US Must Support the Contras To End Communist Oppression

Enrique Bermudez

Enrique Bermudez is a leader of what he terms "the democratic resistance" inside Nicaragua, commonly known as the contras. In the following viewpoint, Bermudez, in an interview with a Heritage Foundation reporter, argues that the Sandinistas betrayed the 1979 Nicaraguan revolution. He believes the only way to honor the revolution is by defeating the Sandinistas and with the help of US aid, to bring true democracy to Nicaragua.

As you read, consider the following questions:

1. What, according to Bermudez, is the goal of the anti-Sandinista movement?
2. Why does Bermudez believe that US money is essential for the contras to obtain their goal?

Enrique Bermudez, *The U.S. and Nicaragua*, The Heritage Lectures, The Heritage Foundation, 1986. Reprinted with permission.

We in the liberation movement do not have enough time to prepare our statement. My feelings, my personal opinion, is that our movement has been misunderstood and the American opinion is not very well informed. We are a democratic movement. We are fighting a war against a totalitarian regime. Few people are aware of what is going on really in Nicaragua.

We, in our movement, the anti-Sandinista movement, seek to establish democracy in Nicaragua. We are trying to achieve a unified front. Our principle has been expressed in many brochures or papers that we have published in the past. Since 1983 we have clearly established what we are fighting for, what we want for Nicaragua.

We are not a political party, we are a movement for democracy. We are not seeking personal power. We want the Nicaraguan people to have the opportunity to express themselves through free elections.

We expect from the United States an understanding of our struggle. We expect you to support us in the same way that President Reagan supports democratic forces or popular forces in the Philippines now and participates also in the establishment of a democracy in Haiti.

Question: Sir, I have a three-part question for you. One, what do you see as the biggest problems for your forces?

Two, what kinds of equipment do you see as necessary to achieve for success on the battlefield?

And three, there are some apparent command and control problems with the forces. What are you doing to rectify those?

Colonel Bermudez: Let me explain. We have been a very dynamic movement. We have pushed for a unified front. But, as you know, in this type of struggle, historically, always there are many divisions. In association with your third point, we have been willing all the time to get together with all the anti-Sandinista groups, to find the way to solve our problems, establish a procedure and go together in this fight, because it is necessary to stay together. No one single movement will have the capacity to defeat the Sandinistas.

The US Is the Main Problem

Our main problem, and this you must understand very clearly, is the United States. In 1984, there was a good momentum. We were pressing hard on the Sandinistas. The political parties were pressuring the Sandinistas as was the Church and all the Nicaraguan sector. When funds were cut off, the Nicaraguan people were very disappointed with the U.S. Anything that Washington does or Congress does affects not only the political sphere but also the labor sector, the Church, and the whole Nicaraguan population. The United States has lost prestige as a trusted ally.

Let me give you an example. Many countries—and I have heard the opinion of many military personnel in Central America—do not trust the United States. They think the United States will abandon them, as they have abandoned other countries. So our main problem is the decision of the United States. People will not get involved against the Sandinistas if they do not see the U.S. support the resistance.

The Sandinistas have exploited that. They have paraded the military apparatus to intimidate the people. You know, they bring the tank through the cities. They bring the helicopter, the artillery. They make a show of the military forces. So any citizen will think twice before he goes to join us.

Contras Support Freedom

Those who argue that to give aid to the Nicaraguan rebels would be a violation of the "principle of a people's right to self-determination" are mistaken. These people seem to ignore or perhaps forget deliberately that self-determination applies to peoples, not oppressive governments that do not legitimately represent the will of the people.

Jaime Chamorro, *The Continuing Crisis*, 1987.

I remember when we started this struggle with no aid from anybody, we had groups, very badly dressed with shotgun or with 22 calibre rifles. And the people did not pay any attention to us. So when we started to receive funds, we emphasized good uniforms, good equipment, and that provoked a very enthusiastic reaction in the population. And this is the reason why we grew up so large and so fast.

Now we are running out of supplies and funds, people are becoming disillusioned. They will be more conscious of Sandinista repression and the Sandinistas, of course, have taken some measures such as forced relocation. They have taken repressive action against those people who they suspect were sympathizing with our forces.

You have heard about the relocating people from the rural areas, to collective farms, in order to control areas they suspect are supportive of us.

Is $100 Million Enough?

Question: If the President were to get his $100 million through Congress, would that be enough for the Contras?

Colonel Bermudez: Yes. Well, our logic is this. We have been able to resist and to keep this pressure on the Sandinistas with almost no help at all. With $100 million we are sure we are going to defeat the Sandinistas very fast.

Of course, we need some anti-aircraft weapons. Definitely, the MI-24 have influenced the tactical situation. For instance, we are operating in Esteli, Jinotega, and Nuevo Segovia, Madriz and Chinandega, which are very well-cultivated lands, and have no dense vegetation to protect forces on the terrain. In that place, the helicopter is very effective. . . .

Question: Colonel Bermudez, could you discuss the Honduras border and how it figures as a Contra sanctuary with all the political aspects?

Colonel Bermudez: Yes. This is a very sensitive issue. Let me say this. Any guerrilla movement against a totalitarian regime like the Sandinistas are creating is totally dependent on internal sources of support. And let me give an example.

Let us make a comparison between the leftist guerrilla in El Salvador and democratic guerrillas in Nicaragua. A guerrilla in El Salvador—which is not a police-controlled population—can change to civilian clothes, go to the city, go to a movie, go to a restaurant, have a good rest. Next day, he will go downtown to a shoe store and he will ask to buy 200 pairs of boots.

The owner of the store will try to convince him to buy 500 and will give him a special price. That has happened with medicine and any article. In Nicaragua, which is totally controlled, you have a rationing card, you have neighborhood committees, so you cannot do that. First of all, there is no medicine in Nicaragua. Medicine is controlled by the government. All the boots are controlled by the government for the army.

Difficult for Guerrillas To Get Supplies

You have to make a written requisition—request—if you want to buy two pair of boots. If you want to buy two pair of boots, you immediately are under suspicion as a Contra and you have to explain why you want the second pair of boots. So in Nicaragua, the guerrilla cannot get supplies.

Question: As you know, one of the chief arguments used by those who are opposed to aid to the Contras is that a majority of the top officers, including yourself, are former members of the National Guard. I wonder if you could give us some ammunition to use against this argument.

Colonel Bermudez: Frankly, this has been a good achievement of the Sandinista propaganda. We have a voluntary army. This is not a conventional army. People do not receive any pay at all. They have their own motivation to fight.

Our leadership is not politically appointed. The regional commanders, the task force commander or small unit commander, are not leaders because somebody appointed them to be a leader. They have gained that leadership fighting. It is not a vacation. They have been fighting against Sandinistas, risking their lives.

We have 71 commanders. We have 17 regional commanders, which are the higher commander. Next is task commander commanding between 200 and 400, a battalion size. Then the unit commander and then groups, which is about between 60 and 100.

We have commanders that were members of the National Guard, we have nineteen. Most of them were soldiers. Some of them were lieutenant, second lieutenant. Two were cadets, and the only colonel is myself. . . .

The former members of the National Guard have their own motivation. I have a list here of 20 who were in the Sandinista army. And I have a list of 32 who were called from different sectors, peasants, most of them, farmers, businessmen, professional, student, and so forth.

Repression in Nicaragua

What happened in Cuba is now happening in Nicaragua. An unmistakable pattern: repression, attacks on the church, the closing down of newspapers, the destruction of independent unions, and the construction of concentration camps and prisons on a scale never imagined. The Sandinista regime has repeatedly hampered the Organization of American States' (OAS) attempts to investigate charges of human rights violations.

The violation of human rights—whether in Kampuchea or Paraguay, Afghanistan or North Korea, whether it be the murder of Baha'is in Iran or the repression of ethnic Turks in Bulgaria—is the rightful cause of all free peoples.

Ronald Reagan, speech given on Human Rights Day, December 10, 1986.

So the participation of former members of the National Guard is voluntary. They were not closely associated with the Somoza regime. They consider themselves professional military persons. A legal instrument that was submitted and approved by the Sandinista junta, by the U.S. government, and by the majority of the democratic members of Congress, it was called the Plan for the Consolidation of Peace and it was sent by the Sandinista junta before they took power to the OAS [Organization American States]. In that plan, they established that the new national army will be composed by Sandinistas and National Guardsmen based upon the principle that not all the members of the National Guard were bad. Now they are exploiting and saying that all the members of the National Guard are bad.

"Our dreams are not of domination, nor of expansion, nor of conquest, but the humble dreams of a humble people aspiring to full justice and full independence."

The US Must Allow Nicaragua To Determine Its Own Government

Sergio Ramirez

Sergio Ramirez, Nicaraguan novelist, short story writer, and essayist, is a member of that country's Governing Junta of National Reconstruction. His books include *To Bury Our Fathers*, and *The Living Thought of Sandino*. In the following viewpoint, Ramirez decries US attempts to overthrow the Sandinistan government and its past support of the dictator Anastasio Somoza. He compares the Sandinistas to the founding fathers of the United States, and explains that like the US, Nicaragua must be allowed to determine its own form of government.

As you read, consider the following questions:

1. How did the US revolution affect Latin America, according to the author?
2. Why, according to Ramirez, is the US supporting the contras?
3. What kind of government does Ramirez say the Sandinistas want?

Sergio Ramirez, "The Revolution as Nicaragua's New Vice President Sees It." Excerpted from *In These Times*, November 14-20, 1984. 1300 W. Belmont, Chicago, IL 60657, (312) 472-5700. Published weekly. Annual subscription: $34.95.

Like the rest of Central America, Nicaragua has been subordinate to the United States, almost since the U.S. emerged as a nation and traded its original project of freedom and democracy for Manifest Destiny.

Our geographic proximity—and the territorial opportunities we offered for providing a course for an interoceanic canal—put Nicaragua in the geopolitical and military sights of successive North American administrations. This proximity and the insatiable thirst for domination encouraged by the imperial idea that the U.S. was meant to perpetually expand its borders have created a fundamental historical contradiction. In order to survive as a nation, Nicaragua has struggled for decades against the imperial ambitions of the U.S.—from 1855, when we were invaded, until 1979, when the Revolution proclaimed true national independence, by way of the actions of General Sandino against intervention in 1927, who organized with arms in hand the ideological principles of this secular struggle, a struggle of all Latin America that we are now waging once more in this small but well-fortified trench.

Since this is also a political and ideological struggle, and the propagandistic imperial arguments only attempt to mask and justify military aggression armed, organized, directed and financed by the Reagan administration, it's worth examining some of the fallacies intoned like songs of death and treachery against our right to independence, and by the light of our reason—which is the reason of a poor people struggling for its national identity against the recurrent attacks of Manifest Destiny—discern the pattern of those lies and sophistries so often repeated:

Exporting Revolution

1. *The Sandinistas' grave mistake in trying to export their revolution.*

Throughout history revolutions have been exportable, if we care to use this mercantile term in speaking of the dynamic whereby ideas tend to circulate across frontiers. There never would have been a French Revolution without the revolution of the 13 North American colonies. Thomas Jefferson's ideas would not have existed without the inspiration of the French encyclopedists. Gen. Lafayette would not have gone from France to fight in the fields of Virginia if he hadn't believed that revolutions have no borders, nor would Benjamin Franklin have spent so many years conspiring in European courts if he hadn't believed his American Revolution was exportable.

The revolution that got the U.S. started as a nation has been the most exported revolution in modern history, and one that used the most imported ideological elements to establish the basis of its thinking, its war of liberation and its new laws.

Faced with the absolutism of the Spanish monarchs in Spanish America, a colonialist absolutism just like that England exercised over its American colonies, our Creole liberators found the most attractive and enlightened formulas for throwing off the colonial yoke in the north: the example of a bloody and relentless war waged by people determined to replace a colonial regime with a new political and social order; the crystallization of European utopian ideas of democracy, which for the first time would be put to the practical test in the New World—a promised land for those philosophical dreams that until then had been so extravagant—a constitutional government with checks and balances. All these were extremist and subversive concepts for the monarchic order, which as they spread clandestinely through Spanish America provoked persecutions, imprisonments and exiles. To read James Madison in those times was a crime of high treason, just as today in Guatemala or El Salvador reading Marx can cost you your life.

Revolutionary Nicaragua a Better Place

What really struck me as revolutionary in the behavior of ordinary [Nicaraguan] people was the total lack of servility. Living in a society that is politically democratic but also highly competitive, with a great sense of status, one that at the same time is emotionally repressive, we have become accustomed to fear, to inhibitions, to artificial smiles, to the anxiety-ridden efforts to please that are the distinguishing characteristic of our insecure fellow citizens. In Managua I felt as if people really acted as if all men were free and equal. The bus drivers, the office workers, the waiters, were friendly and helpful, but they did things with their own rhythm, in their own style, without servile gestures or expressions of any type.

Gabriel Jackson, *The Continuing Crisis*, 1987.

The constitution of the new United States and the new ideas that inspired it traveled by muleback through Central America like contraband, and that emerging republic directed by radical fanatics—extremist exporters of revolutions who believed only in their own model and rejected any other that stood in their way—represented a threat to the internal security and strategic interests of Spain's great New World colonial empire, which was beginning to crack. In 1823, with Central American independence already won, the first federal constitution voted to secure the ephemeral dream of a united Morazan-inspired Central America began word for word as did the constitution edited by Madison in 1787. The U.S. was exporting a model then, and exporting the bloody example that so profound a change could not be carried forward without guns, without crushing the enemy militarily and without emulating the minutemen—guerrilla fighters just as brave as the Salvadoran [revolutionaries]. Faced with the insurgency of a new order based on new ideas, necessarily subversive, the old order and the old ideas were destroyed in war and hundreds of thousands of counterrevolutionary Tories left in a mass exodus for Canada. Revolutions always produce an exodus. . . .

Impossible Not To Export

And so for the Sandinistas—repeating the revolutionary deeds of Morazan in the 20th century—it's impossible not to export their idea of revolution. We're exporting new ideas, ideas of change and renewal, ideas that are establishing a new world. We export the fact that an armed people can, when it decides to, overthrow a tyranny and establish a new world on its ruins. We export the news that in Nicaragua the revolution has brought literacy, land reform, the eradication of polio, the right to life and hope. How can we prevent peasants in some other Central American country from hearing, from knowing, from understanding that in Nicaragua land is being given to other poor peasants like them? How can we keep them from realizing that here children are being vaccinated, while theirs are still dying from gastroenteritis and polio?

Now, as then, the struggle is not between Nicaraguans and Hondurans, but between workers and bosses, between new people and ghosts of the past, between those who are fighting for a better order and those attempting forever to sustain the worse order.

In this sense, we are exporting our revolution.

2. *The Sandinistas have betrayed their revolution.* . . .

When they talk to us Sandinistas of the betrayal of our original project, what are they talking about?

During Ronald Reagan's 1980 election campaign, the spokespeople of the New Right who had already taken ideological control of the Republican Party affirmed that the U.S. would never again commit the mistake of not fighting to the finish for an ally like Somoza, feeling guilty and ashamed for having abandoned him. Later they admitted preferring Somoza a thousand times over the Sandinistas. And still later they armed the old supporters of the Somoza regime, no less than the National Guard, to destroy the Sandinista revolutionary project and retake power with the weapons of counterrevolution.

As for the original project to which the U.S. government refers, it is not ours. Their project, as always, with no changes or variations, is that of the National Guard, which was created in 1927 by the U.S., supported the Yankee occupying army in 1933 and sustained the dictatorship of Somoza for nearly a half century.

The project of the U.S. is the attempt to reinstate the National Guard as the decisive power in the country, faithful to North American interests in the region, just as the army of Honduras is faithful to those interests.

Why do they want the National Guard to occupy again the territory of Nicaragua as it did for 50 years? To give us the constitution of Jefferson and the political model of George Washington?

To realize in Nicaragua the American dream of 1776? That dream does not exist, but the National Guard does, thanks to the efforts of the Reagan administration.

Rejecting Revolution

The miracle workers of the Reagan administration can't really think that we've betrayed the original project of our revolution because at a gut level they reject any idea of revolution. The word revolution is incompatible with their conception of the world; so that the revolution we haven't been able to complete, and which they've tried to take from us, they want to entrust to the colonels and mercenaries of Somoza's Guard, who murdered thousands of young people and peasants, who bombed neighborhoods and villages, who raped women and filled the jails. . . .

The U.S. should return to their original project of freedom and democracy, the project of Washington, Madison and Jefferson—that beautiful project of revolution betrayed by capitalist greed, by wanton accumulation of wealth and by a mistaken expansionist will that has pushed the borders of the U.S. so often toward our

"Our mission will be subversion, sabotage, assassination, and anything else we can think of to preserve democracy in Central America."

© Austin/Rothco.

own, as now once again to the Honduran border.

3. *What the Sandinistas have done is to copy a totalitarian model of revolution. . . .*

For us, the efficacy of a political model depends on its capacity to solve the problem of democracy, and the problem of justice. Effective democracy, like that we're attempting to practice in Nicaragua, means full popular participation, a permanent dynamic of the people's organic involvement in multiple political and social tasks. It means a people who express their opinions and are listened to, a people who contribute, who build, who direct, who mobilize, who attend to communal problems of their neighbors and of the nation; a people active in their own sovereignty, ready to fight in its defense, and also for literacy, for education, for vaccinations. In short, it means a democracy practiced every day, not just once every four years, but also, if given the chance, every four or five or six years when we will have formal elections. It means going to the polls as an entire people, voting consciously and making the best choice, not for a candidate marketed like a brand of soap or deodorant but a conscious leader, with a vote not manipulated by an advertising agency, a vote for change, for improving the country and not for transitional financial interests or military-industrial trusts.

Beyond that, democracy for us is not merely a formal model but a constant process capable of resolving the fundamental problems of development and capable of giving the people who participate and vote the real possibility of transforming the conditions of their lives, a democracy that establishes justice and does away with exploitation.

A political model arises from the necessities imposed by real conditions. Our Sandinista model rises out of the long domination of the U.S. in Nicaragua, a domination that was political and economic as well as military, and at the same time was social and ideological, even cultural. Faced with that domination our model establishes national independence as a vital necessity, and along with it the recovery of our national resources and a will for developing an economic project that, while transforming the country, gives us the opportunity to generate wealth and to distribute it justly.

A Bloody Joke

When people speak of our copying a model, one must keep in mind that what *somocismo* did for half a century was to copy in a servile manner the model imposed by the U.S. Nicaragua was bound to the most radical capitalist model, a market economy that impoverished the country and threw away the chances for its real development; and along with this model of capitalism at all costs, the dependence at all costs on markets, raw materials, means of capital; Nicaragua as a satellite of the U.S., Nicaragua behind a true iron curtain, with thick bars and a triple padlock. And, of course, the Somoza family also imported the political model of elections every four years, which they had there, and a system of two political parties, which they had there, and a legislative system with two chambers, and a supreme court, and a constitution and laws. And it was all a bloody joke.

And that imported, copied, imposed model failed historically, and now we are seeking our own model. We're no longer a satellite of the United States, we're no longer behind the iron curtain of the U.S., and we're free, sovereign and independent, something that was written deceitfully into all the Somoza constitutions, but is true today.

In order to consolidate this national project, this model of our own of a sovereign revolution, we're ready for any challenge and any sacrifice. To make possible that idea and nurse it into ongoing existence, the people of Nicaragua are armed and prepared to defend their project and their model of revolution. And they are prepared to attain a definitive peace that will permit the flowering of that model, which we don't intend to impose on anyone—because they have their real political borders, which are those of Nicaragua. We are not a people chosen by God to fulfill a manifest destiny, we have no capital to export, nor transnational enterprises to protect beyond our borders. Our dreams are not of domination, nor of expansion, nor of conquest, but the humble dreams of a humble people aspiring to full justice and full independence.

That is why we want to live in peace, and grow in peace, and multiply in peace the example of a sovereign people who never thought to ask anyone's permission to make their revolution, and will not ask anyone's permission to defend it.

A free country or death.

Distinguishing Bias from Reason

When dealing with controversial issues, many people allow their feelings to dominate their powers of reason. Thus, one of the most important critical thinking skills is the ability to distinguish between statements based upon emotion or bias and conclusions based upon a rational consideration of the facts.

The following statements are taken from the viewpoints in this chapter. Consider each statement carefully. *Mark R for any statement you believe is based on reason or a rational consideration of the facts. Mark B for any statement you believe is based on bias, prejudice, or emotion. Mark I for any statement you think is impossible to judge.*

If you are doing this activity as a member of a class or group, compare your answers with those of other class or group members. Be able to defend your answers. You may discover that others come to different conclusions than you do. Listening to the rationale others present for their answers may give you valuable insights in distinguishing between bias and reason.

> R = *a statement based upon reason*
> B = *a statement based upon bias*
> I = *a statement impossible to judge*

1. In Peru, extremists tried to sabotage the 1985 elections by unleashing a terror campaign to keep people away from the polls; but only 7% of the registered voters stayed home, proving that the people support the electoral process.

2. If more Central American nations become embroiled in civil wars, the number of Central American refugees is likely to increase.

3. Through improvement of the health and education of its people, Cuba has accomplished substantial economic development during the past fifteen years.

4. It is unlikely that a dictatorship could remain in power for twenty-six years without political prisoners and political prisons.

5. Unlike dictatorships which simply weaken if they try to reform, democracies get stronger—they can change and regenerate.

6. Throughout history revolutions have been exportable; the ideas embodied in one revolution often influence the leaders of others. For example, the early leaders of the French revolution were influenced by the ideas embodied in the American revolution and the Declaration of Independence.

7. To maintain and extend a popular base, Latin American governments will have to prove to their citizens that democracy means not only the end of political brutality but progress in areas such as public health and education.

8. The struggle is not between Nicaraguans and Hondurans, but between workers and bosses, between those who are fighting for a better order and those attempting to sustain the worse order.

9. The sugar companies, by controlling 70% of the arable farmland, monopolized Cuba's chief resource.

10. The Sandinistas managed to deceive national and international opinion because of a very deep-seated malady in Western politics—what is known as the liberal approach to politics.

11. The Reagan administration wants to entrust the Nicaraguan revolution to the colonels of Somoza's Guard, who murdered thousands of young people and peasants.

Periodical Bibliography

The following periodical articles have been selected to supplement the diverse views expressed in this chapter.

Diego Arria — "Why They Paint 'Yanqui Go Home,'" *The New York Times*, June 30, 1985.

Maurice R. Berube — "Assessing a Revolution," *Commonweal*, September 6, 1985.

Foreign Policy and Defense Review — "The Alternative Futures of Latin America," vol. 5, no. 3.

Albert O. Hirschman — "On Democracy in Latin America," *The New York Review of Books*, April 10, 1986.

Brian Loveman — "Military Dictatorship and Political Opposition in Chile, 1973-1986," *Journal of InterAmerican Studies and World Affairs*, Winter 1986/1987.

Jay R. Mandle — "Feasible Socialism and Economic Development," *Socialist Review*, January/February 1987.

Richard T. McCormack — "Obstacles to Investment and Economic Growth in Latin America," *Department of State Bulletin*, October 1986.

Sergio Ramirez Mercado — "On Nicaragua's Resolve," *World Policy Journal*, Spring 1984.

Cecilia Rodriguez — "A Military Menace Hides Behind Latin America's New Democracy," *Los Angeles Times*, November 30, 1986.

George Shultz — "The Resurgence of Democracy in Latin America," *St. Croix Review*, April/May 1985.

World Policy Journal — "On Nicaraguan Democracy: An interview with Clemente Guido, Mauricio Diaz Davila, Sixto Ulloa Dona, and Rafael Solis Cerda, Interviewed by Andrew Reding," Summer 1985.

How Serious Is the Latin American Debt?

Chapter Preface

Many Latin American countries are heavily indebted to the US and to its lending institutions. For some countries the dollar amount is so large that it is virtually unpayable. For Mexico, for example, simply paying the interest on its US debt is so burdensome as to place its economy in serious jeopardy.

Many Latin Americans believe the US should forgive their countries' debts. Some Latin American governments have even threatened to default if the US refuses to do this. They argue that paying the debt diverts resources from feeding and housing their people and results in widespread discontent and potential political instability. In contrast, the US business community believes the Latin Americans are exaggerating their plight to avoid responsibility for paying the debt. Since Latin Americans are the ones to have borrowed the money, they should find a way to repay it without US help.

In the background are the US banks who stand to lose millions of dollars if Latin American nations default. Predictions of the impact on US banks if these threats are carried out range from slight to devastating. The authors in this chapter debate the debts' seriousness and methods of repayment.

"The stimulus to entrepreneurship attendant upon deregulation, and the increased scope for launching small and medium-sized firms, will create jobs."

Freemarket Policies Must Be Implemented

Bela Balassa, Gerardo M. Bueno, Pedro-Pablo Kuczynski, and Mario Henrique Simonsen

Bela Balassa is professor of political economy at Johns Hopkins University and consultant to the World Bank. Gerardo M. Bueno is a senior research fellow at El Colegio de Mexico. Pedro-Pablo Kuczynski is co-chairman of the First Boston International Bank in New York and a former Minister of Energy of Peru. Mario Henrique Simonsen is director of the Graduate School of Economics at the Fundacao Getulio Vargas and is a former minister of finance and minister of planning in Brazil. The following viewpoint is excerpted from a report sponsored by the America Society and written jointly by this team of authors from Latin America and North America in order to offer a new growth strategy for Latin America.

As you read, consider the following questions:

1. Why do the authors believe Latin America can make a full economic recovery?
2. What is "outward orientation," according to the authors? What benefits will it have for Latin America?

Latin America's potential for addressing its problems constructively must be assessed. The difficulties are substantial. Many are of long-standing duration. Many have grown much worse in the first half of the 1980s. But we believe that Latin America can meet the challenge successfully for a number of reasons.

First is the enormous potential of the continent, in both human and material terms. Its people have demonstrated considerable entrepreneurial abilities, despite government policies that often discourage their realization. Educational levels are relatively high in many countries. . . .

Second is the actual record of Latin America. Despite its relative decline, economic growth was quite impressive in several Latin American countries following policy reforms in the mid-1960s. And while growth rates declined over the last decade, manufactured exports rose rapidly—especially in countries that promoted exports after the first oil shock in 1973—although none of them matched the export performance of East Asia.

Even in their response to the adversities of the early 1980s, several Latin American countries revealed considerable economic adaptability and political resilience. The region improved its combined current account position by $40 billion from 1981 to 1984, about 6 percent of its gross domestic product. The predicted political instabilities failed to materialize, and democratization proceeded in several countries.

Third, the relatively greater success of other developing countries and regions demonstrates that better results are possible. There is simply no reason to believe that "the Confucian work ethic" or "the Spanish heritage" mean that East Asia can make it while Latin America cannot. In fact, the rapid growth of the "informal sector" in heavily regulated economies, such as Peru, suggests that the problem is not a lack of business acumen but rather an institutional structure that stifles entrepreneurial spirit in these economies. Policies, and the related economic and social structures, matter substantially, as this and many other studies show. . . .

Savings Rates

Fourth, the starting point in Latin America is much better than is frequently realized. Savings rates, despite recent declines, are quite high. Governments are effective providers of social services in Latin America which, despite wide country variations, are comparable to those in other developing countries at similar income levels. The same thing cannot be said about their effectiveness as producers and regulators. Economic infrastructure has been established in the advanced countries of the region. Export expansion has been impressive in several cases: Brazil now sells aircraft to the United States, and Argentina sells turbines for electricity plants in the international market. The successes of the 1960s and 1970s inevitably left positive results, along with the buildup of imbalances and inefficiencies that brought them to a halt. . . .

Global Environment

Finally, improvements have occurred in the global environment which are supportive of reform in Latin America. World inflation is down sharply and seems likely to remain there; this promises greater stability and obviates the need for industrial countries to adopt restrictive economic policies. World interest rates have declined, cutting the cost of debt service and promoting more rapid growth. The fall in the price of oil, while hurting Mexico, Venezuela, and Ecuador, brings substantial direct benefit to the rest of the region and indirect benefit to all its countries by further checking inflation and enhancing prospects for faster growth in the world economy. The large decline in the exchange rate of the dollar brings major benefits to the region. . . .

Promoting Economic Growth

If Latin American nations are serious about promoting real economic growth with a thriving private sector in the vanguard, they must: reduce public consumption, decrease government investment expenditures, curtail the expansion of state enterprises, and divest of these companies wherever politically feasible. In addition, governments should deregulate or at least ease the regulation of money, credit, exchange rates, price controls, wage rates, licensing systems, and trade performance requirements. In tax policy, real reduction in rates should take place, with the greatest reduction going to the most productive sectors and income groups; tax codes should be simplified and the efficiency of tax collection improved substantially; and tax incentives should be structured to promote investment, savings, cost-effective technology, and hard-currency earnings.

Jerry Haar, *Latin America: Dependency or Interdependence?,* 1985.

Our proposed strategy contains three central elements for the Latin American countries themselves: outward orientation of the economy, with emphasis on exports and efficient import substitution; the generation of adequate levels of savings, primarily from domestic sources but from abroad as well, and their efficient investment; and a reorientation of the role of government toward its demonstrated comparative advantage of providing services and a framework for economic activity, limiting its role as regulator and producer. The critical fourth element is supportive policy by the industrial countries, notably the United States. The four parts interrelate closely, and all are essential to launch a successful

193

development strategy for Latin America.

Outward orientation is a system of incentives that stimulates exports and efficient import substitution. Only such a focus will enable the countries of the region to achieve self-sustaining growth and simultaneously to service their external debt, because only such a strategy will generate both the needed foreign exchange and the essential stimulus to domestic production.

Outward orientation is the keystone of the strategies of virtually all the "success stories" cited above—in East and Southeast Asia, in Latin America in certain periods, in Turkey, and elsewhere. Even where success has been limited, as in Africa, relatively outward-oriented countries have done much better than the inward-oriented. . . .

Increasing Exports

Internationally acceptable export incentives are also an essential component of a strategy of outward orientation. Export credit must be available on competitive terms. Imported inputs for export production should be freed from all duties and indirect taxes. Export promotion measures, including information services and trade fairs, can be useful.

Policies of outward orientation aimed at promoting exports and efficient import substitution, while essential, make up only part of the proposed strategy. The rationalization and modernization of the domestic economy further require *generating higher levels of savings*, primarily domestic but also from abroad, and especially *using all savings available much more efficiently* than in the past. . . .

Export expansion will generally promote savings, as a higher than average share of export earnings is normally saved. A resumption of growth will itself generate increased savings and could launch a virtuous cycle between the two. But a key part of the proposed strategy is the adoption of new measures to promote higher levels of savings and more efficient investment patterns. . . .

The Role of the State

The third central theme of our proposed strategy is *reforming the role of the state in the economic life of Latin America.* Public dissaving via budget deficits is one aspect of this problem. But the problem runs much deeper, indeed to the core of the economic difficulties of the region.

Due in part to the historical heritage of Latin America, the role of the state has become pervasive in most of its countries. Correspondingly, the private sector has been weakened as the state has assumed increasing importance. Part of the blame lies with the private sector itself: its leaders have all too often turned to the state in times of trouble, thereby adding to the expansion of state power. The time has come to begin reversing this trend, as an essential part of a new growth strategy. . . .

This environment of pervasive overregulation is an important element in creating inefficiency in most Latin American economies. The expanding "informal sector" is perhaps the most obvious result. But lacking access to the facilitative aspects of the law, and to credit and insurance, its opportunity to grow and create jobs is limited. Thus entrepreneurial initiative is discouraged.

This same regulatory environment raises prices internally and discourages the flexibility and adaptability needed to achieve international competitivenesss and successful outward orientation. Markets abroad will not wait for licenses to be issued and regulations complied with. Meanwhile, somebody else gets the business.

Free Economies Guarantee Freedom

The United States has convincingly proved that the best scenario to create wealth lies wherever individual self-interests are freely allowed to take risks and reap rewards in a market economy. It also shows that when free economies are firmly entrenched, political freedoms become inevitable.

Learning from this example, Latin American leaders should now move boldly to help remove all barriers and obstacles to a free market in the region. For once Latin American economies are unshackled, their rapid recovery would soon silence all critics and skeptics. And the ensuing popular support would add irresistible momentum to an irreversible historic trend; a trend toward the eventual integration of all America.

Jose Rivas-Micoud, *The Freeman*, March 1987.

Substantial deregulation is thus a central feature of our proposed development strategy. The state should set the legal framework, assuring private property rights and avoiding abuses of individual freedom. It should adopt a coherent and effective growth strategy, as proposed here, and macroeconomic and microeconomic policies to carry out that strategy. It should promote more equitable distribution of income through improved provision of basic services and the establishment of a policy environment that facilitates the growth and productivity needed to create more and better paying jobs. And it should do all this to the maximum extent through the adoption of laws and regulations which are applied universally, eschewing case-by-case decision-making to the maximum extent possible. Indeed, the trend toward political democratization requires such changes—and is fundamentally incompatible with the traditional heavy hand of state regulation throughout Latin America.

Reforms are also needed to reduce the state's role as a producer, and to begin the inevitably lengthy process of revitalizing the

195

private sector. Public utilities and some state enterprises in basic industries have proved to be efficient in some countries. But the proliferation of state enterprises in the potentially competitive sectors has come to involve substantial inefficiencies. It also conflicts with outward orientation because state firms typically come to rely heavily on the favoritism of the state itself to assure their domestic market shares, discouraging them from competing for markets abroad and instead furthering high import protection to enable them to sell at home.

It is obviously impossible to privatize all state enterprises in the competitive sector overnight, even if that were deemed desirable on economic efficiency grounds. Private capital and management skills are simply not available in sufficient amounts. Some firms, however, can be sold off. A clear movement toward privatization should be set in motion. . . .

The Importance of Change

Economic reform is imperative in Latin America. A new approach is essential to promote broad-based, self-sustaining growth along with continued servicing of the external debt. A strategy centered on outward orientation, new market incentives for savings and investment, and a fundamental shift in the role of the state can resolve the dilemma.

Adoption of such a strategy will require numerous changes, structural as well as immediate, in both the external and domestic economic policies of the Latin American countries. The prospects for such reform, however, are encouraging. The record of Latin America in the past, and of many other developing countries at present, shows that such policies can succeed. The world environment is improving. Policy changes in the needed direction are beginning to occur within Latin America and in a complementary direction in the industrial countries. The previously entrenched forces of resistance to reform seem to be yielding in the face of crisis.

"What can be gleaned from the Chilean and Argentine experience is that implementing [free-market policies] or similar programs will foreclose any possibility for . . . economic development."

Freemarket Plans Will Not Resolve Latin America's Economic Problems

Robert Pollin and Eduardo Zepeda

Robert Pollin teaches economics at the University of California-Riverside. Eduardo Zepeda teaches economics at the Metropolitan Autonomous University-Ascapotzalco, Mexico City. In the following viewpoint, Pollin and Zepeda argue that the free-market policies encouraged by the US and the International Monetary Fund (IMF) austerity programs will not work in Latin America.

As you read, consider the following questions:

1. Why do the authors argue that comparisons between Latin America and Southeast Asia are misleading?
2. What did freemarket policies do to the economies of Chile and Argentina, according to the authors?
3. What is the authors' solution to the Latin American debt problem?

Robert Pollin and Eduardo Zepeda, "Latin American Debt: The Choices Ahead," *Monthly Review*, February 1987. Copyright © 1987 by Monthly Review Inc. Reprinted by permission of Monthly Review Foundation.

Since August 1982, when Mexico announced its inability to make interest payments on its outstanding debt of $90 billion, tremendous hardship has been imposed on the indebted countries through austerity programs devised by the International Monetary Fund (IMF) and, more recently, the Latin governments themselves. Amidst an almost constant swirl of activity—new pronouncements, policy twists, and even news of occasional economic upturns—the burden of the debt drags on. While the manifestations of the crisis have been most dramatic in Mexico, Argentina, and Brazil—Latin America's three largest and most heavily indebted countries—the suffering in fact has been widespread, in Latin America and beyond. Even the U.S. economy has been harmed, most seriously through the shrinkage of what had been a huge Latin market for U.S. exports.

One major change has occurred. It has become apparent that Latin America's creditors—the international bankers and their allies in governments and international lending institutions—have become willing to make small concessions in exchange for basic restructuring of the Latin economies. More specifically, they are calling for Latin American countries to become bastions of free-market capitalism, with minimal government, open borders for multinationals, and free trade serving as guiding precepts. In other words, while previously the debate over the debt was shrouded in a pretense of technical neutrality, it has now become an openly politicized struggle over the nature of Latin America's economic development path. . . .

Economic Mistakes

The IMF was never ambiguous in its intention to cut back sharply on public enterprise, government subsidies, price controls, and deficit spending. But it did not recognize that these public-sector activities provide the primary basis for effective demand in all Latin economies. Severe reductions in such programs inevitably raise havoc with domestic markets. The IMF argues that domestic firms should shift to an export orientation after the public sector contracts. But this ignores what almost all economists recognize, that capturing export markets requires time and sustained promotional effort, even after a country's products have become more competitive through devaluation. This situation especially holds for most products of Latin America, which for a generation have been geared to domestic markets and protected from international competition. Latin firms therefore faced moribund markets as an unavoidable consequence of severe government cutbacks. Investment in the region plummeted as a result, falling by 44 percent in Mexico, 37 percent in Argentina, and 17 percent in Brazil between 1981 and 1984. At the same time, acute inflationary pressures were also generated through the devaluations and slashing of price controls and subsidies. In 1981-84, average annual inflation rates were 667 percent in Mexico, 362 percent in Argentina and 141 percent in Brazil. . . .

The Baker Plan and Its Progeny

The growing opposition in Latin America has aroused deep concern within the creditors' cartel and its governmental supporters. The Reagan administration was the first to respond aggressively to this development with its "Baker plan," named for U.S. Treasury Secretary James Baker who first presented it in October 1985 at a joint annual meeting of the IMF and World Bank. In unveiling the plan, Reagan administration officials made no secret that their primary motive was to thwart the growing Latin American opposition. As David Mulford, Baker's Assistant Treasury Secretary for International Affairs explained, it is "far better for us to take the initiative rather than be taken on the defensive." . . .

Repudiate the Debt

The conditions being what they are, the debt can neither be reclaimed, nor repaid; the debt has become a political problem, and that is the light in which it must be seen; the Latin American countries cannot hope to find a realistic and reliable way out of the existing situation, unless the problem is closely tied in with the establishment of a new international economic order; no time must be lost in starting a campaign for a democratic way out of the crisis, an impetus should be given to national development, payment of the debt should be repudiated, and the imperialist diktat rejected.

World Marxist Review, August 1986.

By introducing the Baker plan, the Reagan administration was implicitly conceding that the IMF austerity approach had failed. The U.S. officials contended that, by contrast, the Baker plan would work because it is not an austerity policy, but rather a strategy for promoting economic growth in the indebted countries. The contention is that growth will accelerate in the indebted countries when the proposed market-oriented reforms are implemented, and this in turn will enhance their debt-servicing capacity. Indeed, in official discussions of the plan and in the mainstream press, an interesting linguistic innovation has occurred: a "pro-growth" economic policy has become *by definition* one which dismantles state intervention and delivers the economy, via the "free market," to private capital. . . .

Through devaluation and wage/price controls, proponents of these plans contend that inflation and capital flight could be stifled without requiring further cuts in public spending. An improved business climate would then be established, encouraging more investment both from domestic capitalists and multinationals. With inflation and capital flight down and investment growing, the countries' ability to service their debt should then strengthen.

Both programs did succeed in dramatically lowering inflation. In Brazil's case, moreover, sharp increases in consumer spending and output did follow. But this was largely because consumers began purchasing heavily in anticipation of a revival of inflation after the lifting of price controls. Neither program, however, managed to encourage investment growth, since the controls restricted potential profit opportunities. Moreover, neither country has succeeded through these programs in reducing its debt burden: debt servicing relative to exports, at 51 percent in Argentina and 35 percent in Brazil in 1986, represents no improvement from previous years. In addition, the controls themselves began to unravel by the fall of 1986, creating widespread disillusionment. Both countries thus entered new rounds of negotiations with creditors by the end of 1986, with no significant gains to show for their anti-inflationary programs. In Brazil's case, the government is now demanding major concessions on debt payments and is threatening a partial or full debt moratorium if the concessions aren't granted. . . .

Debt Concessions Needed

It is now apparent that the Latin economies cannot reasonably function without concessions on the debt, regardless of what other policy initiatives are pursued. This has been the lesson of the anti-inflationary programs in Brazil and Argentina, which are disintegrating under the burden of the debt. From the Mexican agreement, it is clear also that the creditors' cartel will insist on free-market restructuring before even minor concessions are granted. The creditors' demand for free-market policies is further underscored by the increasing prominence they attach to debt/equity swap arrangements. In short, it is now clear that unless the Latin governments are willing to dismantle their public sectors, welcome free trade, and actively encourage multinational investors, the Reagan administration and creditors' cartel are prepared to allow their economies to smother under the debt burden. . . .

Freemarket Policies in the Third World

The major question then becomes: What do such free-market policies portend for the debtor countries? Administration officials point to alleged "economic miracles" in South Asian countries, such as South Korea, as evidence that the future under free-market capitalism would be bright indeed. But this comparison is groundless. However one may assess the experience of the South Asian economies, it is certain in any case that their rapid growth was not achieved by practicing laissez-faire. . . .

To understand what actually occurs when a third world country pursues Baker type "structural reforms," one should rather examine the experiences of Chile and Argentina after military governments came to power in these countries in 1973 and 1974 respectively. For almost a decade, vigorous free-market policies were actually practiced in both countries. To begin with, state spending and regulation of market activity were sharply reduced, and the economic and political position of the domestic capitalist class was strengthened. In addition, both countries opened up their economies by eliminating both protectionist barriers to imports and subsidies to domestic export industries, and by providing substantial incentives for foreign investors.

The results of these authentic free-market experiments are well-known: they were both disastrous. Both countries, first of all, experienced sharp declines in living standards as real wages fell and unemployment rose. In addition, in both cases the distribution of income became significantly more unequal, output and investment fell sharply, and potential future output was lost due to the decimation of industry. Both countries did manage to increase exports over this period, as severe wage reductions and exchange rate devaluations lowered prices charged by the exporting firms. But imports increased even more. This was due first to the decline of local production and the consequent need to purchase necessary goods from abroad at prices that were inflated because of the devalued currencies. Demand for luxury imports also increased because the wealthy were capturing an increasing share of the national income. The balance of payments deficits were thus exacerbated in both countries, and this in turn contributed to their debt crises of the 1980s.

State-Centered Economies

Why did this occur? Clearly, in these countries, just as in South Korea, the state had been the center of the economy. It was the largest employer and the primary source of effective demand. It was also responsible for planning and financing of investment activity and support for export and import-competing industries. When the state's dominant role is rapidly withdrawn from such economies, the market is simply not capable of taking its place. Power of this kind may be ascribed to the market in conservative economics textbooks, but there is no evidence that the textbook model accords with reality.

In short, what can be gleaned from the Chilean and Argentine experiences is that implementing the Baker plan or similar programs will foreclose any possibility for decent economic development, just as did the IMF austerity policies. Indeed, rhetoric and minor concessions aside, Baker-type plans turn out to be virtually

201

identical to that of the IMF: the bottom line in both cases is a simple insistence that Latin governments, at whatever cost, swear allegiance to free-market capitalism.

The Need for a Debt Moratorium

James Baker and others have argued that the Latin governments will embrace free-market restructuring because, as Baker put it, "there is no alternative." In fact, however, a debt moratorium is an obvious alternative, though it is not surprising that Baker chooses to ignore it. As Castro, the U.S. bishops, and increasingly the Brazilian government contend, a great deal can be gained from a moratorium now. It would bring immediate and deserved relief from the punishing austerity of the past four years; it would allow the domestic industries to recover some momentum; and it would also, ultimately, force more reasonable financial agreements from the creditors' cartel. Of course the cartel would initially react with tremendous hostility to a moratorium. But the reaction would not be universally shared in the developed countries. U.S. exporters, for example, would clearly welcome the revival of the huge Latin market. It is now also clear that the banks themselves—whose profits have actually been rising since the onset of the debt crisis—could weather a moratorium without requiring a massive government bailout. . . .

In the present circumstances, at least as much as in any of these historical cases, it is clear that progressive forces in Latin America and elsewhere need to fight for a moratorium as a first step toward halting free-market restructuring and capturing the initiative in the struggle for Latin America's future.

"More significant . . . than even the shambles of the Mexican economy is the ballooning political crisis."

Mexico Is on the Verge of Economic Collapse

Sol Sanders

Sol Sanders began learning about Mexico in the late 1940s when he worked as a reporter on the United Press Latin American desk in New York. He has written extensively on Mexico for both scholarly journals and popular publications. In the following viewpoint, Sanders maintains that Mexico's combined political, social and economic crises are leading to the ultimate demise of its current structure. The US needs to pay more attention to Mexico, he contends, to avoid the inevitable impact Mexico's destabilization would have for the US.

As you read, consider the following questions:

1. Why does the author argue that Mexico's political structure is in desperate need of revision?
2. Why is Guatemala a threat to Mexico, according to Sanders?
3. Why does the author believe that Mexico is headed toward chaos?

Sol Sanders, *Mexico: Chaos on Our Doorstep.* Lanham, MD: Madison Books, 1986. Reprinted with permission.

For more than a half century the United States has been able to treat Mexico, to use Sen. Patrick Moynihan's famous phrase from another context, with "benign neglect." But a sea of change has taken place in U.S.-Mexican relations. The old relationship— a virtual ignorance of Mexico on the U.S. side of the border, and a controlled resentment of North Americans by Mexicans—has metamorphosed into a new and more volatile ambiguity. The traditional lack of understanding, in a new world where the interrelationship has become so much more intense, could easily develop into a confrontation—even should both governments do their best to try to diffuse it.

U.S. policy has been ostrich-like in the face of four disastrous trends that have overtaken the Mexican polity:

1. The demographic and historical currents that point toward instability.

2. The unsettling geopolitical situation in the Caribbean and Central America which redounds onto Mexico.

3. The chronic but escalating economic crisis.

4. The merging of the growing influence of Marxist-Leninism with the traditional autocracy on Mexican institutions, including the all-powerful presidency.

All these point to the likelihood of a coming destabilization in Mexico, inimical to the United States. . . .

Lower Living Standards

Mexico is no longer as isolated as she once was; her calls for pluralism in other countries—a ploy so often directed at the U.S. by Communist fellow-traveling Mexican intellectuals—is beginning to boomerang. The concentration of all power in Mexico City, which was effective with a smaller and more isolated population, makes it increasingly difficult to implement decisions in cities of over a million, some a thousand miles from the capital. The system is, moreover, crippled by corruption. That corruption, as old as the Conquest and the ruthless sacking of the Aztec capital by the Spaniards, exceeded all bounds in the last administration. President José López Portillo personally may have stolen as much as $3.5 billion, more than the total reserves of many smaller countries. All this might have been tolerable had the bubble of oil riches—which Mexicans were led to believe would solve all their problems—not burst. The falling real price of energy meant not only that all Mexicans had to face lowered living standards, but the whole "solution" of their international debt crisis, trumpeted around the world as the model for other creditors, collapsed. . . .

Today, Mexico has a running sore along her southern border where Guatemalan Communist guerrillas squat along the 1,500-mile isolated and jungled frontier and operate against non-Communist Guatemala, the largest of the Central American states.

Not only are they based on Mexico's territory, but it is often with the aid and comfort of Mexican nationals, not the least important being local Catholic clergy of the liberation theology persuasion. This situation has the approval, of course, of Mexican leftists— even of some factions of the ruling party. And the federal government in Mexico City has tolerated the situation, impotent to do much else.

Mexico's Inefficient Government

Today the government is by far the largest employer in the country, and according to several estimates accounts for half of Mexico's GNP. Besides owning and managing the all-important petroleum industry, it presides over an eclectic conglomerate consisting of textile mills, most of the movie industry, real estate companies, luxury hotels, lumber mills, sugar refineries, and virtually every other type of business imaginable. It even runs a golf course.

Since the state's involvement to this degree has mushroomed in the last decade or so, there is little systematic information about its efficiency relative to the private sector. Nonetheless, horror stories have begun to emerge that underscore what a white elephant government administration has been. Public enterprises are said to suffer a whole host of maladies: inadequate definition of objectives, poor organization, underutilization of resources, lack of cost control, poor coordination with other government enterprises and bureaucracies. Whispers of corruption also abound. The latest of these cite personal loans to bureaucrats that are many times higher than their annual salaries.

Forrest D. Colburn, *The New Leader*, January 13, 1986.

Denying the thesis that in the contemporary world situation all regional conflicts tend to become a part of the superpower confrontation, the standard Mexican rationalization is that the revolutionary movements in Central America are only latter-day manifestations of the same currents that drove Mexico's own earlier revolution, and that they will, in time, become "domesticated." But the truth is that Mexico neither has the will nor the power to police that border. And it is certainly arguable that any Mexican government (even one backed by U.S. power) could fend off a campaign of guerrilla subversion waged against it from a Communist Guatemala. It is the classic guerrilla situation where the Communists exploit various elements: old resentments against a central government, an extremely difficult terrain, a frontier that artificially bisects kindred peoples, and smuggling and clandestine migratory crossings dating back over the centuries.

Mexico, too, has had internal changes—political, social, and economic—which have impacted on the bilateral U.S.-Mexican relationship, first and foremost the incredible demographic explosion. The Mexico of the Revolution of 1910-1922 of 15 million people has mushroomed to 80 million in 1985 with the expectation that it will exceed 100 million people before the end of the century, and perhaps 130 million in the ensuing decade.

It is doubtful that any regime could have handled this expansion with equanimity; that is, it would have been difficult under the best of conditions for Mexico to maintain both stability and material progress for its people. There is growing evidence that the present Mexican regime has not been able to accomplish the latter and the former is increasingly in question. Statistics in Mexico, as has been said about all Latin America, are poetry. But there is every indication that even before the onset of the current international debt crisis, the per capita income in Mexico was dropping rapidly. And the need to rein in the roaring inflation through austerity—or permitting the alternative of run-away inflation— promises that all Mexicans will see their living standards fall rapidly in the immediate future. Nor is there much hope that even the long-term pattern can be reversed, for it would require, as a minimum, an early and complete about-face in the government's economic and political strategies. . . .

Outdated Electoral System

More significant, however, than even the shambles of the Mexican economy is the ballooning political crisis that the nation faces. Contrasted with the enormous economic and social changes is the regime's failure to evolve a political process fit for a major, modern state with a large and diverse population living in a country devilishly designed by nature with a proliferation of climates and peoples. The regime's failure is fuel for the growing indignation of a small but burgeoning lower middle class that has a new set of values derived from its exposure to the world outside Mexico. A decentralization and a distribution of power is absolutely essential, and, although Mexican politicians pay lip service to the idea, the traditional centralization of the regime continues apace. . . .

But is this not all a domestic Mexican situation that precludes the U.S., especially given the history of Mexican-U.S. antagonistic relations, from a close examination much less an attempt to influence events there?

Given the intimacy of our relationship, there is no way that Americans will be able to avoid the impact of a Mexican breakdown. To think otherwise is to lull ourselves into a false sense of security, one that has been carefully nurtured in our psyche since we withdrew our troops from the horrendous engagement in Southeast Asia in 1973. . . .

Cognizance of Mexico's difficulties remains miniscule relative to the enormity of the implications a possible Mexican destabilization implies for the U.S. The financial crisis of 1981-1982 indicated what could lie in store for Mexico—and for the U.S. Greedy and foolish New York and regional bankers had lent Mexico upwards of $100 billion based on unrealistic estimates of oil and its rapid development. . . .

What simply was not being faced—in Mexico or in Washington or in New York—was that something fundamental had changed in Mexico . . . that the famed Mexico Model was badly flawed if not totally inoperative, and that the old order in Mexico was tottering.

Mexico's Patterns Continue

Nothing seems to go far toward breaking the old Mexican pattern of maldistribution of wealth or bridging the vast chasm between rich and poor. Meanwhile the population keeps growing at a rate of 2 million annually. That increases pressure on authorities to deliver more jobs and social services. It also increases U.S. worries about a tide of illegal aliens.

John S. DeMott, *Time,* June 13, 1983.

In fact, a fossilized regime—created in 1922 for some 15 million Mexicans—no longer could cope with the growing sophistication and frustration of a population nearing 80 million. The regime's vaunted corporate state, in which the various groupings in the "revolutionary family" had pretensions to represent all the constituencies in the nation, was no longer working. A halting and insincere movement toward political pluralism by López Portillo was taken up briefly by De la Madrid in an attempt to prop up the system. But free elections for municipalities boomeranged for the first time in the history of the country when the PRI lost one election after another in the spring and summer of 1983. De la Madrid had to pull down the riot shutters with a resounding political thud to save the "face" and perhaps the future of the PRI when reformist critics within the PRI elite had to face the very real prospect of being voted out of power were elections to be fair.

This is the background that makes certain that the U.S. increasingly must look to the south with growing anxiety. A Mexican regime which continues to be unable to solve its domestic problems will become a major preoccupation of the U.S., dwarfing many other older concerns in Washington. It could fundamentally shift America's post-World War II concentration from Western Europe and East Asia to Latin America.

Among many old hands who have dealt with Mexico and Latin America, there is an abiding hope that the fatalism which permeates Mexican society, a heritage perhaps from its Indian origins, will somehow, along with the mystique of the PRI and its incredibly flexible and pragmatic system (a special product of the Mexican ethos), permit the regime to muddle through. But there is, realistically, less and less hope that it will.

What would the PRI's failure mean for the U.S.? One obvious and immediate concern is that destabilization, sporadic violence, and civil conflict in Mexico would within weeks send *millions* of refugees scurrying across the largely undefended 2,000-mile land border into the Southwest. The thought of moving across that frontier in the event of a breakdown in the country is ingrained in the Mexican psyche today as is another—if contradictory—belief, held by many of the middle class: that should the worst overtake their country, somehow or other, Uncle Sam would descend like the Virgin of Guadalupe and miraculously rescue them. Unfortunately, there is much more realism associated with the first concept than with the second.

Washington, notoriously unable to focus on any foreign policy issue until it is in full crisis, is still blithely able to avoid formulating a comprehensive policy toward Mexico. After the 1981-1982 financial crisis, because of domestic U.S. pressures stemming mainly from the banking community, Washington willy-nilly moved into a long-term strategy of massive support of the PRI regime. . . .

Propping Up Mexico

There may have been no alternative to current U.S. policy, that is, no alternative but to wait and pray that somehow the PRI would weather this crisis as it has so many others. The Mexican moderate and conservative opposition is weak, fragmented, and unrealistic in its views of the current situation. The Mexican Left is dominated by a small but influential Communist movement, almost impervious to the disenchantment and a new sense of reality of some of the most devout fellow-travelers and even within the Communist parties of Western Europe.

Nor is there any hope that the present Mexican regime would permit a peaceful transfer of power to an opposition group, whatever its capabilities. What could well be in the offing is a new period of chaos in Mexico. That seems the likeliest scenario because of the weakness of both the Communist Left, despite its enormous inroads among intellectual elite, and the conservative Right. Neither seems able to build an alternative regime for the country. The question of whether the PRI has not outlived its time, of whether U.S. support, however extensive, and however well intentioned, will be enough to bolster it, has hardly been whispered. But in the months and years ahead, it will be asked.

"In terms of economic policy we [Mexico] have probably done more to reform our public finances and reduce subsidies than others."

Mexico Is Not on the Verge of Economic Collapse

Manuel Comacho Solis

Manuel Comacho Solis is the secretary of Urban Development and Ecology of the Mexican Federal Government. In the following viewpoint, Solis takes issue with US predictions that Mexico is careening toward social and economic collapse. He argues that Mexico has been an independent and democratic nation longer than any other Latin American country, proving that Mexico's government has continued to be innovative and representative of the people.

As you read, consider the following questions:

1. What is behind US predictions of Mexico's economic collapse, according to the author?
2. Why does Solis believe it is difficult for US citizens to understand Mexico?
3. Do you agree with Solis, that criticism of Mexico is based on misunderstanding? Why or why not?

Manuel Comacho Solis, in a speech given to the Wilson Center Annual Meeting on Mexico-U.S. Relations in Washington, DC on November 12, 1986.

We have seen a new round of apocalyptic predictions regarding Mexico. These have been coupled with several measures which will certainly not benefit our economy.

Regarding the harsh language: Mexico is presented as being close to ungovernable, inefficient in its economic management, incapable of modernizing its commercial relationships and its political regime. Mexico is shown as a nation incapable of facing corruption and drugs; unable to guarantee its future stability.

Regarding the measures, we see an increase in protectionism, taxes on oil imports, threats of massive migrant worker deportations and proposed economic sanctions tied to anti-drug results.

I could use this key forum to give a series of numbers and arguments on the many things Mexico has done to face its multiple problems. Few regimes have had to face such adverse conditions in the past few years. . . .

I could also start by pointing out that the strength of the anti-Mexican arguments lose their content when you look at your own reality or to what is happening in most countries. In terms of economic policy, we have probably done more to reform our public finances and reduce subsidies than others.

While your budget deficit has been increasing, we have cut ours drastically, or to give a further example, while your agricultural subsidies tripled, we have reduced ours and faced large social costs.

Drug Wars

With regard to the fight against drugs, you know that a few blocks from here [Washington, DC] one can be approached by people trying to sell almost any drug. Some banks and other businesses are used to launder close to 50 billion dollars per year. In many states, there has been a virtual elimination of penalties for marijuana use and drug enforcement agencies have asked other nations not to use noxious chemicals which would hurt consumers when they spray crops. An agent, who is a victim of the fight against narcotics, is turned into a martyr, when, already over 400 Mexican soldiers and policemen have died.

Regarding democracy, all of us appreciate the richness of the United States' political system, its liberties, the degree of community participation, its federalism. But there still remain many irregularities, such as close political ties to business interests, excessive campaign costs, political bosses and many other forms of non-competitive political control, particularly in poor urban areas or in less developed states.

Our foreign policy may differ from yours, but we can also cite multiple examples of U.S. interventions which have been counterproductive or political models which have not resolved what they were set up to resolve. We remain convinced, that despite periods when it seems that negotiations are ineffective, escalation and radicalism are still less effective.

I could try to answer every argument, or say that I simply do not find many of them convincing, because you also share and are a part of these same problems. But I do not think that you, or anyone else, has the right, if they are truly tolerant, to think that they are morally better and that everyone else is completely mistaken. This path would get us nowhere. We do not want to fall into a discussion in which you would passionately go on defending your country and its policies and I would, with decision and reason, also defend mine.

This is why I think it would be more constructive to seriously address the subject of the Mexican political system and to point out what, in my judgment, are mistakes of interpretation. Mistakes which, if left uncorrected, could only further complicate the relationship between our countries.

Mexico: A Finely Tuned Clock

If Washington insists on underlining Mexico's present regional impotence; if it continues systematically to disqualify, reject, or wear down every Mexican attempt to further its current goals in Central America; if it leaves Mexico no choice but to withdraw from all international activity and simply to manage its day-to-day affairs with the United States, then Mexican instability may become a real danger. . . . This instability is much less likely to take the form of a left-wing drift or takeover than of the slow breakdown of the finely tuned, delicately crafted, clockwork-like mechanisms that have guaranteed Mexico's political stability since the 1930s.

Jorge G. Castañeda, *Foreign Policy*, Fall 1985.

I will skip the recurrent failures of the predictions that have been made since the consolidation of our regime. Ours is the one in Latin America, that has preserved a constitutional order and freedom for the longest time. The prophecies on its unviability and its unavoidable breakdown are not new. They occurred in the 20s and 30s. There were more, 15 years ago, and four years ago. They have always proved mistaken.

The important question is whether these approaches derive from an adequate and responsible analysis or not. And above all, to clearly state our own point of view.

The interpretations of Mexico have changed. First, it was said that the opposition by the National Action Party—an important and necessary one within our multiparty system—was to play the key role in allowing an alternation of parties. This would become the basis for bipartisanship. The facts have shown how weak this analysis and proposal were.

Since this did not occur, there is an increasing resort to arguments and fears on the supposed ungovernability of Mexico.

What is behind it? The vision that what is convenient to the U.S. is either: A process of democratization similar to that of the U.S.; or if that fails, an increasing reliance on authoritarian control as a safeguard to protect vital U.S. interests. Both visions lack an understanding of the Mexican reality and are contrary to a mature and beneficial bilateral relation.

For Mexico, the values and procedures for its democratization are in its Constitution. The viable democratization strategy runs through both liberal and social channels. In Mexico, since its birth as an independent nation, there has always been a will for democracy. The revolution of 1910 started over an electoral and anti-reelection battle. And, we could not have achieved and maintained stability for over half a century without advancing in the formation of consensus and the perfecting of electoral procedures.

It was through a political reform in 1977 that Mexico was able to resolve the problems of clandestine Marxist groups by incorporating them into legality and into Congress. Now, these organizations act within the law. They march and protest, try to grow, but always within the limits established by the constitutional order. . . .

Reforming Electoral Procedures

At the most convenient time for Mexico, President de la Madrid sent to Congress a bill to reform the electoral procedures, to establish a grand jury for solving disputes and to establish open and proportionate rules for campaign financing.

This reform shows, once again, the capacity of the Mexican regime to modernize itself and adapt its procedures to the changes in society and the regional and urban characteristics of our country.

This reform will bring institutional changes, new equilibria between the political parties, more resources to opposition groups and a new opportunity to continue our democratic development.

We have not limited ourselves to the electoral process. Mexico has been strengthening the decision making capability of local and state governments, the intensity of debates within Congress and the resources available to the judicial system.

In relation to the Presidential powers, these have been evolving and have changed in the way they are exercised. They have based themselves increasingly on dialogue and consultation, but without restricting the power required in a developing country with as many problems as Mexico. They have guaranteed the cohesion, direction and efficacy of government. Some have absurdly proposed a parliamentary regime. This is completely unviable.

During the last years, the processes for social participation that used to be customary on the farms, in the life of small towns and

212

in the city's suburbs, have acquired new meanings. They have now been translated into new formulas for social concert, without which it would have been practically impossible to solve major problems such as the reconstruction of Mexico City or industrial reconversion programs.

Mexico's History

It may be difficult for you to understand the fundamental characteristic of our history: The importance we give to our nationalism and our independence. The problems on your border and the political conflicts in this country are very different from ours. To us, there could be no cultural integration without our nationalism. The necessary counterweight between a more developed north and a rural south, or between the cities and the countryside would not be possible.

Mexico Is Successful

Mexico's political system, like that of every other country in the world, emerged within a specific context that defined its traits and peculiarities. It should not be surprising, for instance, to find Mexico's government as promoter and direct participant in the economic realm, as far back as the middle of the 19th Century. At a time when most of the industrialized nations were pursuing free-market policies as the key to development, Mexico's government was forced by reality to pursue a different course, one that has given it more than half a century of stability and economic growth. Throughout that period, there were many arguments that Mexico would not be successful in its path to development. Despite the current difficulties, reality has clearly proved otherwise.

Luis Rubio, *Los Angeles Times*, December 21, 1986.

No social basis of support, no political organization or basic consensus would exist that could guarantee a lasting stability and permanent liberties and security: There could be no nation.

It is not only surprising, but also irresponsible that some supersede the equilibrium of a nation of eighty million people, one of the most complex in the world because of its history, its cultural diversity and its needs, with a game of pressures and bets so as to gain minor advantages.

Trying to alter our political equilibria could only awaken what we call "El Mexico Bronco," that is, the rough Mexico. The one with radicalisms and violence.

We were born and rose from those social upheavals. We know what the hardening of positions and intransigency can lead to: They only generate rebellion, intolerance and violence. We are just as knowledgeable of the extreme weakness which comes from atomizing power as we are of the dynamics of hard line positions. It is by dominating both of these that we built our nation.

Our experience tells us that there are better ways to solve conflicts than confrontation. Other formulas that require less sacrifice. And, most important, that provide the space and time that our country needs to solve its most urgent problems and to sustain its process of modernization. A process with its own rhythm, maintained for five decades at a pace required by the growth of our population.

"The Latin American debt is unpayable and should be canceled."

The Latin American Debt Should Be Canceled

Fidel Castro

Fidel Castro has been the premier of Cuba since his rise to power in 1959. An avowed Marxist-Leninist, he has often said that he would spread "the Cuban revolution" to the rest of Latin America. In the following viewpoint, he expands on this notion by arguing that Latin American countries must unite and refuse to pay back their acquired foreign debt. Only then, he believes, can these countries break the oppressive economic bond they have with the West.

As you read, consider the following questions:

1. Castro states that canceling the debt would not solve *all* of Latin America's problems. What does he believe it *would* accomplish?
2. Why does Castro believe that it is impossible to pay back the debt?
3. In what sense does the author believe the debt represents an opportunity for Latin America?

Fidel Castro, in an interview conducted by Regino Diaz, editor of the Mexican newspaper *Excelsior*. Reprinted from the *Granma Weekly Review*, April 7, 1985.

We consider that the fundamental premise for the Third World countries' independence, sovereignty, and development—and even for their right to make social changes—is the disappearance of the iniquitous system of exploitation through which the Third World countries are victimized. That is, we consider the struggle for the new world economic order . . . to be the most essential thing in the short term. Marx himself always considered economic development to be a premise for socialism. Experience forced a number of countries, Cuba among them, to take the socialist road of development. Each people should decide for itself what it wants to do. I am absolutely convinced that for the peoples of the Third World, who have a great variety of systems and forms of government, different degrees of development of their productive forces, and the most diverse forms of political and religious beliefs, development is their most important current task and a vital priority for all, without exception, in which they can unite in a common struggle. . . .

I consider the struggle for the new world economic order to be the most important thing the Latin American and Third World countries can do now, because it can lead to the creation of conditions needed for real independence, real sovereignty, and even the right to carry out social changes—and not only the right but the objective possibility of doing so.

There is one essential thing: the cancelation of Latin America's foreign debt in itself won't solve our problems; it would only offer a few years' respite.

Economic Situation Bleak

There are several countries in Latin America in which if you canceled their debts tomorrow you'd have solved practically nothing. Problems have become so serious in some countries—Bolivia, for example—that canceling their debts wouldn't have any impact. They might be able to count on an additional $200 million, or $250 million, or $270 million, which was their favorable balance of trade, but the problems that have accumulated in those countries are so serious that $270 million wouldn't even give them a "breather." I've been told about installations at which it costs $16 to produce a pound of tin, while the present world market price is $5 a pound.

There are some countries where canceling the debt would undoubtedly provide a respite; it would give a respite to Argentina, Uruguay, Brazil, Venezuela, Colombia, Ecuador, Peru, and—yes—Mexico. Mexico isn't one of the countries with the most difficult situations but it would surely provide a respite for Mexico, too.

Now then, we should be aware of the fact that there can be no final solution for our problems as long as the ominous law of sustained deterioration of the terms of trade remains in effect, as long

216

as the industrialized capitalist powers continue to impose the protectionist policies, as long as the practice of dumping subsidized products in order to grab markets and depress the prices of the exports on which many Third World countries depend continues, as long as monetary policies are imposed by means of which a powerful industrial country determines the interest to be paid and we are lent money at one value and expect to repay it at a higher value, as long as the capital we need for development is drained away, and as long as models and methods such as the ones recommended by the [free-market advocate] Chicago School are imposed. . . .

Repaying the Debt Is Impossible

I believe that this is the time to wage this struggle. Such a serious crisis situation has been created that the Third World countries are being forced to think, to unite, and to seek solutions, regardless of their political stands and ideologies, as an elementary matter of survival.

Paying the Debt Is Impossible

It is impossible that the outstanding principal of Third World debt will ever be repaid. Simply deferring interest payments and principal to the transnational banking circuit and seeking for rescheduling agreements would perhaps mitigate the bleeding and the pain. It can by no means stop the hemorrhage.

In fact neither can the principal nor the interest ever be repaid. Nor is it desirable that the debt (interest and principal) should be repaid. Debt repudiation stands out as the only ethically feasible and rational solution for the Third World. Moreover what our analysis exemplifies is that such measures as compensatory finance and the advocacy of interest rates reduction, while noble in their aims, cannot even begin to aspire to tackle a problem of such magnitude.

Frederick Clairmonte and John Cavanagh, *The National Reporter*, Spring 1987.

I believe that the Latin American countries need to wage that struggle and that, fortunately, they have excellent conditions for waging it. The struggle to solve the problem of the debt will benefit all the Third World countries—not just the Latin American countries, but all the developing countries in Asia and Africa, as well. I feel that the debt should be canceled. Mathematically it can be shown that it is unpayable.

The problem no longer involves the amount of the debt, but the interest that is paid on it.

I base my view on four hypotheses, all based on the assumption that the debt won't grow.

First hypothesis: that a ten-year grace period is granted for paying the capital; that, during that period, the interest will continue to be paid, as it has been thus far; and that ten years will then be given for the amortization at an interest rate not exceeding 10 percent. Latin America would have to pay $400 billion in the first ten years and an additional $558 billion in the next ten years. In twenty years, Latin America would have transferred $958 billion—nearly $1 trillion in U.S. terms, or $1 billion in English terms—to its creditors. That is, nearly a trillion dollars would leave these countries, in spite of their enormous accumulated social problems, their enormous economic problems, and the development they will have had to forgo. In twenty years, they would have to extract nearly $1 trillion from the modest economies and send it to the industrialized capitalist countries. Is this possible? Is it conceivable? And this, I repeat, is assuming that the debt won't grow and that the interest rate doesn't go over 10-percent during the amortization period. Is this conceivable, especially if the other problems I have mentioned—unequal exchange, protectionism, dumping, and so on—are taken into account? No.

Second hypothesis: that the formula of paying a maximum of 20 percent of the value of each country's exports and each year is applied and that interest rates don't go over 10 percent. The exports of Latin America as a whole are already close to but haven't reached $100 billion. Let us even assume that even if those exports surpass that figure, no more than $20 billion will be paid each year. In that case, we would pay $400 billion in twenty years, and, at the end, we would have a debt of $1.16185 trillion—that is, after we had paid $400 billion, our debt would be triple what it is now.

Third hypothesis: that a ten-year grace period is granted, including the interest; an additional ten years is granted for its amortization; and the interest doesn't go over 10 percent in any given year. This would undoubtedly mean a ten-year respite. In twenty years $1.44731 trillion would have to be paid.

Fourth hypothesis: that the interest rate is lowered to 6 percent; a ten-year grace period is granted, including the interest; and an additional ten years is given in which to pay. This would certainly be the kindest of the four formulas, but in twenty years $857.471 billion would still have to be paid.

Debt and Interest Show Hopelessness

I have put forward four hypotheses. In all, I have assumed that the debt would never exceed 10 percent, and all of them show that the debt and its interest cannot be paid.

Based on reality, on all the problems I've mentioned, it is simply impossible to pay the debt. It can't be done from a practical standpoint—our economies couldn't survive it—and it could never

For God's sake, man, pull yourself up by your bootstraps!

BANKS

solve the problem of development. The debt is an economic and a political impossibility. It is also a moral impossibility. The immense sacrifice that would have to be demanded of the people and the blood that would have to be shed to force them to pay that immense sum of money—which, to a large extent, was drained away, misspent, or embezzled—would be unjustifiable. The debt has already taken its first toll in blood in the Dominican Republic, where dozens of poor people were killed. Any attempt to pay the debt under the present social, economic, and political circumstances in Latin America would cost our suffering and impoverished nations rivers of blood, and it could never be done. Our peoples are not to blame for underdevelopment or for the debt. Our countries are not to blame for having been colonies; neocolonies; banana republics; or coffee, mining, or oil republics whose role was to produce raw materials, exotic products, and fuel at low cost and with cheap labor. . . .

As a result of all these mathematical calculations and moral, historical, political, and economic reflections, I have come to the conclusion that the Latin American debt is unpayable and should be canceled.

"The lending countries must reinitiate a lending program to Latin America and maintain consistent macroeconomic policies that allow the debtor countries to service their debt."

The US Must Aid Latin America in Repaying the Debt

J. Antonio Villamil

J. Antonio Villamil is a senior vice president and corporate economist in Miami. In the following viewpoint, he argues that many Latin American countries are teetering on the brink of economic disaster while struggling to uphold democratic governments. The US must aid these countries in repaying their debts, he believes, in order to maintain political stability.

As you read, consider the following questions:

1. Why does the author believe that increased lending to Latin America is the key to solving the debt crisis?
2. What are some of the policies that Villamil believes would allow debtor countries to repay the debt?
3. What is "the second crisis" that the author fears might affect Latin America?

J. Antonio Villamil, "Is Latin America Headed for Another Debt Crisis?" Reprinted from USA TODAY MAGAZINE, January 1986. Copyright 1986 by the Society for the Advancement of Education.

Since the Latin American debt crisis erupted in August, 1982, the countries of the region have made significant progress in economic stabilization. However, to maintain and extend this progress, the lending countries must reinitiate a lending program to Latin America and maintain consistent macroeconomic policies that allow the debtor countries to service their debt. Serious political pressures on the new Latin American democracies could result if economic difficulties continue without an end in sight, which would not be to the benefit of the lending nations.

To understand the Latin American debt issue, one must understand its origins. During the middle 1970's, real Eurodollar rates averaged around 3.5%, encouraging Latin American and other developing nations to borrow at low or negative rates, *vis-a-vis* inflation. Beginning in 1979, when the U.S. shifted to a monetarist Federal Reserve policy, the real Eurodollar rates averaged around seven percent, double that of the mid-1970's. This rise in interest rates made commercial banks more hesitant to lend to developing nations, contributing to the drying up of credit. These two factors significantly squeezed many of the delicate Latin American economies.

A second facet of the debt crisis concerns how many Latin American nations have structured their economies. They have pursued an inward-led development strategy—*i.e.,* governments encouraged production for the local market, involved themselves in large capital projects, and engaged in market protection. This is in sharp contrast with many Far East nations, which have geared their economies for export.

Debt/Export Ratios

A comparison of debt/export ratios (the relationship between total external debt and total exports) between some Latin American countries and Korea underlines this point. Argentina's debt/export ratio is 442%; Brazil's 347%; Chile's 420%; and Mexico's, 302%—as compared to Korea's 110% debt/export ratio.

Moreover, this ratio is growing in the aforementioned Latin American countries. Argentina's debt/export ratio has grown nearly 30% since 1981; Brazil's, about 12%; Chile's, nearly 80%; and Mexico's, about 10%. Clearly, these nations have not geared their economies to exporting, as many Far Eastern nations have.

Many of the Latin American countries have made strides in improving their exporting capacities. A primary example of Latin America's economic recovery may be found in the region's balance of payments. The yearly trade deficit for Latin America averaged a relatively large $10,000,000,000 in 1980 and 1981. In 1984, Latin America had a combined trade surplus of $37,000,000,000—up 20% over the prior year's surplus.

Improvement of the external accounts of Latin America has been accomplished through a combination of appropriate exchange rate management and tight monetary and fiscal policies under the International Monetary Fund programs. The costs of external stabilization have been, however, quite significant in terms of forgone economic growth. At present, per capita income in Latin America is lower than it was in 1979. Furthermore, investment as a percentage of gross domestic product—the source of future income growth—declined from a strong 22% of GDP in 1981 to only 15% in 1984. In essence, the cost of external stabilization has been primarily borne by the productive sectors of the economy.

To improve the longer-term debt-servicing capacity of Latin America, investment expenditures must revive. Otherwise, shrinking productivity capacity will adversely impact income and export growth—leading to an even more formidable external debt-servicing burden. A necessary condition for "investment-led" growth requires restarting foreign commercial bank lending to Latin America. This is necessary for improving the liquidity position of private companies and for financing export-oriented projects. Thus, increased, rather than decreased, net lending to Latin America is the key for avoiding a second, and perhaps more virulent, recurrence of the external debt-servicing crisis of late 1982 and early 1983.

We Want Promises

Latin America's economies are caught in a vicious circle. Because they are devoting so much of their savings to debt service, they are undercutting their ability to invest, to grow and to generate additional earnings to improve their credit-worthiness.

This situation is intolerable, economically and politically.

The exhilaration engendered by the revival of democracy is beginning to give way to dissatisfaction. In several countries, the new governments are being pressed by labor union resistance, public demonstrations and opposition victories in by-elections. A scrawl on a wall in Lima summed up the growing popular sentiment: "We've had enough crisis. We want promises."

Abraham F. Lowenthal, *Los Angeles Times,* February 11, 1986.

Since foreign commercial banks provide about 60% of net new lending to Latin America, appropriate financing mechanisms must be developed so that countries of the region can regain access to international private capital markets. An impediment to this process is the U.S. budget deficit. Because of its deficit, the U.S. has become a net capital importer, drawing funds out of these developing countries and competing on capital markets for funds. This distortion in the international economy will have serious repercussions if it continues.

Three developments in the U.S. since the late 1970's have hurt the Latin American countries' ability to service their debt: the American shift to monetarist policies in 1979 to wring out inflation; the combination of increasing interest and dollar exchange rates; and declining commodity prices. Each of these events were interrelated, and drove up drastically the cost of Latin American debt-servicing. A one percent rise in U.S. interest rates adds about $2,000,000,000 in servicing costs to the region. The rise in the value of the dollar *vis-a-vis* Latin American currencies also decreased those nations' ability to service their debt. Finally, the steep decline in commodity prices, a prime money earner for the Latin nations, has also hurt Latin American economies.

These three factors have resulted in a shift from too much lending to the developing countries in the middle and late 1970's to too little lending beginning around 1980 and continuing to the present. This swing in total net foreign bank lending to Latin America has been dramatic—and shows little sign of reversal. In 1982, for example, total net foreign bank lending to Latin America was a large $24,300,000,000. In 1982, the figure was only $400,000,000, and in 1984 it was a negative $3,700,000,000. This situation is not sustainable in the long run as Latin America, an underdeveloped region, requires net infusions of foreign capital to supplement domestic savings for investment. The U.S., for example, was a large net foreign debtor during the second half of the 1800's as it financed part of its development with foreign capital.

Take Each Country Individually

A second condition for avoiding another debt-servicing crisis in Latin America is to treat each country differently in debt-rescheduling exercises and new money facilities. Each country of the region has different external debt-servicing capacity and is at different stages of adjustment. Countries such as Peru and Bolivia, for example, will require significant debt relief as the levels of external debt are very high relative to economic size and export-generating potential. Argentina can not productively utilize external capital until it brings down hyper-inflationary conditions. On the other side of the spectrum, Brazil, Colombia, Mexico, and Venezuela have manageable long-term external debt-servicing burdens, and can productively absorb moderate net increases in external debt for financing trade and viable projects.

The U.S.'s macroeconomic policies could significantly assist economic adjustment in Latin America. The latter primarily borrows in dollars, and U.S. interest rates significantly impact the cost of servicing dollar-denominated debt. As mentioned, U.S. interest rates have a sharp impact on debt-servicing costs. Thus, a significant reduction in the structural budget imbalance in the U.S., with subsequent declines in U.S. real interest rates, would allow the region to divert part of its interest payments on external debt to domestic investment. Indeed, improvement in American macroeconomic policies would be the best "aid program" that we can give to the region.

What Must Be Done

Many Latin American nations need to do more to get their own houses in order as well. A primary difficulty in many Latin American nations is inflation. Argentina is the most visible example, where prices in many stores are changed several times a day. Inflation erodes domestic savings, undermines the value of the currency, and destabilizes the economy, making foreign lending unattractive. Latin American nations must also make more productive use of the capital loaned. In some countries, loaned

Jean Plantu, *LeMonde*, Paris. © 1987 Cartoonists & Writers Syndicate.

funds were used on spurious projects of little lasting productive value for either export or domestic consumption. Finally, Latin American countries should open their doors to foreign investment. Jobs created by foreign investment would assist governments in reducing unemployment, raising the per capita standard of living, and expanding the tax base.

From a political standpoint, it is in the best interests of the lending nations in general, and the U.S. in particular, to aid the Latin American nations in economic recovery. The democracies that have been established in the last decade remain tenuous in most cases, and prolonged economic distress could result in a return to the totalitarianism that has plagued the region. Argentina has already shown signs of civil strife, and other nations may follow.

In summary, avoiding another debt-servicing crisis in Latin America requires the reestablishment of net foreign bank financing to the region. It also requires a country-by-country approach to debt-restructurings and new money facilities. These two conditions have not been met at present. It is politically astute for the lending nations to aid Latin American recovery in order to preserve their democratic governments, but they have not done so. The possibility exists, therefore, that a second crisis could appear in the not too distant future with political, as well as economic, ramifications.

a critical thinking activity

Distinguishing Primary from Secondary Sources

A critical thinker must always question sources of information. Historians, for example, usually distinguish between *primary sources* (a "firsthand" or eyewitness account from personal letters, documents, or speeches, etc.) and *secondary sources* (a "secondhand" account usually based upon a "firsthand" account and possibly appearing in a newspaper or encyclopedia).

A man's description of his imprisonment in Chile is an example of a primary source. A news report about a government crackdown which includes this man among those who have been unfairly convicted would be an example of a secondary source.

Interpretation and/or point of view also play a role when dealing with primary and secondary sources. For example, the newswriter who mentions this man among a number of dissidents locked up one weekend may include his/her own view on the rightness of the law or the likelihood of the man's being guilty. Even the primary source must be questioned as to interpretation or underlying motive. The convict might be a revolutionary stressing the cruelty of the present system or he might be a petty criminal trying to legitimate his behavior.

This activity is designed to test your skill in evaluating sources of information. Pretend that your teacher tells you to write a research report on the economic situation in Latin America. Listed below are a number of sources which may be useful in your research. Carefully evaluate each of them. Then, *place a P next to those descriptions you believe are primary sources.* Second, *rank the primary sources* assigning the number (1) to what appears to be the most objective and accurate primary source, the number (2) to the next most objective, and so on until the ranking is finished. *Repeat the entire procedure, this time placing an S next to those descriptions you feel would serve as secondary sources and then ranking them.*

If you are doing this activity as a member of a class or group, discuss and compare your evaluation with other members of the group. If you are reading this book alone, you may want to ask others if they agree with your evaluation.

_____ 1. a paper presented at the World Economists Conference entitled: "Latin American Economics for the 1990s" _____

_____ 2. a chapter from a book called *US Involvement in Latin America: 1890-1935* _____

_____ 3. an editorial calling for an end to contra aid from a former contra leader _____

_____ 4. an analysis of Mexico's economic policies written by an American banker _____

_____ 5. a summary of recent Latin American events in *Newsweek* _____

_____ 6. Augusto Pinochet, in a televised interview, describing how he turned Chile's lagging economy around _____

_____ 7. a song by Bruce Cockburn describing the squalid living conditions of Latin America _____

_____ 8. a *New York Times* article summarizing evidence that militant subversive groups are financed by the Soviet Union _____

_____ 9. a letter from Brazil's foreign minister to the US Congress asking that Brazil's foreign debt be forgiven _____

_____ 10. an American documentary on how US corporations have changed Latin American society _____

_____ 11. an article in *Fortune* detailing how Latin American nations should handle their debts _____

_____ 12. a lecture by a Guatemalan professor on the effects of a reduction in American economic aid to Guatemala _____

227

Periodical Bibliography

The following periodical articles have been selected to supplement the diverse views expressed in this chapter.

Peter Bauer   "Accounts Receivable," *The New Republic*, June 15, 1987.

Pablo Gonzalez Casanova   "Foreign Debt, Foreign Intervention and Democracy," *Contemporary Marxism*, 14.

Jorge G. Castenada   "Mexico at the Brink," *Foreign Affairs*, Winter 1985/1986.

Rafael Hernandez Colon   "Sharing the Burden of Latin Debt," *The New York Times*, April 16, 1987.

Robert M. Dunn Jr.   "How To Help Latin Debtor Nations," *The New York Times*, June 26, 1987.

Jaclyn Fierman   "Fast Bucks in Latin Loan Swaps," *Fortune*, August 3, 1987.

Carlos Fuentes   "The Real Latin Threat," *The New York Times*, November 5, 1985.

John A. Gavin   "Mexico, Land of Opportunity," *Policy Review*, Winter 1987.

James S. Henry   "Where the Money Went," *The New Republic*, April 14, 1986.

Kenneth P. Jameson   "Mortgaging a House of Cards," *Commonweal*, February 27, 1987.

Morton Kondracke   "The Machine and the Tiger," *The New Republic*, February 23, 1987.

John J. Lafalce   "The Third World Debt Crisis," *Vital Speeches of the Day*, January 1, 1987.

Penny Lernoux   "Tio Sam's Big Financial Stick," *The Nation*, March 22, 1986.

Arthur MacEwan   "Latin America: Why Not Default?" *Monthly Review*, September 1986.

The New Republic   Dear Brutus," March 16, 1986.

Bernard Nossiter   "The Blood and Stone Principle," *The New York Times*, March 19, 1987.

Organizations To Contact

American Enterprise Institute for Policy Research
1150 17th St. NW
Washington, DC 20036
(202) 862-5800

The Institute is a conservative think tank that researches a number of issues, including foreign policy and defense. It publishes the monthly *Economist,* and the bimonthly *Public Opinion,* as well as books and monographs.

American Friends Service Committee
1501 Cherry St.
Philadelphia, PA 19102
(215) 241-7000

The AFSC is a Quaker organization that believes in the dignity and worth of every person. The Committee lobbies the US to stop financing anti-Sandinista groups and to stop forcing Honduras and Costa Rica to oppose Nicaragua, while suggesting the US give genuine support to the initiatives of the Contadora group.

American Security Council
Box 8
Boston, VA 22713
(703) 547-1776

The Council pursues a national strategy for peace through strength. It offers back issues of its newsletter, *Washington Report.*

Americas Society
680 Park Ave.
New York, NY 10021
(212) 249-8950

The Society is an organization on Latin American affairs and culture in the United States. It publishes *Review* on Latin American literature and the arts.

Association of American Chambers of Commerce in Latin America (AACCLA)
1615 H St. NW
Washington, DC 20062
(202) 463-5485

AACCLA represents the common aims and views of binational business interests of its members in the United States and host countries. It explains the important place of the private sector in economic progress. It publishes the quarterly *AACCLS Outlook* and brochures.

Cardinal Mindszenty Foundation
PO Box 11321
St. Louis, MO 63105
(314) 991-2939

This anti-communist organization was founded in 1958 to conduct educational and research activities concerning communist objectives, tactics and propaganda through study groups, speakers, conferences and films. It publishes the monthly *Mindszenty Report.*

CAUSA International
401 Fifth Ave.
New York, NY 10016
(212) 684-6122

CAUSA International is an educational organization which promotes an examination of values and a moral renaissance in the West, as well as the liberation of people from communist regimes. CAUSA International sponsors the International Security Council as a program for providing critical information and insight on security issues to citizens who are concerned about their nations' well-being. They publish a quarterly magazine, *CAUSA*, a lecture manual, and position papers.

Center for Inter-American Relations
680 Park Ave.
New York, NY 10021
(212) 249-8950

The Center is a group interested in furthering hemispheric cooperation. It seeks to educate American citizens about the societies of the Western Hemisphere. It publishes the monthly *Agenda*, as well as the *Annual Report*.

Center for International Policy
236 Massachusetts Ave. NE, Suite 505
Washington, DC 20002
(202) 544-4666

The Center is a research organization concerned with the impact of US foreign policy on human rights and socioeconomic conditions in the Third World. It publishes the *International Policy Report* six times a year, as well as frequent spot reports.

Central America Resource Center
1701 University Ave. SE
Minneapolis, MN 55414
(612) 379-8799

The Center is an organization dedicated to justice for the people of Central America. They support their right to self-determination and they recognize the need for fundamental economic, political, and social change. The CARC believes US policy must be changed to one which respects the basic rights and needs of Central American people. The Center publishes a directory of curricula, classroom resources, audio-visuals, and books on Central America, and also the *Executive News Summary*, a monthly digest of news articles on Central America.

Christian Anti-Communism Crusade
PO Box 890
227 E. Sixth St.
Long Beach, CA 90801
(213) 437-0941

The Crusade sponsors antisubversive seminars "to inform Americans and others of the philosophy, morality, organization techniques, and strategy of Communism." It publishes the semimonthly *News Letter*, as well as books and pamphlets.

Civilian Material Assistance
PO Box 22790
Memphis, TN 38112
(901) 452-0856

Civilian Material Assistance is the oldest and most active organization supporting the FDN Freedom Fighters of Nicaragua (contras). CMA provides non-lethal assistance to the contras and their families to promote the preservation of democracy and to liberate oppressed people from communist rule. It publishes the newsletter, *Halt*.

Coalition for a New Foreign and Military Policy
720 G St. SE
Washington, DC 20003
(202) 546-8400

The Coalition works for a peaceful, non-interventionist, and demilitarized US foreign policy. It wants to reduce military spending, protect human rights, and promote arms control and disarmament. A subscription to *Coalition Close-Up*, published quarterly, and other publications, is included in its annual $20 membership.

Council of the Americas
680 Park Ave.
New York, NY 10021
(212) 628-3200

The Council is made up of US corporations with direct investments or other business interests in Latin America. It seeks to contribute to the development of commerce and industry in the respective countries of the Western Hemisphere. It publishes the monthly *Agenda*.

Council for the Defense of Freedom
1275 K St. NW, Suite 1160
Washington, DC 20005
(202) 789-4294

The Council works against communist aggression and for US national security. It maintains a library and a speakers bureau, as well as publishing the weekly *Washington Inquirer*, the monthly *Bulletin*, and monographs.

Department of Defense
Office of Public Affairs
Public Correspondence Division
Room 2E 777
Washington, DC 20037

Write for a list of publications.

Embassy of Nicaragua
1627 New Hampshire Ave. NW
Washington, DC 20009
(202) 387-4371

The Embassy opposes US covert activity in Nicaragua and defends its sovereignty, independence, and territorial integrity. The Embassy publishes a variety of government documents available to the public.

Guatemalan Human Rights Commission
PO Box 91, Cardinal Station
Washington, DC 20064
(202) 529-6599

The Commission works to inform the US public about alleged human rights violations in Guatemala. It publishes the monthly, *Information Bulletin*.

The Heritage Foundation
214 Massachusetts Ave. NE
Washington, DC 20002
(202) 546-4400

The Foundation is dedicated to limited government, individual and economic freedom and a strong national defense. It supports US involvement in Central America to stop communist influence in the area. It publishes The Heritage Foundation *Backgrounder,* The Heritage *Lectures,* and *Policy Review.*

Inter-American Commission on Human Rights
Organization of American States
1889 F St. NW
Washington, DC 20006
(202) 458-6000

The Organization serves to promote cooperation among the American Republics and is a regional agency of the United Nations. The Commission's principal function is to promote the observance and protection of human rights. It monitors the human rights situation in the member-countries by examining denounced violations, on-site inspections, and other procedures. It publishes documents that are available on request.

North American Congress on Latin America, Inc.
151 West 19th St.
New York, NY 10011
(212) 989-8890

The Congress is an independent research organization founded to document US corporate, military, and political activities in Latin America and to relate those to conditions in the US. It publishes an influential bimonthly newsletter that focuses on Central America, *Report on the Americas,* and pamphlets and books.

Organization of American States
17th and Constitution Ave. NW
Washington, DC 20006
(202) 458-3000

The multi-national Organization was founded to achieve an order of peace and justice among the American Nations, to promote their solidarity, and to strengthen their collaboration. It publishes the bimonthly *Americas.*

Washington Office on Latin America (WOLA)
110 Maryland Ave. NE
Washington, DC 20002
(202) 544-8045

The Washington Office on Latin America seeks to encourage US policies which promote human rights and to strengthen democratic trends in Latin America. It is committed to the belief that 1) the US and Latin America are tied by geography and history; 2) that US policy has a great impact on Latin America; and 3) that the American public wants to know about and supports US policies which are conducive to the betterment of Latin America. It publishes a monthly newsletter.

Bibliography of Books

P. Ananyev, et al. — *The Economies of the Countries of Latin America.* USSR: Progress Publishers, 1984.

Christian Anglade and Carlos Forth, eds. — *The State and Capital Accumulation in Latin America.* Pittsburgh, PA: University of Pittsburgh Press, 1985.

Tom Barry — *Guatemala: The Politics of Counter-insurgency.* Albuquerque, NM: The Inter-Hemispheric Education Resource Center, 1986. Available from The Resource Center, Box 4506, Albuquerque, NM 87196.

Tom Barry — *Roots of Rebellion: Land and Hunger in Central America.* Boston: South End Press, 1987.

Tom Barry and Deb Preusch — *The Central America Fact Book.* New York: Grove Press, 1986.

Humberto Belli — *Breaking Faith: The Sandinista Revolution and its Impact on Freedom and Christian Faith in Nicaragua.* Westchester, IL: Good News, 1985.

Charles Bergquist — *Labor in Latin America: Comparative Essays on Chile, Argentina, Venezuela and Colombia.* Stanford, CA: Stanford University Press, 1986.

Karl Berman — *Under the Big Stick: Nicaragua and the United States Since 1848.* Boston: South End Press, 1986.

Cole Blasier — *The Giant's Rival: The USSR and Latin America.* Pittsburgh, PA: University of Pittsburgh Press, 1983.

Cole Blasier — *The Hovering Giant: US Responses to Revolutionary Change in Latin America.* Pittsburgh, PA: University of Pittsburgh Press, 1986.

Cynthia Brown — *With Friends Like These.* New York: Pantheon Books, 1985.

Roger Burbach and Patricia Flynn, eds. — *The Politics of Intervention: The United States in Central America.* New York: Monthly Review Press, 1984.

Teofilo Cabestrero, ed. — *Blood of the Innocent: Victims of the Contras' War in Nicaragua.* Maryknoll, NY: Orbis, 1985.

Fidel Castro — *History Will Absolve Me.* Secaucus, NJ: Lyle Stuart, Inc., 1984.

Cesar N. Caviedes — *The Southern Cone: Realities of the Authoritarian State.* Totowa, NJ: Rowman and Allanheld, 1984.

Joshua Cohen and Joel Rogers — *Rules of the Game: American Politics and the Central America Movement.* Boston: South End Press, 1986.

Joseph Collins, Frances Moore Lappe, and Nick Allen — *What Difference Could a Revolution Make?* San Francisco, CA: Institute for Food and Development Policy, 1982.

Department of State — *Democracy in Latin America and the Caribbean: The Promise and the Challenge.* Special Report No. 158, March 1987. Available from United States Department of State, Bureau of Public Affairs, Washington, DC 20520.

Department of State	*Human Rights in Castro's Cuba.* Special Report No. 153, December 1986.
Chistopher Dickey	*With the Contras: A Reporter in the Wilds of Nicaragua.* New York: Simon & Schuster, 1986.
Martin Diskin, ed.	*Trouble in Our Backyard.* New York: Pantheon Books, 1983.
Jose Napoleon Duarte	*Duarte: My Story.* New York: G.P. Putnam's Sons, 1986.
Esperanza Duran, ed.	*Latin America and the World Recession.* Cambridge, England: Cambridge University Press, 1985.
Dieter Eich and Carlos Rincon	*The Contras: Interviews with Anti-Sandinistas.* San Francisco: Synthesis, 1985.
Mark Falcoff	*Small Countries, Large Issues.* Washington, DC: American Enterprise Institute for Public Research, 1984.
Mark Falcoff, Joseph Grunwald, and Howard Wiarda	*The Crisis in Latin America: Strategic, Economic, and Political Dimensions.* Washington, DC: American Enterprise Institute for Public Research, 1984.
Eduardo Galeano	*Memory of Fire: Faces and Masks.* New York: Pantheon Books, 1987.
Guillermo Toriello Garrrido	*A Popular History of Two Revolutions.* San Francisco: Synthesis, 1985.
Altaf Gauhar, ed.	*Regional Integration: The Latin American Experience.* Boulder, CO: Westview Press for the Third World Foundation for Social and Economic Studies, 1985.
Morris B. Goldman, ed.	*Debt/Equity Conversion: Strategy for Easing Third World Debt.* Washington, DC: The Heritage Foundation, 1987.
Lawrence Harrison	*Underdevelopment Is a State of Mind: The Latin American Case.* Lanham, MD: University Press of America, 1985.
Jack W. Hopkins, ed.	*Latin America: Perspectives on a Region.* New York: Holmes and Meier, 1987.
Christopher A. Kojm	*The Problem of International Debt.* New York: H.W. Wilson, 1984.
Lester Langley	*Central America: The Real Stakes.* New York: Crown Publishers, Inc., 1985.
Alvin Levie	*Nicaragua: The People Speak.* South Hadley, MA: Bergin & Garvey, 1985.
Robert Emmet Long, ed.	*Mexico.* New York: H.W. Wilson, 1986.
Kevin J. Middlebrook and Carlos Rico, eds.	*The United States and Latin America in the 1980's.* Pittsburgh, PA: Pittsburgh University Press, 1986.
Kent Norsworthy and William I. Robinson	*David and Goliath: The US War Against Nicaragua.* New York: Monthly Review, 1987.
Michael Novak	*Will It Liberate?: Questions About Liberation Theology.* Mahwah, NJ: Paulist Press, 1986.
Michael Novak and Michael P. Jackson	*Latin America: Dependency or Interdependence?* Washington, DC: American Enterprise Institute for Public Policy Research, 1985.

Philip O'Brien and Paul Cammack	*Generals in Retreat: The Crisis of Military Rule in Latin America*. Manchester, England: Manchester University Press, 1985.
Mario Payeras	*Days of the Jungle: The Testimony of a Guatemalan Guerrillero, 1972-1976*. New York: Monthly Review Press, 1983.
Douglas Payne	*The Democratic Mask: The Consolidation of the Sandinista Revolution*. New York: Freedom House, 1985.
Barry Rubin	*Modern Dictators: Third World Coup Makers, Strongmen, and Populist Tyrants*. New York: McGraw-Hill, 1987.
Sol W. Sanders	*Mexico: Chaos on Our Doorstep*. Lanham, MD: Madison Books, 1986.
Stephen Schlesinger and Stephen Kinzer	*Bitter Fruit: The Untold Story of the Coup in Guatamala*. Garden City, NY: Anchor Books, 1983.
George Shepherd and Ved P. Nanda, eds.	*Human Rights and Third World Development*. Westport, CT: Greenwood Press, 1985.
Wayne Smith	*The Closest of Enemies: A Personal and Diplomatic Account of US-Cuban Relations Since 1957*. New York: W.W. Norton, 1987.
Stockholm Institute of Latin American Studies	*The Debt Crisis in Latin America*. Stockholm, Sweden: Latinamerika Instutet i Stockholm, 1986.
Jan F. Triska	*Dominant Powers and Subordinate States: The United States in Latin America and the Soviet Union in Eastern Europe*. Durham, NC: Duke University Press, 1986.
Robert Wesson and Heraldo Muñoz, eds.	*Latin American Views of US Policy*. New York: Praeger, 1986.
Richard Alan White	*The Morass: United States Intervention in Central America*. New York: Harper & Row, 1984.

Index

236

237

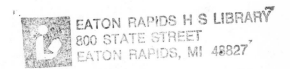